The Complete Book of
Wildlife & Nature
Photography

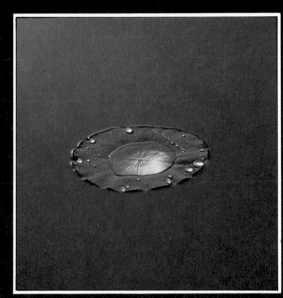

The Complete Book of
Wildlife & Nature
Photography

Michael Freeman
Consultant Nigel Sitwell

SIMON AND SCHUSTER · NEW YORK

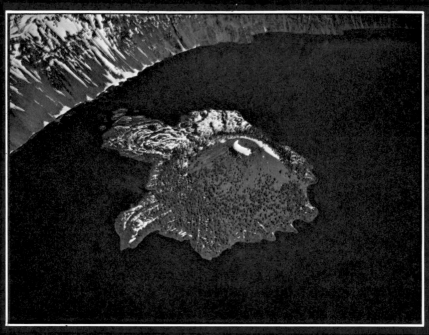

Half-title page: White ibis,
Florida Everglades.

Title page: Johnston
crocodile, Queensland,
Australia (J-P.Ferrero), lotus
leaf, in the lower Amazon.

This page: Crater Lake,
Oregon.

An Adkinson Parrish Book
Copyright © 1981 by Adkinson Parrish Limited

Published by Simon & Schuster
A Division of Gulf & Western Corporation
Simon & Schuster Building, 1230 Avenue of the Americas
New York, New York 10020
SIMON and SCHUSTER and colophon are trademarks of Simon & Schuster

Designed and produced byAdkinson Parrish Limited, London

Managing Editor	Clare Howell
Art Editor	Christopher White
Editor	John Roberts
Illustrators	Richard Blakeley Phil Holmes
	Dave Pugh Ken Stott

Phototypesetting and illustration origination by
Siviter Smith Limited, Birmingham

Printed and bound in Great Britain by

Hazell Watson & Viney Ltd, Aylesbury, Bucks

1 2 3 4 5 6 7 8 9 10
Library of Congress Cataloging in Publication Data
Freeman, Michael, 1945–
The complete book of wildlife and nature photography
Includes index
1.   Photography of animals   2.   Photography of birds
3.   Photography, Submarine   I.   Title
TR 727.F72   778.9′3   81-5237
ISBN 0 671-41255-8   AACR2

Contents

INTRODUCTION

As human development encroaches steadily on the world's wild places, threatening the survival of species after species of animal and plant, it has actually stimulated a new, sharper interest in nature. The wilderness areas and their inhabitants begin to seem more precious when their continued existence can no longer be taken for granted. Thankfully, the vigorous campaigning of conservation organisations in recent years has helped to make more and more people aware of, and interested in, the natural world. In one form or another, the enjoyment of wild places, animals and plants has become a major form of recreation for millions. National parks, sanctuaries and reserves have never been so popular as they are now.

Photography has a unique place in this surge of interest in wildlife. As a creative expression, the photograph can reveal beauty or significance that might otherwise go unnoticed. In capturing hidden details or the rare and exotic, the camera can display the richness of nature to a wide audience who may never have the opportunity to see these things for themselves.

With modern equipment, virtually the whole range of wildlife is accessible to the photographer—at all levels of scale, right down to the sub-microscopic, and also including areas such as animal behaviour that once required highly specialized technique and knowledge. The camera is one of the naturalist's chief research tools, revealing actions and patterns of behaviour that were hitherto unknown. High-speed flash and remote-sensing equipment have revealed the aerodynamics of an insect's wing beat, while the scanning electron microscope can achieve not only enormous magnifications but also resolution and depth of field that bring a new dimension to the close-up world of insects. Finally infrared and image intensifying equipment have begun to open up new possibilities in nocturnal photography.

Although they are expensive and specialized, techniques such as these have broken new ground in natural history. And with the benefits of advanced technology, most photographers can tackle subjects that might have seemed impossible a few decades ago. Motor drives, essential for fast action sequences, are almost accepted as standard accessories, and modern portable flash units have brought precision and reliability to close-ups and night photography. No longer is the simple recording of an animal's appearance the objective of wildlife photography. Photographers are searching for added interest in their subjects, whether it is the behaviour of an animal, drama in a landscape, or composition and harmony in close-up work and photomicrography. Above all, the best nature and wildlife photographs stand as photographs in their own right—fresh exciting and stimulating pictures.

The scope of the subject, and of this book, is enormous. Simply put, it is the world where man has not yet put his mark. Complex, infinitely diverse, it encompasses everything from the sweeping landscape to the intimate details of the smallest creatures. For any photographer, it contains enough material and fascination for a lifetime.

A recently discovered species of varanus lizard basks on a rock in the mountains of Western Australia (J-P. Ferrero). Nikon with 24 mm lens, Kodachrome 64, 1/60 sec at f16.

The animal kingdom

The range of photographic opportunities offered by the many thousands of animal species is as great as the variety of ecological niches they occupy. From swamps sweltering in immense humidity and heat to freezing, windswept mountain-sides—the world offers such a complexity of habitats that the number of different forms of animal life seems almost without limit. New species are still regularly being discovered. So, for the photographer, this is a subject area of immense richness. For many types of wildlife, only the most straightforward equipment is needed—a modest telephoto lens in the case of the three illustrations on these pages—under-lining the principle that in wildlife and nature photography it is usually the context of the shot that takes pride of place, rather than an excess of creative technique.

Captured with a medium telephoto lens, a pygmy marmoset in the upper Amazon rainforest is aware of the camera, but at sufficient distance to remain undisturbed.

A Mississippi alligator rests still in the shallows of a backwater swamp.

Regrettably rare in the wild, the tiger remains one of the most attractive of all animals to photograph. This superb specimen was photographed by Jean-Paul Ferrero from the back of an elephant in the Kanha National Park, India.

The close-up view

At a scale that is rarely appreciated with a casual glance, insects, small flowers and other close-up subjects inhabit a world that photography is uniquely equipped to reveal. The combination of a close-focusing lens and a well defined frame that eliminates distraction helps to narrow the concentration towards details that often have an un-expected beauty. Camera technique at these scales of reproduction needs precision—the tolerances of lighting, focus and depth of field are slender. The subjects themselves may need a delicate approach in addition to the technical skill required to capture them effectively on film, but the reward can be images of extraordinary quality.

The fragile beauty of wildflowers is a fine subject for photography. The isolated and framed photographic image reveals details in this greater stichwort, found in Savernake Forest, England, that could easily be missed with the naked eye.

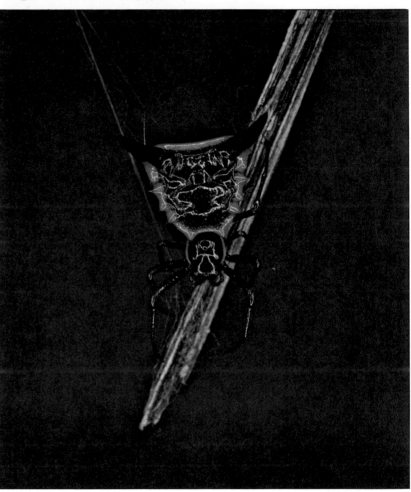

The strange, exotic fascination of small creatures can be most effectively captured with close-up photography, although shallow depth of field and insufficient light are problems that have to be overcome. This horned spider was photographed in the Guiana highlands of South America.

An example of the dramatic
images to be found in the
miniature world of close-up
photography—a mosquito is
silhouetted against the
setting sun.

The world of birds

Birds have long been favourites with wildlife photographers. Their variety is immense, their behaviour fascinating, and they cover the entire globe. They can be found in the heart of cities and in the densest jungles. Their great mobility makes them frequent visitors to every type of habitat, and the gregarious nature of many species means that they can often be found together in huge numbers, providing the photographer with some of the great spectacles of the natural world. Bird photography requires a sense of action, with split-second timing combined with thorough planning to ensure the best camera position. It may even be worth taking to the air as well—for a participant's view of flight.

Single birds in flight can often be photographed effectively from the ground with a telephoto lens. Here, the subject is an open-billed stork. Be careful not to underestimate the problems of focusing and exposure with this approach to bird photography.

A flock of white ibis flies over the Florida Everglades. For this type of shot, seeing birds truly in their own air-borne environment, aerial photography can be a successful technique.

The natural landscape

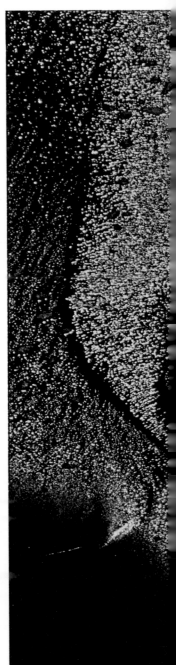

The majesty of nature is amply demonstrated by these Arizona buttes, photographed against the evening sky.

One of the classic themes of photography, landscape offers more scope for personal interpretation than any other subject. By definition, it is not limited to any single element of the natural environment, but takes in the whole—or whatever part of it the photographer decides. Landscape can be approached in as many ways as there are photographers. Ranging from the grand vista of a vast wilderness to the intimate detail of a weatherbeaten stone, the landscape photograph is best when it conveys a definite sense that the image shows a very particular place seen through the eyes of one individual photographer.

Details of inanimate nature can also provide original and unexpected views. This glistening sand in a spent wave was found at Point Lobos, California.

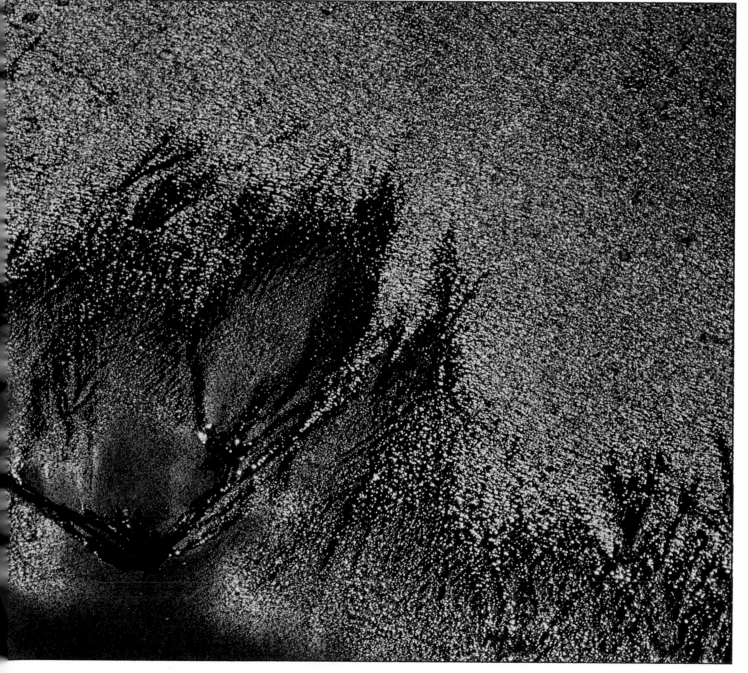

EQUIPMENT

One of the features that distinguishes wildlife and nature photography is the extent to which the subject matter influences the way of working. The behaviour of an animal or the annual cycle of a plant virtually determines the techniques to be used by the photographer. Many creatures, for example, cannot be approached closely, calling for long distance work with a telephoto lens. Others can only be photographed from concealed positions, which involves the use of hides and sometimes remote control accessories. Whereas many other photographic subjects, such as people or still-life, offer the possibilities of looser interpretation and more freedom in technique, the need to show specific characteristics of animals, plants and other nature subjects usually gives the photographer less choice.

As a result, wildlife photography has traditionally been dominated by technique and special equipment. Custom-made versions of cameras, lighting equipment and remote control devices feature prominently in early writing on the subject, and this, probably more than anything else, has tended to discourage beginners. Now, however, most of these technical limitations have faded with the rapid improvements in basic photographic equipment.

What has happened is not that the need for special equipment has diminished, but that the cameras, lenses, lighting and accessories now supplied for regular photography fulfil most of the special require-ments of wildlife and nature subjects. Long telephoto lenses and macro lenses are common, while efficient, self-regulating flash units have made accurate lighting in the field straightforward and uncomplicated.

The relative importance of equipment in photography is a contentious problem. Special equipment undoubtedly makes certain photographs possible, and photography is, after all, based on the use of technology. However, equipment, which should be made to serve the needs of the picture, frequently tends to take over as an obsession. Many people replace an interest in photography with a love of gadgetry, frequently without being conscious that there is a difference between the two. By immersing themselves in the imaginative demands of the equipment, they often lose sight of the real aims of photography—to produce stimulating and informative images. Achieving good pictures calls for a balanced view, with the final print or transparency as the only important result and equipment merely as a useful tool in producing it.

A phelsuma lizard through
the viewfinder of a 35mm
single lens reflex with the
prism head removed.

Camera systems

In nature and wildlife photography the range of subjects is so great, and photographic style so varied, that virtually all types of camera can be used. Some, however, are better suited to particular tasks than others. When you are choosing equipment, the type of work you intend to concentrate on will determine the format and type of camera you buy.

The three most important film sizes are 35mm (24 × 36mm picture area), roll film (principally 6 × 6cm and 6 × 7cm) and sheet film (most commonly 9 × 12cm and 18 × 24cm, although several other sizes are available). The cameras designed for these formats have characteristics that impose a style on the photographs taken with them. 35mm cameras, for example, are ideally suited to fast action photography–they are highly portable and can be operated very quickly. Because of this, they have become the most popular camera for the mass photographic market, and consequently they have received the major effort in technological development. A further advantage of the relatively small film size is that great depth of field is possible in 35mm photography. Not only does this make it possible to combine sharply focused foregrounds and backgrounds in landscape photographs, but it is also extremely valuable in macro-photography.

The history of sheet film is as old as photography itself. The earliest cameras were designed for single shot plates of quite large format, and modern view cameras differ little in design, which in principle is simple and straightforward. A view camera, whether a traditional mahogany and brass field camera or an advanced monorail studio model, is essentially a flexible light-tight 'box' with a lens panel at the front and film holder at the back.

Other cameras can be reduced to this basic description, but in the case of the view camera the simplicity of the system has been deliberately preserved. Its design is the most adaptable and versatile possible. When it is important to record the maximum detail, and when careful consideration rather than a fast reaction is needed, it is ideal. The bulk and slowness of operation, however, make it generally unsuitable for photographing active wildlife.

Roll film, with a picture area 6cm across, is something of a compromise between 35mm and sheet

View cameras are precision instruments that make fine detail and a high degree of control over the image possible. Compared with a motor driven 35mm SLR, they are extremely slow to use, particularly on location. They are well suited to landscape photography, however, provided that there is no need for a large number of shots. A 5×4 in (9×12 cm) model was used for this shot of Double Arch in Arches National Park, Utah (far right).

Camera suitability

	35mm VIEWFINDER CAMERA	35mm SLR CAMERA	ROLL FILM: TWIN LENS REFLEX	ROLL FILM: SLR	VIEW CAMERA: FIELD MODEL	VIEW CAMERA: TECHNICAL MODEL	VIEW CAMERA: MONORAIL	MOTOR DRIVE	AUTOMATIC WINDER	REMOTE CONTROL FACILITY	PANORAMIC CAMERA	UNDERWATER CAMERA OR HOUSING	HIGH SPEED CAMERA
FIELDWORK													
STALKING	b	a	c	b	d	d	d	a	a	d	d	a	a
HIDES	b	a	a	a	d	d	d	b	b	a	d	d	b
BIRDS IN FLIGHT	c	a	d	b	d	d	d	b	a	d	d	d	a
FLOWERS	b	a	b	a	b	c	c	d	c	d	c	d	d
INSECTS AND SMALL ANIMALS	c	a	c	b	c	d	d	a	a	a	d	d	a
THE ENVIRONMENT													
LANDSCAPE	b	a	b	a	a	c	c	d	b	d	a	d	d
TREES	b	a	b	a	b	d	c	d	b	d	d	d	d
VOLCANOES AND GEYSERS	b	a	b	a	c	d	d	b	b	d	b	d	c
WEATHER	b	a	b	a	b	d	c	d	d	d	c	b	c
SPECIAL CONDITIONS													
POLAR	b	a	b	a	b	d	c	d	d	b	a	d	c
MOUNTAIN	b	a	b	b	c	d	c	b	b	b	a	d	c
DESERT	b	a	b	b	c	d	c	b	b	b	a	d	c
RAINFOREST AND SWAMP	b	a	b	b	d	d	d	b	b	b	c	b	c
SEA AND SHORE	b	a	b	b	c	d	d	b	b	b	b	a	c
UNDERWATER	b	a	d	a	d	d	d	d	a	d	d	a	d
NOCTURNAL	b	a	b	a	b	d	c	c	b	d	d	d	d
UNDERGROUND	b	a	c	b	d	d	d	b	b	d	d	a	d
AERIAL	c	a	c	c	d	d	d	b	b	d	d	d	d
STUDIO WORK													
CAPTIVE SETS	b	a	b	a	b	b	b	b	b	d	d	d	b
ZOOS	b	a	b	a	c	d	c	b	b	d	d	d	c
INSECTS AND SMALL ANIMALS	b	a	c	a	c	d	d	b	b	b	d	d	a
PHOTOMICROGRAPHY	d	a	d	c	c	b	b	d	d	d	d	d	c
FOSSILS	b	a	b	a	a	a	a	d	d	d	d	d	d
MINERALS AND ROCKS	b	a	b	a	a	a	a	d	d	d	d	d	d
FLOWERS	b	a	b	a	a	a	a	d	d	d	d	d	d

Key: **a** ideal, b suitable, c can be used with a little difficulty, d unsuitable.

film. Cameras made for it are designed to preserve the ease of operation of 35mm models while being able to record more detail on the larger film size. To a limited extent, however, the development of camera and film technology in the last decade has reduced the value of this intermediate size.

The most famous of all modern roll film cameras, the Hasselblad, was specifically designed for nature and wildlife photography, the aim being to combine a large film size (almost four times the picture area of 35mm film) with the obvious advantages of a single lens reflex design and rapid film advance. The development of extremely fine grained 35mm colour films such as Kodachrome, however, means that under the right conditions as much detail can be recorded on a 35mm frame as on 6 × 6cm. In addition, while it used to be difficult to reproduce 35mm transparencies satisfactorily in magazines and books, the precision of the latest scanning reproduction equipment has elevated 35mm to the standard professional format for hand-held work. Roll film cameras have an important place, but this is tending towards specialized and static types of photography, chiefly in the studio.

Apart from these basic camera systems, there are a number of highly specialized formats and designs intended for specific purposes. Panoramic cameras use either rotating or oversized lenses to use up to three or four times the length of film for a single shot. High-speed cameras use a variety of mechanical and electronic devices to increase shutter speed. Purpose built underwater cameras use 0 ring seals and non-corrosible materials.

Each type of photography has sponsored the development of its own specialized equipment. Advice on using such aids will be given in this book where appropriate to the branch of wildlife or nature photography under discussion.

For most active wildlife photography, 35mm is the most useful format. For portability, ease and speed of use, a 35mm camera with interchangeable lenses is the best possible equipment. When stalking, or with fast moving subjects, or in any situation where the shooting conditions are uncertain, it is a natural choice. In this example, stalking a tiger from the back of an elephant called for fast reactions, as the animal was unlikely to remain in shot for long (J-P. Ferrero).

Most medium format cameras use a 6×6cm format, which has the advantage of a larger area of film than 35mm – more than three times the size – but the disadvantage of being a difficult shape to compose within. The majority of subjects suit a rectangular format, either horizontal or vertical, so that in most shots some of the picture area is wasted. Medium format cameras are slower and less convenient to use than 35mm, and so are better suited to situations that do not change rapidly. In this photograph of massed river turtles, speed of operation was not important, and the square composition is effective.

Lenses/the principles

Manual/automatic 35mm SLR   Automatic 35mm SLR

	Standard 50mm (39°)
	Wide-angle 28mm (67°)
	Extreme wide-angle 20mm (84°)
	Fish-eye 16mm full-frame (137°)
	Long-focus 105mm (20°)
	135mm (15°)
	200mm (10°)
	300mm (7°)
	Extreme long-focus 400mm (5°)
	600mm (4°)
	800mm (3°)
	80mm–200mm (23°–10°)
	180mm–600mm (11°–4°)
	Macro 55mm
	200mm Medical

Ultimately, the quality of the photographic image depends on the optical quality of the lens used. Of all equipment, the lens deserves the greatest care in selection and use and top priority when apportioning expenditure. All good camera systems have the facility for interchanging lenses, so the special properties of different lens design can be chosen to suit particular photographic subjects.

Covering power

Every lens forms a circular image that is generally sharpest in the centre, deteriorating towards the edges. Clearly, the diameter of the sharp image must be at least as large as the film format, so that a lens for a 35mm camera must cover a circle of at least 43mm diameter (the diagonal of the film size). A lens for a 6 × 6cm camera must have a greater covering power–at least 85mm diameter. For most system cameras, lenses are designed to fit specific models, but with view cameras the choice of lenses is normally up to the photographer.

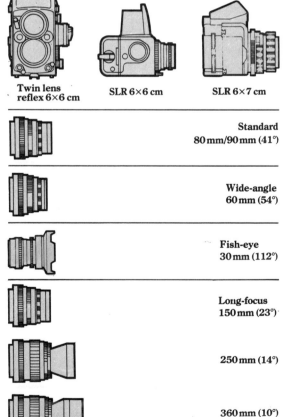

Twin lens reflex 6×6 cm   SLR 6×6 cm   SLR 6×7 cm

	Standard 80mm/90mm (41°)
	Wide-angle 60mm (54°)
	Fish-eye 30mm (112°)
	Long-focus 150mm (23°)
	250mm (14°)
	360mm (10°)
	500mm (6°)
	Macro 140mm (24°)

The lens charts (left) show the main groups of lenses available for 35mm and medium format cameras, and representative examples of each.
The focal length determines both the degree of magnification and the angle of view. Standard focal lengths (that is, equal to the diagonal of the film format) are the basis for calculating these: a 200mm lens on a 35mm camera, for example, has a focal length four times that of the standard 50mm, and as a result gives an image that is magnified four times and covering a quarter of the field of view. A 600mm is more extreme, giving 12 times the magnification with only a 4° view.

The angles of view here, shown in brackets, are calculated along the horizontal side of the frame, rather than along the diagonal. For the medium format cameras, the angles are calculated for a 6×6 cm format; on the larger 6×7 cm format the angles of view would be slightly greater.

Focal length

The focal length, normally given in millimetres, is the measure of how far behind the lens the image is formed. A so-called 'standard' lens has a focal length similar to the diagonal of the film format (43mm rounded up to 50mm for 35mm film, 85mm for 6 × 6cm) and has an angle of view that generally appears to be the same as the human eye. This is a subjective comparison, as the human eye records details differently from a camera, but the perspectives and coverage of a standard lens approximate to what we are accustomed to seeing.

Long-focus lenses have narrower angles of view, and thus magnify the image. They can be used to select small parts of a scene and to record details smaller than the unaided eye can distinguish.

Design improvements have made it possible to shorten the physical length of long-focus lenses. Telephoto design incorporates converging and diverging elements to shorten the light path and so focus closer to the lens, while catadioptric lenses 'fold' the light path with mirrors.

Short-focus lenses have the opposite effect, reducing the size of the image by covering a greater angle of view. They are consequently known as wide-angle lenses. Fish-eye lenses, which can cover extremely wide angles–sometimes over 180°–have a very distinctive 'barrel' distortion, which curves all lines near the edge of the frame.

Light gathering power

The quantity of light that a lens can accept determines how it can be used in low light conditions. Improvements in lens design and the development of new types of glass have been responsible for the steady improvement in the maximum apertures of fast lenses. Several normal lenses have apertures of f1.2, and a 400mm long-focus lens that opens up to f3.5 is available.

Lens suitability

	Mirror lens	Very long focus lens (600mm and above)	Long focus lens (300mm–500mm)	Moderate long focus lens (100mm–250mm)	Standard lens (45mm–55mm)	Telephoto zoom	Normal zoom	Wide-angle zoom	Wide-angle lens (28mm–35mm)	Extreme wide-angle lens (15mm–24mm)	Full-frame fish-eye lens	Circular image fish-eye	Macro lens	Medical-Nikkor	Perspective control lens	Night lens	P-C lens
FIELDWORK																	
STALKING	b	c	a	a	c	a	b	d	d	d	d	d	d	d	d	d	b
HIDES	a	a	a	a	c	a	b	d	d	d	d	d	d	d	d	d	d
BIRDS IN FLIGHT	b	c	b	b	d	b	d	d	d	d	d	d	d	d	d	d	d
FLOWERS	d	d	c	b	b	b	b	b	b	b	c	d	a	a	c	c	c
INSECTS AND SMALL ANIMALS	d	d	d	b	b	c	c	d	d	d	d	d	a	a	d	c	d
THE ENVIRONMENT																	
LANDSCAPE	b	b	b	b	b	b	b	b	b	b	b	b	b	d	b	b	b
TREES	b	b	b	b	b	b	b	b	b	b	c	c	c	d	a	d	b
VOLCANOES AND GEYSERS	b	b	b	b	b	b	b	b	b	b	b	b	b	d	b	b	b
WEATHER	b	b	b	b	b	b	b	b	b	b	a	a	b	d	c	d	b
SPECIAL CONDITIONS																	
POLAR	b	b	b	b	b	b	b	b	b	b	b	b	b	b	b	b	b
MOUNTAIN	b	b	b	b	b	b	b	b	b	b	b	b	b	b	b	b	b
DESERT	b	b	b	b	b	b	b	b	b	b	b	b	b	b	b	b	b
RAINFOREST AND SWAMP	b	b	b	b	b	b	b	b	b	b	b	b	b	b	b	b	b
SEA AND SHORE	b	b	b	b	b	b	b	b	b	b	b	b	a	b	b	c	b
UNDERWATER	d	d	d	d	b	d	d	d	a	a	a	a	d	d	d	d	c
NOCTURNAL	c	c	b	b	b	c	c	c	b	c	c	d	b	c	d	d	a
UNDERGROUND	d	d	c	b	b	c	c	c	b	b	b	b	b	b	d	d	a
AERIAL	d	d	d	c	b	c	c	c	a	a	c	d	b	d	d	d	b
STUDIO WORK																	
CAPTIVE SETS	d	d	d	b	b	d	b	b	c	d	d	d	a	a	d	b	c
ZOOS	a	a	a	a	b	a	b	c	c	d	d	d	b	c	c	d	b
INSECTS AND SMALL ANIMALS	d	d	d	b	b	c	c	d	d	d	d	d	a	a	c	c	c
PHOTOMICROGRAPHY	Only the microscope lens should be used																
FOSSILS	d	d	d	b	b	c	c	d	d	d	d	d	a	b	d	b	c
MINERALS AND ROCKS	d	d	d	b	b	c	c	d	d	d	d	d	a	b	d	b	c
FLOWERS	d	d	c	b	b	b	b	b	c	c	d	d	a	a	d	c	c

Key: **a** ideal, b suitable, c can be used with a little difficulty, d unsuitable.

Lenses/long-focus, macro and wide-angle

The two chief characteristics of wide-angle lenses are great depth of field and a wide field of view, making them useful for broad shots of a habitat, in particular for those with a subject in the close foreground. In this way, subjects can be related to their surroundings. Here, by stopping down to f16 with a 20 mm lens, the whole image was sharp from the skyline to the cacti less than a metre from the camera.

Because of the special nature of many wildlife subjects, certain lenses are particularly suitable. As most large animals do not allow close approach, a lens that magnifies their image is especially useful, whereas wide-angle lenses are generally successful for broad, environmental shots. The majority of creatures are small however, so much wildlife photography involves close-up work. These three lenses—long-focus, wide-angle and macro—should form the basis of the wildlife photographer's equipment.

Long-focus lenses

These are the work horses of wildlife photography in the field, and are absolutely essential for dealing with any but the smallest creatures. Basically, any focal length more than twice that of the format's standard lens is a long-focus lens, and the longer the focal length, the more extreme the effects. Long focal length can only be achieved at the cost of added weight and bulk and the loss of light-gathering power—and the best long-focus lenses are always expensive.

Long focus lenses have three important qualities. Firstly, they magnify. A 200mm lens on a 35mm format camera has four times the focal length of the standard 50mm lens, so it projects a four-times enlarged image on the film. For the wildlife photographer trying to approach a wary animal, this is the most important property of the lens—it brings the animal closer.

With a really long-focus lens, such as a 600mm on a 35mm format, the animal's image is magnified 12 times. However, the most powerful of long-focus lenses are not always the best choice. Their weight and bulk make them difficult to use without a firm support—usually a tripod—and their maximum apertures are often so small (as little as f8 or f11) that it may not always be possible to use

shutter speeds fast enough to freeze the animal's movements. Additionally, long-focus lenses magnify faults as well as the image. These include not only camera shake, which is hard to avoid with a heavy lens, but also the optical defects of the lens itself. Only a few types of extreme long-focus lens give as sharp an image as a standard lens, and these tend to be very expensive.

The second important quality of long-focus lenses is their ability to isolate subjects from their surroundings, something that is clearly useful where an animal is found in a confusing mass of vegetation. The animal is isolated by a long-focus lens not only because the angle of view is so narrow (5° across the horizontal side of the image for a 400mm lens on 35mm format), but also because the depth of field is much shallower than for a normal lens. When a 400mm lens is stopped right down to its minimum aperture, the depth of field is very limited, but at the maximum aperture—how long-focus lenses are often used when photographing wildlife—the depth of field covers only a very narrow band. Everything in front of or behind the subject is out of focus, which helps to make the animal stand out clearly from its surroundings.

The third quality is closely related to this shallow depth of field, and has a very specific interest for wildlife photography. Because nearby objects are recorded out of focus as a blur, it is possible to shoot through a thin screen of vegetation with only limited interference to the image. In this way, branches and bushes can be used as cover when stalking. To do this successfully, the lens must be at its widest aperture.

Macro lenses

Most lenses are designed to give their sharpest image when focused at distances approaching infinity. At very close distances, the lens elements

have to be moved so much further away from the film that focusing becomes impractical. Partly because of this, most lenses are restricted in how close they can be focused. A typical 50mm lens on a 35mm camera will not focus any closer than 45cms (17ins), while a 300mm lens may have a close limit of more than 4 metres (13 feet). Macro lenses, however, are specifically designed to work at close distances. Their optical performance is best close-to and the lens barrel is arranged so that focusing can be as close as 24cms (9½ins). For nature and wildlife photography they are ideal, and they have the added bonus of functioning perfectly well at distances up to infinity.

Most macro lenses are available in standard focal lengths (around 50mm) and also slightly longer (around 100mm) to give a greater working distance between the lens and subject. This greater lens to subject distance of the long-focus models is particularly useful when working with small creatures that may be disturbed by too close an approach. It also tends to produce a more pleasing perspective.

Wide-angle lenses

Although wide-angle lenses are not normally used in wildlife photography, they are able to give a panoramic view with sufficient depth of field to bring both foreground and background sharply into focus. In landscape photography, therefore, they have an important place. They are also useful in any situation where the subject has to be shown as part of its larger environment—wild flowers, for example.

The most extreme wide-angle lenses produce such strong distortion that they can dominate the picture with their own properties. Fish-eye lenses, for example, can produce striking images, but need to be used with caution.

A macro lens is probably the second most useful lens in wildlife and nature photography after the long-focus lens. Its main features are an optical design that is most efficient in close-up and a close focusing mount that gives magnifications up to half life size. Close-up shots in the field, such as these spiders, are thus possible without additional extensions or supplementary lenses.

A special advantage of long-focus lenses in wildlife photography is concealment. Because depth of field is very shallow, especially at maximum aperture, foreground objects normally appear as a blur. The foliage used as cover in this shot of painted storks is thrown so much out of focus that it interferes very little with the image.

The greater magnification achieved with a lens of long focal length makes it possible to take photographs from a distance. Long-focus lenses are thus essential equipment for the many instances when an animal cannot be approached closely. An additional effect is foreshortening—the compression of planes that with some subjects, such as this mass of northern elephant seals, can give extra graphic interest to the shot (F. Gohier).

Lenses/additional

While the three most useful lenses for wildlife and nature photography—long-focus, wide-angle and macro—will be adequate for most situations, other lenses also have their place. In some cases, these are common parts of the photographer's equipment, but some lenses are specialized in function and will consequently be used less often. These lenses also tend to be expensive, so it is wise to think carefully before investing in them. It may be that a good photographic store locally will have a hire department from which they can be obtained on a temporary basis. Unless you expect to use them again and again, this will probably be the wisest approach.

Standard lenses

By definition, the standard lens gives a normal perspective and angle of view, one that does not seem unusual or obtrusive. For subjects that are accessible and not too small, the normal lens is a natural choice for making straightforward photo-

graphic records. It is therefore ideal in the studio, and for many static subjects in the field.

The 'normal' focal length for any film format is generally held to be the diagonal of the film frame, although this is not a hard and fast rule. For a 35mm format the normal focal length is 43mm (rounded up to 50mm or 55mm), for 6 × 6cm 85mm, for 6 × 7cm 92mm, for 9 × 12cm 300mm, and so on. The high quality of most macro lenses is worth considering when looking for a standard focal length lens. Many professionals use a 50mm or 55mm macro lens in place of that usually supplied by manufacturers.

Zoom lenses

A zoom lens has a variable focal length and can take the place of several lenses. An 80–200mm zoom, for example, has the properties of both a slightly larger than standard and of a long-focus lens—with any stage in between. The focus does not need adjustment when the focal length is

Because many wildlife and nature subjects need special techniques to approach and photograph them, standard lenses, which give a 'normal' view, have a relatively low usefulness, particularly as a macro lens can usually stand in quite effectively for them. Nevertheless, for a subject such as this rainforest river bank, which has no problems of access or scale, a standard lens is the natural choice.

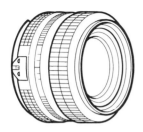

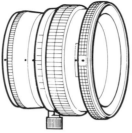
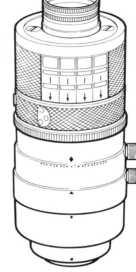

Standard lens: its 50 mm or 55 mm focal length gives a view corresponding to that of 'normal' human vision. A macro lens is often a better choice.

Night lens: with an aspherical front and large maximum aperture, giving exceptional performance in low light.

Perspective control lens: normally used for architecture, it can correct converging verticals when photographing tall trees.

Medical lens: with a built-in ringflash, it is ideal for photographing close-up subjects in constantly repeated, even lighting.

There are a great many different lenses available for use with 35 mm systems. As well as the three most useful types described on the previous pages, four examples are illustrated here. The photographer would be wise to consider carefully before buying these lenses as their use will be more limited in wildlife and nature photography—unless you concentrate on a particular type of subject.

changed, which makes it a useful lens in field-work when you suddenly need a different lens to capture a shot.

The infinitely variable focal length often allows you to fill the frame exactly as you want to, but there is the disadvantage that zoom lenses, transmitting less light, are not as fast as fixed lenses of equivalent focal length.

Perspective-control lenses

To photograph the entire height of a stand of trees from close to, it is usually necessary to point the camera upwards. If the trunks are straight and parallel, as in a pine forest, they will appear to converge. This is a perfectly normal feature of perspective, but in a photograph may appear awkward and unsatisfactory.

A specially designed lens can overcome this, simply by having great covering power and lens elements that can be shifted laterally. By pointing the camera horizontally, thereby recording the verticals with their normal, acceptable appearance and shifting the lens laterally upwards, the edge of the lens's field of view can be used to include the higher part of the subject without distortion.

Night lenses

Another specialist lens design is useful for photography in conditions of extremely low light. The maximum aperture of night lenses is very wide indeed, usually f1.2, so that they have excellent light-gathering power. In addition, these lenses have an aspherical front element which reduces the flare from light sources included in the frame. This is more useful for night or twilight scenes with streetlights included than for wildlife and nature photography. For low levels of illumination, this type of lens is unsurpassed, but they are very expensive.

Medical-Nikkor

This unusual lens, designed specifically for use in the medical profession, is an interesting

Although medical lenses are designed chiefly for medical purposes, these specialized lenses are also very useful for wildlife close-ups, particularly when the main intention is to achieve a shot rather than to make subtle alterations to the lighting. Combining a macro lens and a ringflash, a medical lens is extremely simple to use. The shadowless lighting reveals all the details of a subject—here a horned viper—although the flat illumination can become monotonous if used often.

choice for some wildlife close-up work. Intended for use in parts of the body where access is restricted (perhaps during an operation) with the least complication, the Medical-Nikkor incorporates its own ringflash, which produces almost shadowless lighting. The resulting effect does not suit every subject, but at least gives a clear illumination of all its parts, even in difficult circumstances.

The Medical-Nikkor is designed in such a way that no complicated flash calculations are necessary. According to the magnification desired, a particular supplementary lens is fitted, and the subject is brought into focus by moving the entire lens and camera.

Supports and accessories

Most wildlife and nature photography involves fieldwork, and this carries with it the need to keep down the weight and bulk of the equipment to be carried. This is nearly always a problem—for, to be effective, camera supports must be solid and well constructed. For any field photography other than with the camera hand-held, the need for firm, reliable support has to be set against the difficulties of carrying it. It is no surprise therefore that wildlife and nature photographers choose a wide variety of solutions. Camera supports are not restricted to tripods, although these are the most common, and the selection illustrated here shows some space saving adaptations as well as the conventional answers.

Wildlife subjects that call for good support include flowers, very small creatures, birds and animals photographed from hides, some landscapes, and anything that has to be photographed with a lens with a very long focal length. Supports have two functions: to hold the camera steady against movement that could blur the image, and to maintain a precisely framed picture. Even with electronic flash, which removes the problem of camera shake, there is often an advantage in having a fixed viewpoint—to hold focus in close-ups, for example. In studio work, there is no good reason not to use a tripod.

As for accessories, there is no possibility of carrying everything that might be useful, and packing for any field trip calls for a ruthless exclusion of anything that is not strictly necessary. Stalking in particular can only be done successfully with the very minimum of weight. There is obviously little sense in taking so many accessories that you cannot move silently or quickly. Take only those items that you are fairly certain you will need, and follow the advice given for specific subjects, conditions and techniques as discussed in subsequent sections of this book.

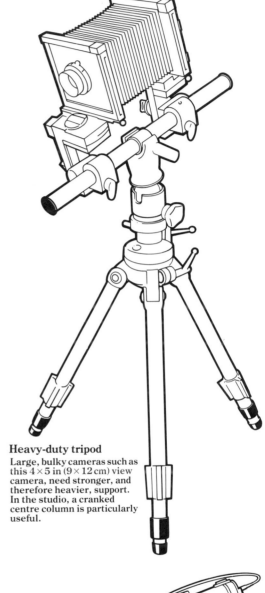

Heavy-duty tripod
Large, bulky cameras such as this 4×5 in (9×12 cm) view camera, need stronger, and therefore heavier, support. In the studio, a cranked centre column is particularly useful.

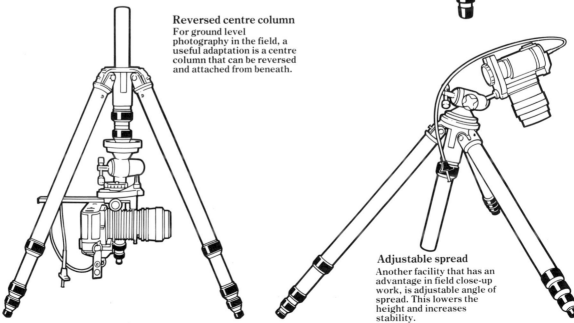

Reversed centre column
For ground level photography in the field, a useful adaptation is a centre column that can be reversed and attached from beneath.

Adjustable spread
Another facility that has an advantage in field close-up work, is adjustable angle of spread. This lowers the height and increases stability.

Accessories suitability

	Tripod	Pocket tripod	Monopod	Rifle stock	Close-up lens	Extension rings	Bellows	Cable release	Reversing mount	Magnifying viewfinder	Speedfinder	Studio flash	Portable flash	Ringflash	Flash meter	Light meter	Reflectors	Clips and clamps	Tape measure
FIELDWORK																			
STALKING	c	b	a	a	d	d	d	c	d	d	a	d	c	d	d	a	d	d	d
HIDES	a	d	d	c	d	d	d	a	d		a	d		d	d	b	d	d	d
BIRDS IN FLIGHT	d	d	b	a	d	d	d	d	d	d	d	b	d	d	d	b	d	d	d
FLOWERS	a	a	c	d	a	a	b	a	a	a	a	b	d	a	b	a	a	a	a
INSECTS AND SMALL ANIMALS	b	b	b	d	a	a	a	a	a	a	a	b	d	a	a	b	b	c	a
THE ENVIRONMENT																			
LANDSCAPE	a	b	b	c	d	d	d	a	d			b	d	d	d	b	d	b	d
TREES	a	b	b	c	d	d	d	a	d			b	d	d	d	b	d	b	d
VOLCANOES AND GEYSERS	a	b	b	c	d	d	d	a	d			b	d	d	d	b	d	b	d
WEATHER	a	c	b	c	d	d	d	b	d			b	d	d	d	b	d	b	d
SPECIAL CONDITIONS																			
ARCTIC	b	b	b	b	b	b	b	b	b	b	b	d	b	b	b	b	b	b	b
MOUNTAIN	b	b	b	b	b	b	b	b	b	b	b	d	b	b	b	b	b	b	b
DESERT	b	b	b	b	b	b	b	b	b	b	b	d	b	b	b	b	b	b	b
RAINFOREST AND SWAMP	b	b	b	b	b	b	b	b	b	b	b	d	b	b	b	b	b	b	b
SEA AND SHORE	b	b	b	b	b	b	b	b	b	b	b	d	b	b	b	b	b	b	b
UNDERWATER	d	d	d	d	a	a	d	d	d	d	a	d	a	d	a	a	c	d	c
NOCTURNAL	b	b	d	d	b	b	b	b	b	b	a	d	a	b	a	d	c	b	b
UNDERGROUND	a	b	d	d	b	b	b	b	b	b	b	d	a	b	a	b	c	b	b
AERIAL	d	d	d	d	d	d	d	d	d	d	a	d	d	d	d	b	d	d	d
STUDIO WORK																			
CAPTIVE SETS	a	a	d	d	a	a	b	a	b	b	b	a	b	b	a	b	a	a	a
ZOOS	b	b	b	b	b	c	d	b	d		b	d				b	d	d	d
INSECTS AND SMALL ANIMALS	a	a	d	d	a	a	a	a	a	a	a	b	a	a	b	a	a	a	a
PHOTOMICROGRAPHY	a	d	d	d	d	b	d	a	d	a	b	b	b	b	c	d	d	d	d
FOSSILS	a	b	d	d	a	a	a	a	a	a	b	a	a	b	c	a	a	a	a
MINERALS AND ROCKS	a	b	d	d	a	a	a	a	a	a	b	a	a	b	c	a	a	a	a
FLOWERS	a	a	d	d	a	a	b	a	b	a	b	a	b	b	a	a	a	a	a

Key: **a** ideal, b suitable, c can be used with a little difficulty, d unsuitable or unnecessary.

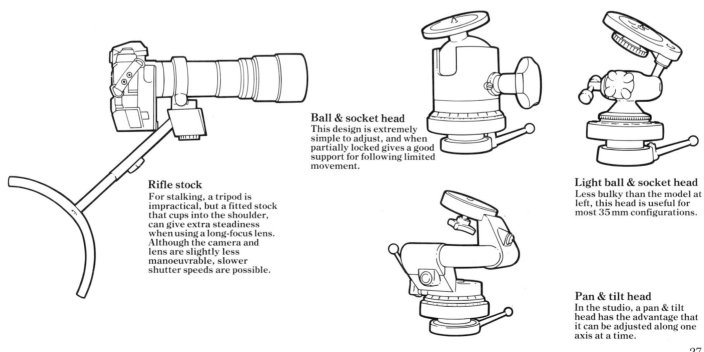

Rifle stock
For stalking, a tripod is impractical, but a fitted stock that cups into the shoulder, can give extra steadiness when using a long-focus lens. Although the camera and lens are slightly less manoeuvrable, slower shutter speeds are possible.

Ball & socket head
This design is extremely simple to adjust, and when partially locked gives a good support for following limited movement.

Light ball & socket head
Less bulky than the model at left, this head is useful for most 35 mm configurations.

Pan & tilt head
In the studio, a pan & tilt head has the advantage that it can be adjusted along one axis at a time.

Film and filters

With the exception of a few specific subjects where tradition and creative opportunities have helped black-and-white film to retain some importance, there is probably a greater bias towards colour in wildlife and nature photography than with any other category.

Ultimately, however, it is the final use of the photographs that determines which of the three major film types—colour transparency (also known as reversal), colour negative and black-and-white negative—is best suited to the subject. Colour transparencies are intended for projection, and are also the standard type used for publishing. If you intend to submit photographs to wildlife magazines or books, then transparencies are the first choice. They also have an important advantage over colour negatives where precise colour rendition is important, as when photographing flowers or butterflies. A colour transparency is a one step process, whereas colour negatives need to be printed, leaving the printer a surprisingly free interpretation of the image. This is not to say that transparency film is inherently more accurate—it is equally prone to colour imbalances due to manufacturing faults, poor storage or misuse.

If colour prints are the final form in which you want the image, then colour negatives give the highest quality. Prints can be made from transparencies, but lack the definition and subtle gradations of those from original negatives. The advantages of colour negatives are that many prints can be made from a single negative, and that negative material is more tolerant of exposure errors.

In all areas of photography, black-and-white is being used less and less, which is in many ways a pity, as in skilled hands it is capable of a great range of expression. Because the powerful sensory element of colour is absent, the form of the image becomes more important. Also, the tonal gradation, through an infinite series of greys, can be controlled with great precision, and it is not surprising that the one area of nature photography where personal expression is the key quality—landscape—is also a stronghold of black-and-white photography.

Film speed and grain

High resolution needs fine grain, and if it is essential to see every detail a film such as Kodachrome 25 or Panatomic-X is a good choice. However, fine grained films are inevitably slow, and for low light conditions, or when a very high shutter speed is needed, or when the maximum aperture of the lens is quite small (as with a very long focal length lens), they are not very suitable. Fast films—ASA 400 is the most common rating—have a coarser grain structure, so that resolution often has to be compromised in many active wildlife situations. Nevertheless, film manufacture is constantly improving, and films such as Ektachrome 400, Fujichrome 400, Kodacolor 400 and Tri-X can give remarkably good results, even when substantially enlarged.

Manufacturing differences

Between major makes of film of the same type

there are detailed differences. Ektachrome 400, for example, has a bluer cast than its competitor Fujichrome 400, but gives more natural results in tungsten lighting. The best approach to selection is to try different makes, compare the results, and then keep to the one you prefer. You will thus become familiar with the characteristics of one film under different conditions, and so have greater control. Among colour films, the most significant diference apart from speed and grain is between those that can be processed by yourself or at an independent laboratory, and 'non-substantive' films such as Kodachrome which can only be processed by the manufacturer. The latter have a less obvious grain structure. In black-and-white, the major difference is between conventional silver halide emulsions and the new chromogenic films, such as Ilford XP-1 and Agfapan Vario-XL, which can be used fast or slow, depending on the choice of the user.

Special films

Some films designed for specific types of photography are sensitive to different wavelengths or use dyes in unconventional ways. Black-and-white infrared film, when used with filters to cut out visible light, renders living vegetation almost white, blue sky black, and virtually eliminates haze in distant views. In its colour version, with the recommended yellow filters, healthy vegetation appears red, and this can be used to produce some unusual images. Photomicrography film has the high resolution and high contrast needed when working with semi-transparent subjects.

Filters

Although an increasing number of special effects filters are popular, in wildlife photography, where the actions and features of the subject are the main interest, there are few good reasons to use them. There are other filters, however, that have more specific applications and these are standard items of equipment.

Polarizing filters deepen blue skies and reduce reflections, such as from the surface of water.

Colour balancing filters adjust the film's response to the changing colour temperature of daylight—on a clear sunny day, illumination in the shade is distinctly blue, for example.

Colour correction filters overcome colour imbalances due to manufacturing deficiencies or abnormally long exposure.

Graduated density filters darken a part of the picture, such as the sky, without affecting the remainder.

When using black-and-white film, there are two particularly useful types of filter.

Polarizing filters reduce reflections.

Colour contrast filters block the light from specific colours and thus alter the relationship between tones. A yellow filter, for example, partly blocks the passage of blue light, and can be used to darken the appearance of a clear sky. Similarly, a green filter lightens the appearance of vegetation, and darkens the appearance of red flowers or red rocks.

35 mm: the small size of this cassette-loaded film requires great enlargement for even small prints. On the other hand, it allows for the most versatile and portable of all equipment.

6 × 6 cm: the standard medium format, using 120 roll film. Excellent enlargement is possible and the film is ideal for relatively static subjects.

70 mm: a sprocket film for use in medium format cameras. Fewer film changes are needed than with 120 roll film, and motor drives can be used.

6 × 7 cm: a medium format variation using a slightly greater length of 120 roll film for each frame. Many photographers find the oblong frame more satisfactory (J. P. Ferrero).

5 × 4 inch (12 × 9 cm): one of several sheet film sizes. The large image includes great detail and is ideal for great enlargement and minutely textured results. Heavy and awkward cameras restrict its use.

BASIC FIELDWORK

Wildlife photography requires two basic areas of skill—an understanding of wildlife behaviour and a thorough knowledge of camera handling. For successful photographs you have to work to perfect both. Even the most skilled fieldcraft is wasted if you make a mistake with one of the camera settings, while photographic expertise alone will not place you in the best position for a shot of an alert animal.

Because wildlife photography can, at its most professional, seem highly technical and time consuming, the first major step is to gain confidence. This only comes with success, so that initially it is important to choose a situation where the animals are easily accessible. At a zoo you familiarize yourself with animals, but they seldom behave naturally in confinement and you will not be able to learn very much that is useful. The ideal place to start is an established wildlife sanctuary, and some of the most interesting ones are briefly described at the end of the book. The quality of the access to the animals you can expect, however, varies throughout the world. Countries with large undeveloped regions and a commitment to conservation may have abundant wildlife reserves—the United States is a notable example.

Look for well organized reserves that are knowledgeably staffed and which balance the interests of wildlife and tourist. Parts of Florida's Everglades, for example, have nature trails in the form of boardwalks over the swamps. The animals are so accustomed to these that a large number of species can be seen at close quarters on even a casual walk.

With these ideal opportunities, you need not feel so anxious about simply getting any shot on film, and can work at making the best photographic use of your subject. If the animal is particularly approachable, experiment by altering your position for more effective composition and lighting. Fast reactions will eventually come with practice, so rather than risk early mistakes, take things slowly.

Spend time observing the animal. Watch its behaviour, learn its motives, and try to capture its most interesting actions. An animal engaged in an identifiable activity makes a more interesting photograph than a static portrait. Also, explore the relationship between the animal and its habitat. Vary your shots to include those that show the animal in detail, filling the frame, and also those that place it in its environment as a setting.

A bull moose fording the
Madison River in the
Yellowstone National Park,
Wyoming.

Stalking

Some of the best wildlife shots are those that reveal the behaviour rather than just the appearance of animals. A working knowledge of the species being photographed is very useful, enabling the photographer to plan expeditions to coincide with particular phases of an animal's behaviour. By choosing the rutting season and heading across country for the shade of a group of Eucalyptus trees where kangaroo are likely to congregate to escape the heat of the sun, the photographer achieved this shot of the famous sparring between male red kangaroos (J-P. Ferrero). Nikon with 400 mm lens, ASA 64, 1/125 sec at f8.

With all but the smallest creatures, there are two basic approaches to wildlife photography in the field—stalking and the use of hides. Stalking involves opportunistic shooting, and although it needs practice and patience to be successful, it does involve less equipment and physical preparation than hides. The results are less predictable, and there is usually a higher failure rate, but for most beginners the prospects of stalking are less daunting than the hardships of carrying, constructing and waiting in a hide. Its uncertainties also make it quite exciting.

Animal behaviour

The techniques of stalking with a camera are very similar to those of a hunter, and borrow a great deal from the behaviour of the animals themselves. Before all else, you should have a working knowledge of the animals you intend to photograph. You should know their pattern of activity and preferences, when and how they breed, their feeding habits, when they are most likely to be approachable—in short, their general range of behaviour throughout the year and throughout the day.

If this is not familiar to you, research will be needed. If you are about to work in an established and well organized wildlife reserve, there will probably be literature available locally and wardens or rangers who can help you. This applies to every field of wildlife photography, but in stalking it is the key to finding your subjects in the first place.

Many animals are particularly active around dawn and sunset. This will not only affect the time of day that you plan to go stalking, but also your choice of equipment and film—the lower light levels may mean that you need fast film and fast lenses. If your subject is an animal that feeds in groups rather than singly, you are less likely to come across it simply by wandering through a suitable part of its territory. In an area that has pronounced wet and dry seasons, such as the monsoon parts of Asia, the distribution of water will often determine how easy it is to approach the animals. In the dry season, water can be limited to just a few sites, and there will be greater wildlife concentrations at this time of year than at any other.

These are only a few examples of the kind of detail that can make the difference between success and failure. There is a large element of luck in all forms of wildlife photography, but knowing animal behaviour improves your chances greatly, particularly when stalking.

Most birds feed shortly after sunrise and before sunset, and many have regular feeding areas. Although deserted during the day, this marshland bordering the Myakka River in Florida was very likely to be visited early and late by white ibis. If you are familiar with the topography of the area, you can plot the likely locations in advance, as in this case. Feeding times have an additional advantage for the stalker, as the animals or birds are preoccupied. Here, it was possible to approach to within about 60 feet (19 metres) over fairly open ground.
Nikon with 400 mm lens, Kodachrome 64, 1/125 sec at f5.6.

During the dry season, water-holes can provide excellent photographic opportunities as animals (here, Burchell's zebra in a parched East African game reserve) will almost certainly congregate there in substantial numbers (S. and D. Simon).
Pentax with 200 mm lens, Kodachrome 64, 1/250 sec at f8.

Stalking/understanding animals

One of the major concerns in wildlife photography is to avoid being noticed. You may have to pay special attention to noise, movement or smell, depending on the species you are trying to photograph.

How animals and birds perceive

As a rule, the particular sense that an animal or bird relies on must have evolved to suit its way of life. Knowing something about its habits and patterns of activity will suggest whether it relies on hearing, sight or smell. Active predators, for example, usually need good vision for the final stages of capture. Animals living in areas with limited visibility, such as thick forest, commonly use their hearing more than their vision.

Birds

Vision Practically all birds have much better sight than humans. Most important of all, their resolution of detail tends to be higher; a typical hawk has eyes with the retinal cells packed together eight times more densely than a human. Most species can distinguish colour differences, although nocturnal birds, such as owls, sacrifice much of this in favour of good vision in dim light. The majority also have a wide angle of view, with the eyes situated well to the side of the head. Some, such as ducks, have 360° vision.

What is still not known, however, is how the visual information is processed by the bird's brain. Nevertheless, from practical experience it seems that most birds, like most animals, tend to ignore motionless objects. Movement is a key element in the way they perceive, hence the importance of 'freezing' when stalking if your prey catches sight of you.

Hearing Most birds have better hearing than humans, and nocturnal species tend to rely on it quite heavily. However, in flight the rush of air and the bird's own wing movements probably reduce sensitivity to sound. There is some evidence that birds sense extremely low frequency sound, which can carry over great distances.

Smell As a rule, the sense of smell tends to be of little importance to birds, probably because in flight and at any altitude above the ground faint smells are impossible to detect. Exceptions to this rule are ground-dwelling birds such as the wild turkey, which has high scent sensitivity.

Mammals

Vision Most animals are at least partly nocturnal, and tend not to rely as much on sight as on other senses. Additionally, except for the higher primates and some rodents, they are virtually colour-blind. There are, however, significant exceptions, particularly those mammals, such as cats, that use speed to capture prey or those that use it to escape, such as deer. It is helpful to learn the characteristics of individual species before relying on their poor eyesight for your concealment.

Hearing Hearing is nearly always well developed, and animals with large cupped ears, such as deer, have very good directional sensitivity.

Smell Practically all mammals have such a strong sense of smell that it is out of all comparison with that of human beings. Whereas our olfactory tissue occupies a small part of the upper nasal passage, the tissue of most mammals is folded and convoluted so as to expose a very large area to the air—in some species, the olfactory tissue surface is several times greater than the outside body area. As a rule, mammals use their sense of smell more than any other sense.

Different birds have different visual capabilities, and the photographer will improve his chances by appreciating the characteristics of his particular quarry.

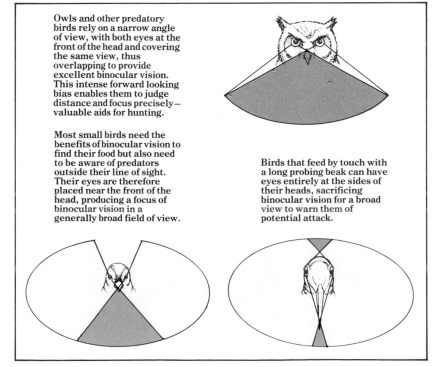

Owls and other predatory birds rely on a narrow angle of view, with both eyes at the front of the head and covering the same view, thus overlapping to provide excellent binocular vision. This intense forward looking bias enables them to judge distance and focus precisely—valuable aids for hunting.

Most small birds need the benefits of binocular vision to find their food but also need to be aware of predators outside their line of sight. Their eyes are therefore placed near the front of the head, producing a focus of binocular vision in a generally broad field of view.

Birds that feed by touch with a long probing beak can have eyes entirely at the sides of their heads, sacrificing binocular vision for a broad view to warn them of potential attack.

The visual perception of mammals such as these Asian buffalo, photographed in Assam, India, is limited. Their hearing and sense of smell, however, are acute. They tend to establish a mental safety perimeter and as long as the photographer remains beyond this minimum distance they will not bolt, even though fully aware of his or her presence (J-P. Ferrero).
Nikon with 400 mm lens, ASA 25, 1/125 sec at f5.6.

When stalking birds, it is nearly always essential to have cover, as most have keen eyesight and can scan a large part of their surroundings without moving their heads. This reddish egret perched on the branches of a mangrove tree in the Caribbean was photographed through a light screen of leaves. With a long focus lens at full aperture, the leaves formed effective cover without spoiling the image.
Hasselblad with 500 mm lens, ASA 64, 1/250 sec at f8.

This barred owl (left) was discovered by chance perching on a branch in Corkscrew Swamp, Florida. Although very shy of humans, owls do not have very good daylight vision and can be approached as long as complete silence is maintained.
Nikon with 400 mm lens, ASA 64, 1/60 sec at f5.6.

Stalking/The technique 1

The pale skin of the face and the backs of the hands can make a photographer very conspicuous to wildlife, even at great distances.

A dark woollen helmet can reduce the visibility to a limited extent.

Streaks of dark make-up break up the light areas of hands and face, merging with the background and providing effective camouflage.

Complete make-up is more effective still, but is perhaps only suitable for the extremely dedicated.

Following the example of military practice, complete camouflage – with netting and foliage – can turn the photographer into a walking hide. In the right circumstances, this approach can be very effective indeed.

The techniques of stalking mimic the actions of many animals, and you can improve your own fieldcraft by watching the way, for example, that a deer moves and behaves. Its actions are motivated by the need for self-defence but it still uses stealth and alertness in ways that you can copy.

To begin with, prepare yourself so that you do not appear conspicuous. If you are particularly dedicated, proper camouflage may enable you to approach your subject very closely, although you should be aware of exactly what the particular animal can perceive.

On most occasions you may not want or be able to go to such lengths. Nevertheless, follow the basic principles of avoiding anything bright or gaudy. Use drab clothing and wear nothing that is likely to glint in sunlight. If you wear spectacles,

make sure that any bright metal parts are taped over. If you have a fair complexion, your face can be surprisingly conspicuous at a distance. In cold weather, a woollen balaclava can cover much of it, but otherwise you might consider putting on a few streaks of dark make-up or even dirt.

Scent can be a problem with many mammals, though seldom with birds. One of the main elements in human scent is butyric acid, and dogs, for example, are about a million times more sensitive to this than human beings. Clothing helps a little, but more important is to move your body around as little as possible, and to stay downwind from the animals you are stalking. Avoid using any strong artificial scent, such as deodorants, aftershave or even mouthwash.

One of the basic stalking techniques is a smooth,

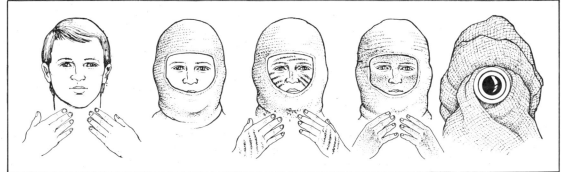

Giraffe and other large subjects may not require a close approach for a dramatic shot. The inclusion of the setting as they were feeding in the late evening even added drama to the scene (S. and D. Simon). Pentax with 180 mm lens, Kodachrome 64, 1/250 sec at f8.

noiseless walk. Most walking involves jerky, unnecessary movement—the torso moves from side to side, arms swing, feet slap on the ground. All these actions have to be avoided when stalking and replaced with a more economical, gliding motion. Watch a domestic cat stalking a bird—when it moves, it does so smoothly, and its head and most of its body remain still. It appears to glide forward, and unless you are paying direct attention, you may not even notice that the cat is moving at all.

Practise rolling your feet—place the heel on the ground, and then roll the remainder of the foot in a curve, using the outside of the foot and the ball. It may feel unnatural at first, but it is smooth and quiet. Choose carefully where you place your feet, avoiding dead leaves and twigs. At the beginning, this may mean that you spend a lot of time looking at the ground and missing opportunities, but with practice you can learn to use your peripheral vision while looking ahead.

If you do snap a twig, freeze. Any animals nearby will be alerted by the noise, but the natural reaction of most animals is not to bolt immediately but to stay still and observant, waiting for any further sign that a predator is nearby. To be safe, wait a few minutes. After this time, most animals will have satisfied themselves that the noise was a false alarm and return to their activity.

Keeping still is probably the greatest skill in concealment. Practise it consciously, and you may be surprised at how difficult it is to avoid small movements, jerks and twitches. Absolute stillness often produces a physical strain, and this alone can start nervous actions, like tapping fingers and shifting to more comfortable positions.

If you can learn to stay absolutely motionless for several minutes, you will have a great advantage in the field. Stalking is not all movement, and there are occasions when the best stalking method may be simply to sit quietly. Choose a comfortable position and concentrate on blending with your surroundings. You may even be rewarded by the close approach of an animal that has failed to recognize you. Keeping still has the extra advantage of allowing your scent molecules to dissipate in the air, making you less noticeable to animals with a good sense of smell.

Lightly wooded country, with frequent clearings and enough room to walk easily between trees, is a particularly common stalking environment. Moving from tree to tree makes the best use of the available cover, and by standing motionless it is quite easy to blend in with their vertical pattern. A more acute problem, particularly with an animal that has good hearing, such as this white-tailed deer, is the noise of walking over forest litter —dead leaves and twigs— which can only be solved by watching where you put your feet and by moving smoothly. Nikon with 180 mm lens, Kodachrome 64, 1/60 sec at f2.8.

Some animals allow a close approach, although it is important to be able to anticipate their behaviour to take advantage of this. This Australian sea-lion was photographed as it cried in defence of the pup (J.-P. Ferrero). Nikon with 24 mm lens, Kodachrome 64, 1/125 sec at f11.

Preoccupied with the prey, this lioness could be approached more closely than otherwise—from the safety of a jeep (S. and D. Simon). Pentax with 180 mm lens, Kodachrome 64, 1/250 sec at f8.

Stalking/the technique 2

Open ground stalking

Approaching an animal across open ground is the most difficult problem of all. Even with great skill, it is very risky, and there are no certain methods. Accept that there is a strong possibility that you will not be able to get close enough, but try some of the following tricks.

1. Use the animal's own pattern of activity by moving only when it is busy. When feeding, for example, most animals pause frequently to check their surroundings. At these times, stop moving, and start again only when the animal is preoccupied once more.

2. Move directly forward, but very smoothly, without any unnecessary movement, to create the illusion that you are not moving at all.

3. If the animal spots you, and is suspicious, start moving to one side. Avoid any eye contact. With luck, it may think that you, as a potential predator, have not seen it and that for now it is safe.

In the example shown here, the problem is to approach some deer feeding in a water meadow in wooded country. Before beginning the approach, plan the route to make use of the available cover—boulders and fallen trees. Avoid being silhouetted against the skyline and stay in the shadows where possible. A decision has to be taken about how close to try to go. It may be wiser to use a long lens rather than pushing forward the final yards.

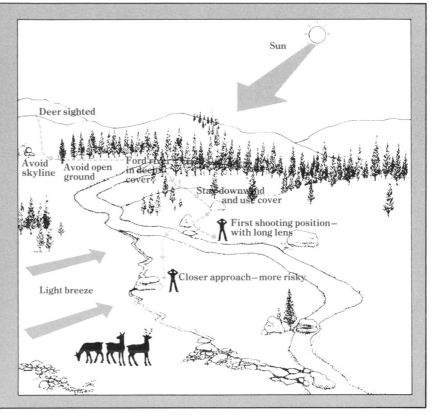

The camera introduces an additional problem in stalking—it is noisy, unnatural and has bright reflective parts. There is not a great deal that you can do to reduce the noise. A blimp, or soundproof container, obstructs camera handling, and you really do need rapid access to the camera's controls when stalking. On the other hand, it is a good idea to tape over the chrome parts of the equipment to make them less noticeable. It is doubly important to stay in the shade and avoid the risk of sunlight glinting off the lens surface or other bright, reflective parts of the camera.

If you are choosing a camera with stalking in mind, consider noise and ease of operation—ideally it should be quiet and rapid. A rangefinder camera, such as the Leica, fulfils both of these needs, but unfortunately has the great disadvantage of not showing the exact picture in the viewfinder. With a long-focus lens there is too great a risk of incorrect framing or incorrect focusing for it to be a serious contender. Among 35mm single lens reflex cameras there is a noticeable difference in noisiness, but most makes are well suited to this kind of work. Larger formats, such as 6×6cm, are much bulkier and usually have louder shutters.

Be prepared for instant shooting. The uncertainties of stalking mean that you must seize picture opportunities at once, and this requires that everything on the camera, from the choice of lens to aperture setting, must be worked out in advance. You may have no more than a second or two in which to take a shot and there could be no time even to adjust the exposure, let alone change the lens.

The subject's own activities can help the photographer. When occupied with some purposeful activity, most birds and animals are less likely to notice the approach of an intruder. In this example, a great egret was busy gathering nesting materials, and when it paused to check the surroundings the photographer stayed still, moving only when it resumed its activities. Intervening leaves provided cover. Nikon with 300 mm lens, Ektachrome 64, 1/250 sec at f8.

Approaching a wary animal when there is little cover can be difficult. These red kangaroo, photographed in New South Wales, Australia, were stalked slowly in a car over open ground. A long lens was used so the approach would not have to be too close (J-P. Ferrero). Nikon with 400 mm lens, ASA 64, 1/250 sec at f8.

Stalking/choice of lens

Choosing the right lens for the situation is never easy. The kind of terrain that you are in will give you some idea of what focal length you are likely to need. Long-focus lenses are nearly always best because of the difficulties of approaching most wildlife closely, but there is always the risk of an unexpected encounter right in front of you. One answer is to carry a second camera, loaded and pre-set, with a normal or moderate long-focus lens, or you may prefer to use a good zoom lens.

Another factor that may prevent you from using a really long lens—such as a 400mm for a 35mm camera—is the light level. If you are in a forest, or if sunset is approaching, a long lens may not have a sufficiently large aperture. Long-focus lenses rarely exceed f5.6, which may require a shutter speed too slow for hand-held use. Using a faster film is a partial solution, although fast films usually have more noticeable graininess. Your final choice of lens and film will depend on the particular situation as well as your ability to take hand-held shots at slow speeds.

One way of anticipating different situations is to carry two cameras, each with a different long-focus lens. The first choice would probably be a long telephoto lens, shown here fitted to a camera body with a motor drive. However, for unexpectedly close encounters, and for low light conditions in shade or at the end of the day, a medium telephoto lens is also at the ready. With interchangeable lenses, an additional precaution is to use one camera body with a fine grained film and the other with a fast film.

For animals that will allow a close approach, such as this Indian monkey with her baby, above, a moderately long focal length—between 150 mm and 200 mm on a 35 mm camera—will give the best chance of good framing in most situations. As there is often no chance to change lenses when you come across an animal suddenly, the choice of lens has to be anticipated in accordance with the likely subjects.

For the majority of stalking situations, a telephoto lens with a long focal length is the most important item of equipment. Catadioptric mirror lenses, which also have long focal lengths, are more awkward to hold by hand, and their fixed aperture is inconvenient when adjustments have to be made quickly. The small group of chamois in the Alps at far left, for example, would certainly not tolerate a close approach, which would in any case, be difficult and slow over the rough and exposed terrain. A 400 mm lens on a 35 mm camera was essential (J-P. Ferrero).

The baby fur seal photographed in New Zealand, left, is an example of an animal which can be closely approached. Coupled with its relatively large size, this makes the use of a standard lens (50 mm or 55 mm on a 35 mm camera), with its close approximation of human vision, possible (J-P. Ferrero).

Stalking/long-focus technique

It is immensely valuable to be able to use a camera at slow shutter speeds, and you can improve your performance with practice. With a 400 mm lens on a 35 mm camera, most manufacturers recommend that a tripod be used at speeds less than 1/500 sec, but by holding the camera in certain ways and by controlling your breathing, you will find that 1/125 sec is quite manageable. On occasions, you may even manage a sharp photograph at 1/60 sec.

At these speeds it is unwise to rely too much on your ability to hold the camera steady, but by taking a number of shots you can increase your chances of getting a clear photograph. This 'bracketing' is a professional trick that is worth adopting—if the picture is likely to be a good one, consider film as cheap. Remember, however, that even at 1/125 sec, any but the slowest movements of an animal will record as a blur, so you should take care to wait for moments when the animal is almost still.

Using a long-focus lens is similar to firing a rifle—steadiness and timing are all-important. Bulky tripods are not essential, for a tree or rock can also offer support—either jam the camera up to the surface, or lean your body against it. When there is no support, it is steadier to kneel, resting an elbow on the knee, or to lie down.

If there is no time to get into one of these posi-tions, put one leg in front of the other, lean forward and brace your elbows against your chest. Try out various positions like these before going out in the field, and notice how some stances give you better balance than others. Also practise controlling your breathing. It is steadiest to draw a fairly deep breath, then to exhale slightly just as you squeeze –never jab–the shutter release.

Having selected the equipment, and knowing the limitations under which you can use it, antici-pate the shots you are hoping for. Always cock the shutter immediately after taking a shot so that you are prepared for the next. Apart from this, there are three critical camera settings—shutter speed, aperture and focus. On most occasions when stalking an animal, you will need the fastest shutter speed possible. This will be determined by the aperture setting, which will normally be at its widest. Although a large aperture inevitably means shallow depth of field, particularly with a long-focus lens, this will not necessarily be a dis-advantage. The subject will stand out more clearly from its surroundings, and intervening foliage will become less obtrusive, even an out-of-focus blur. Remember that a single lens reflex camera dis-plays the image in the viewfinder at maximum aperture, and the actual photograph may look more confused than you see it.

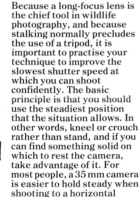

Because a long-focus lens is the chief tool in wildlife photography, and because stalking normally precludes the use of a tripod, it is important to practise your technique to improve the slowest shutter speed at which you can shoot confidently. The basic principle is that you should use the steadiest position that the situation allows. In other words, kneel or crouch rather than stand, and if you can find something solid on which to rest the camera, take advantage of it. For most people, a 35 mm camera is easier to hold steady when shooting to a horizontal format rather than a vertical one.

Standing: the least stable position. Place one leg in front of the other for improved balance.

Kneeling: rest your elbow on your knee for support. Pause to steady your grip after focusing.

Squatting: a stable position with practice. Both elbows can rest on the knees to support the camera.

Improvised support: rocks, logs and other potential supports can give cover when stalking as well as providing stable camera platforms.

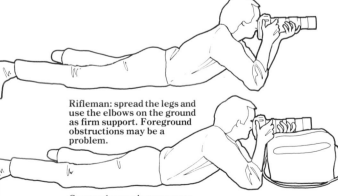

Rifleman: spread the legs and use the elbows on the ground as firm support. Foreground obstructions may be a problem.

Camera bag: using a camera bag or any other available object can give useful support when shooting from a prone position.

Shoulder stock: specially designed pistol operated long-focus lenses can give a steady hold—particularly when used with a shoulder stock.

Good lighting conditions help when using long-focus lenses. Relatively fast shutter speeds can be combined with large apertures to avoid the risk of camera shake. These nesting gannets would not have allowed closer approach, and the cliff they inhabited in any case made shooting difficult. Nikon with 400 mm lens, ASA 64, 1/125 sec at f8.

Where the setting makes it possible to silhouette a subject, shooting into the sun makes handling a long-focus lens simple. These open-billed storks suited this treatment—the gap between their bills shows up best in outline—and the high shutter speed and small aperture solved the problems of steadiness and depth of field. To obtain a strong silhouette with some tone in the sky, as in this photograph, follow the camera's TTL meter reading. For more detail in the subject, increase the exposure by one or two stops. Avoid looking directly at the sun through the lens—the magnification increases the risk of damaging the retina. Nikon with 400 mm lens, Kodachrome 64, 1/500 sec at f32.

Stalking/exposure

When the light levels are low, subjects in uncomplicated settings such as this colony of painted storks in Bharatpur, India, can be photographed against the rising or setting sun. Although sunsets and sunrises have become photographic clichés, the results can still be worthwhile if care is taken over the composition. Nikon with 180 mm lens, Kodachrome 64, 1/125 sec at f4.

A through-the-lens (TTL) metering system is a great advantage when you have to work quickly, but even this can be too slow for some surprise situations. By anticipating sudden opportunities, however, you can pre-set the exposure. If you are stalking in woodland, for example, there may be no more than three general levels of brightness—deep shade, open shade and sunlight. As you walk along, test the exposure settings for each so that, without thinking, you can turn from one to the other at a moment's notice. Keep the shutter speed and aperture set in the most likely combina-

tion. This improves your chances of a good sudden shot by cutting out two of the processes of setting the camera, leaving only the element of focus.

Some cameras have electronic shutters that automatically adjust to the light conditions, giving automatic exposure control. These can be immensely valuable, but remember that their metering systems work best with an average scene. When photographing a small animal brightly lit against a large dark background, for example, automatic metering is likely to overexpose the subject.

Light levels in the shade at
dawn or dusk are so low that
a long-focus lens needs either
a firm support or fast film. In
the case of this limpkin
foraging among cypress roots
in the Suwannee River, the
camera position was a small
wooden jetty. By resting the
lens against a post, and
waiting for moments when
the bird was still, it was
possible to shoot at 1/30 sec
and still have a sharp image.
Nikon with 400 mm lens,
Kodachrome 64, 1/30 sec at
f5.6.

Because the majority of
wildlife subjects that can be
stalked are at their most
active around sunrise and
sunset, low light levels are a
common working condition.
This makes it particularly
important to be able to hold
the camera steady at slow
shutter speeds and also calls
for careful positioning to be
able to make the best use of
the available light. In this
example, about half an hour
before sunset, the approach
was deliberately made from a
direction that would have the
sun to the side of and slightly
behind the deer. The rim of
light around the side of the
animal's head defines it more
strongly than if the sun were
behind the camera, so
making it possible to use a
faster shutter speed.
Nikon with 400 mm lens,
Kodachrome 64, 1/125 sec
at f5.6.

Stalking/focusing and shooting

Focusing can usually be achieved rapidly and without thinking, but with a long focus lens larger hand movements are needed and this takes time. Once again, anticipate situations and have the lens set in advance at an approximation of the required distance. On open plains you will probably be working at long distances, and the focusing ring will be best left at infinity. In forest or scrub, however, you are likely to come across animals at closer range. Be completely familiar with the direction the lens must be turned to focus nearer or further away—it is surprisingly easy, in the heat of the moment, to turn the focusing ring in the wrong direction.

After each sequence of shots, check the film counter. If you have only a few frames left, it may be wise to rewind and start with a fresh roll. The slight wastage is preferable to running out of film in the middle of an exciting burst of action. The number of frames you are likely to need depends on the kind of animal you are stalking. If there is a strong possibility of a useful sequence of pictures—a pride of lions interested in a herd of zebra, for example, could mean an imminent chase—you should make sure that you have at least a dozen frames left. It is not wasteful to replace a partly used roll of film if this gains you a good picture.

Choosing the moment to shoot is the final, and critical, decision. If the animal has good hearing, the noise of the shutter may mean that you will only be able to take one shot. There is no hard and fast rule. In some situations it may be safe to start shooting before you or the animal is in the best position. In others you may feel the risk is too great. Unless you find it too distracting, keep both eyes open when you are shooting to give you a valuable preview of activity and to warn of potential obstructions outside the picture frame. This is the moment that dermines success, and it is here that the final skill, that of judgement, is needed.

In a rapidly changing situation, it may not be sufficient just to preset the aperture and shutter speed (above). Moving across the field of view, and kicking up clouds of dust, this herd of elephants in Kenya called for a changing exposure setting. Under these conditions, through-the-lens metering is the most reliable guide (S. and D. Simon). Pentax with 120 mm lens, ASA 64, 1/250 sec at f4.

Although automatic metering often reduces flexibility by preventing rapid exposure changes to compensate for unusually dark or light backgrounds, when fast reactions are needed it can be invaluable. There may be the opportunity for only one or two shots, as in the case of this jungle cat with its freshly caught prey in Israel, and what little reaction time there is needs to be spent focusing and framing (J-P. Ferrero). Nikon with 400 mm lens, ASA 64, 1/250 sec at f8.

Using foliage as a screen is a standard technique in terrain that is at least partly wooded (top right). For this photograph of an Indian darter, the focus was first set while the bird was only just visible through the trees. The shutter was released as the photographer moved to bring the bird into full view.
Nikon with 180 mm lens, ASA 64, 1/500 sec at f5.6.

On the exposed slopes of a mountain in Glacier National Park, Montana (above), there were two light levels—sun and shade. The exposure would have been wrong if the TTL reading had been followed: the meter would have over-compensated for the dark background, and the goat would have been overexposed.
Nikon with 180 mm lens, ASA 64, 1/250 sec at f11.

Stalking/shooting from vehicles

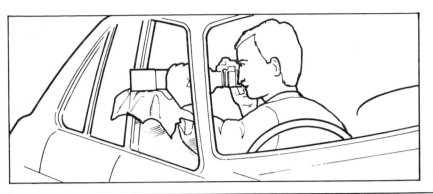

A car or four-wheel drive vehicle may not at first seem like the ideal cover for stalking. It is noisy, smelly, looks completely unnatural, and can only be driven on reasonably smooth surfaces. But at least it does not look like a predator, and many animals and birds do not associate cars with people. In some places, familiarity with moving vehicles has removed fear, so that roadside photography from a car window offers simple but rewarding opportunities. In the game parks of East Africa, for example, it is one of the best methods and is the only safe way of photographing many of the animals.

From the point of view of the wildlife, a car has certain characteristics. One of them is that it normally moves, and another is its engine noise. Stop either of these two suddenly and your subject may take fright. If you spot an animal or bird as you are driving along, come to a halt gently, and switch off the engine before you stop.

Unless it is unavoidable, do not open the car door to get out–you may be ignored inside the vehicle, but once outside you are a recognizable threat. Instead, work from the window, resting your camera on a beanbag or a jacket. This can even be a better support than a tripod, and is certainly faster to set up. When using this method, it is important to switch off the engine. There is less risk of alerting the animal if the car is left running, but the vibrations will ruin the shot.

When driving through wooded country, large birds are surprisingly often spotted in the trees, apparently oblivious to the vehicle's approach. By taking advantage of just such an opportunity, this rare crested serpent eagle (above) was photographed in India (J-P. Ferrero).
Nikon with 400 mm lens, ASA 25, 1/30 sec at f5.6.

Cars are not the only vehicles that can be used to approach timid animals. When travelling by boat on the Periyar lake in southern India, these wild elephants (right) were photographed as they moved slowly off towards the trees (J-P. Ferrero).
Mamiya RB67 with 180 mm lens, ASA 64, 1/250 sec at f8.

Although an unusual form of transport, in some parts of the world an elephant is a vehicle nonetheless. In swampy ground in Kaziranga, Assam, India, this rhinoceros (far right) could be clearly seen through the reeds from the high camera platform of the elephant's back. it would also have been extremely difficult terrain to cross by any other method (J-P. Ferrero).
Nikon with 105 mm lens, ASA 25, 1/125 at f4.

A car can be an effective means of approaching wild animals (left). Use the window, partly wound down, as a support, with a cloth or bean-bag to provide a soft surface to rest the camera on. Switch off the motor to stop vibrations.

In marshes, poling a flat-bottomed punt is one of the quietest and most efficient ways of moving around, and is certainly better than wading, which can be very noisy. By allowing the punt to drift gently through the reeds, it was possible to approach these nesting painted storks to within a few metres. As with other vehicles, the smooth movement appears less threatening than a single human figure.
Nikon with 180 mm lens, ASA 64, 1/125 sec at f5.6.

Stalking/motor drive

A motor drive allows the wildlife photographer to react quickly and fire off a large number of frames. In order not to waste any of this precious advantage, all the camera settings should be, as far as possible, preset, so that you can start shooting without hesitating. The unedited take opposite shows how the technique can work: the location was northern Scotland in late autumn, and even using a fast, ASA 400 film, the light levels on a cloudy afternoon were low enough to be marginal, particularly with a long-focus lens with a maximum aperture of f5.6. The encounter with the stag was sudden, and there was no time to make adjustments. With a moving animal nearly filling the frame, 1/250 sec was the slowest shutter speed to be of any use, and so, irrespective of the light level, this was the setting used.

The motor drive has a special place in wildlife photography, and particularly in stalking. After the basic camera and long-focus lens, it could be considered the most important piece of equipment in the wildlife photographer's case.

Substituting rapid mechanical operation for laborious manual triggering and film winding makes the camera more flexible, better suited to handling the sudden, fast and often unpredictable reactions of wild animals. Motor drives and the more basic automatic winders are now available for most camera systems. They have also become lighter and more compact than the early models, reducing the bulk that was once their chief drawback. Stalking inevitably requires fast reactions, not only up to the moment of finding the animal, but also in adjusting focus, exposure, viewpoint and composition. Anything that frees the photographer's attention from the mechanical actions of winding on is valuable at the crucial moment of shooting.

Most motor drive units can be set either to take single shots or for continuous operation. The danger of continuous operation is that you can quickly use up a roll of film without being aware of it, leaving yourself without enough frames for the next encounter. Many wildlife photographers find that the single shot setting is adequate, unless they are expecting events to happen very quickly. An alternative is to leave the motor drive set for continuous operation and to obtain single shots where required by using the trigger lightly. This takes some practice, but offers a good compromise solution.

When stalking a particularly skittish or alert animal, use the motor drive with discretion. It is even noisier than a manual release, and will startle the animal more easily. It often happens that, as soon as the shutter is released, the animal will react and bolt, and judgement is needed to decide the best moment to shoot. When an animal takes fright, it is bound to head in the opposite direction and will present an unattractive view. When the animal is at rest and still unaware of you, you may find it useful to take one shot for insurance with the

manual shutter release before using the motor drive with its additional noise risk.

The continuous picture sequence is the motor drive's special reward. With the unit set for continuous operation, shooting rates of up to five frames per second are frequently possible. With many motor drives, there is a choice of shooting rates, although the higher speeds are limited to the faster shutter settings. Some motor drives are available with even faster rates, although these tend to require the mirror to be locked up before operation. One new system which promises faster practical rates has a fixed mirror that also passes sufficient light through to the film.

Despite the fact that a motor driven camera behaves in many ways like a ciné camera, do not expect miracles from it. Even at five frames per second, only a small proportion of a fast moving animal's actions will be recorded. At high speeds with a motor drive, you can quickly use up a roll of film, so unless you fit a bulky 250-frame back, it is best to fire short bursts at the peak of action.

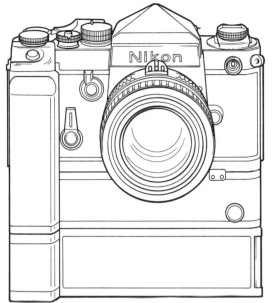

Modern motor drives are manufactured to be compatible with a particular camera system. The Nikon model shown here has single shot and sequence operation up to a speed of five frames per second.

The complete sequence of the fleeing stag produced only a few good shots. Accurate focusing and exposure were both problems. In order to ensure the best possible processing of the roll as it had been shot, a 'clip test' (left) was used. Having finished the roll, another was exposed of the same scene without the stag, at the same exposure setting. An accurate measurement of the exposure suggested that it would give results that were slightly too dark. The laboratory was therefore asked to 'push-process' a short section of the second film (over-developing it) to test the results. This gave good results and indicated the correct processing for the roll with the stag.

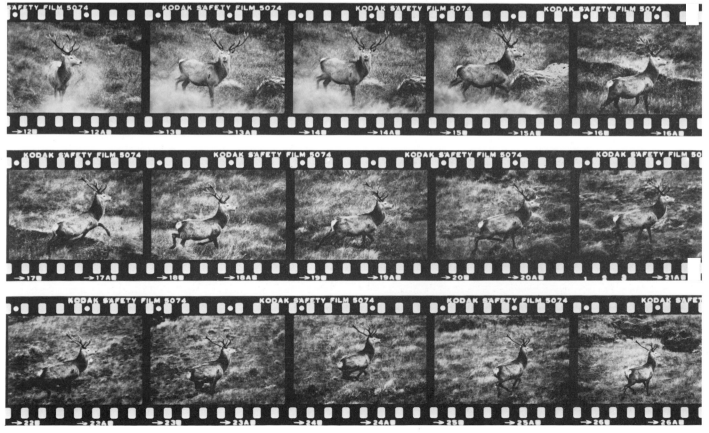

Stalking/moving subjects

This red kangaroo, photographed in New South Wales, Australia, was travelling very fast. In order to show the kangaroo's unique bounding motion, a moderately fast shutter speed had to be used to freeze the animal's movements within the frame. Panning— following the kangaroo in the viewfinder before and after the shot—helped with the achievement of accurate framing and also blurred the background to create a sense of fast movement, without which the shot would have appeared static and unrepresentative of the scene (J-P. Ferrero). Nikon with 200 mm lens, ASA 64, 1/250 sec at f5.6.

Another example of the panning technique used to suggest movement—here an emu. Animals will nearly always run away from the camera when startled, presenting an unattractive rear view. In this case, the photographer remained hidden while an assistant approached the animal from one side. It then fled across the field of view (J-P. Ferrero). Nikon with 200 mm lens, ASA 64, 1/250 sec at f8.

Being able to photograph rapidly moving subjects is a necessary skill when stalking. Although an animal's bolting from the camera presents an unappealing view, there are occasions–when chasing prey, for example–when it might cross the field of view and so offer a worthwhile opportunity for photography.

Capturing a sharp image depends on matching the shutter setting to the speed at which the animal crosses the picture frame. The larger the animal's image in the viewfinder, the more rapid its actions will appear, and the faster the shutter speed you will need. The natural tendency when photographing any moving subject is to follow the movement in the viewfinder. Known as panning, this technique nearly always offers the best solution, making it possible to freeze most of any large animal's actions. The background, by contrast, becomes blurred at all but the fastest shutter speeds, adding a bonus to the sense of motion.

In fact, the impression of speed is every bit as important as a sharp image of the subject. Were it possible to record every element of the picture–the animal and its surroundings–in frozen detail, the static result would almost certainly not be as effective as one with the characteristic streaks of a blurred background. On some occasions, particu-

A quite different way of handling movement is to abandon a literal, representational approach, and aim instead for the sensation of wing or limb movements. By panning this seagull against a dark background of trees and exposing for one second, the effect is a pattern of blurred curves. Because of its special nature, this technique can only be used occasionally. Light subjects against dark backgrounds give the clearest images.
Nikon with 400 mm lens, ASA 64, 1 sec at f32.

When photographing waterfalls, a slow shutter speed can be used to give some sense of the moving water. Here, a compromise setting of 1/30 sec gave some streaking to the spray passing over the rocks, whereas an even slower speed would have lost the character of the water altogether.
Nikon with 400 mm lens, ASA 64, 1/30 sec at f16.

larly with an instantly recognizeable animal, you may even feel justified in using such a slow shutter speed that the leg movements or wing beats are themselves converted into a streaked image. The highly impressionistic effect of using shutter speeds as low as a second gains in sensation what it loses in content.

For most practical purposes, however, recording a large and satisfactorily sharp image of a fast moving animal calls for a shutter speed of at least 1/500 sec. This, together with the lighting conditions and the maximum aperture of the lens, will determine the speed of film that you need. As you will probably have to work with an open aperture, accurate focusing is essential, and the techniques for this are described on the following pages. An additional and important skill is anticipation – judging the path of an animal and where it is likely to enter cover. The more alert you are to the surroundings before you start to shoot, the better prepared you will be.

The best equipment for this kind of work is that which offers the fastest access to the camera controls and allows eye-level viewing. A 35 mm single lens reflex camera, particularly if fitted with through the lens metering and a motor drive, has no rival in this field.

Stalking/birds in flight 1

Photographing birds in mid-air is the most severe test of camera dexterity. Complete familiarity with all the camera's controls is only the starting point, for the photography of flying birds combines many special problems of technique. Shutter speeds must be high, the subject is constantly moving and often changing direction, and long lenses are usually needed if the bird is to appear large in the frame. Above all, split-second reactions are necessary, because the moment for the best shot may be a fleeting one, easily lost if all the camera and lens settings have to be laboriously adjusted in response to it.

You can improve your chances of success by anticipating the path that the bird will follow. It can also be a good idea to choose a windy day, when birds that are flying into the wind will be moving more slowly.

Choice of equipment

The best opportunity of capturing the image of a bird in flight seldom repeats itself, so be prepared, with the right equipment to hand. Viewfinder cameras are generally unsuitable because precise framing is essential. Single lens reflex cameras are easily the most appropriate, although only those with line of sight viewfinders and rectified images should be used. This includes the standard 35mm type but not roll-film cameras fitted with waist-level viewfinders. These reverse the image and

are completely unsuited to following movement. Prism viewfinder attachments are available for some roll-film SLRs. Their bulk, however, generally makes them more difficult to use than the 35mm SLR for this purpose.

Because single flying birds are normally photographed at a distance, long-focus lenses are needed. However, even though it may seem natural to try and fill the frame with the bird, very long focal lengths are not necessarily a good idea. The longer the lens, the less convenient it is to handle and the smaller its maximum aperture will be. Following a fast flying bird with a 600mm lens is not easy, even though the panning motion helps to steady it in the hand. The image is magnified 12 times more than a normal lens, and even a slight vibration of the wrist will throw the bird out of frame. In addition, on most such lenses the focusing ring has to travel a greater distance, making changes awkward. The maximum aperture may be as little as f8, and high shutter speeds will then only be possible by using a high speed, and therefore grainy, film.

Much depends on the circumstances, but many photographers prefer to use a less powerful lens— say 300mm on a 35mm camera—with the certainty of recording a sharp image, even if it is rather small. A negative can easily be cropped at the printing stage, and even with transparencies this is possible, particularly if the picture is being repro-

As birds in flight are usually photographed from ground level, it is advisable to be close to a nesting or feeding site, where the birds will be flying relatively low. With a nesting colony, or any circumstance where birds are found in large flocks, the chances of success are much greater, as individuals tend to follow similar flight paths, giving a number of opportunities to practise framing, focusing and timing. By following previous passes by these spoonbills, it was possible to set the lens focus to the distance at which the birds would fill the frame. Nikon with 500mm lens, Kodachrome 64, 1/250 sec at f5.6.

duced in a magazine or book.

Whatever focal length is used, a matt focusing screen is the easiest. Screens with clear centres are dangerous, because irrespective of how far away the bird is, it will appear sharp when in the middle of the frame, and focusing may have to be done too rapidly for split-image focusing to be accurate.

Films can be chosen for resolution or speed, but not both together. The films that give the sharpest image are the slowest—Kodachrome 25, for example—whereas high-speed films have a coarser, more grainy appearance. Because low power, long-focus lenses generally have larger apertures than those with much longer focal lengths, they can be used with slower, less grainy films even at high shutter speeds. There may be little to choose between the images from, say, a 180mm f2.8 lens used with ASA 64 Kodachrome (which has particularly good resolution) and a 400mm f5.6 lens used with ASA 200 Ektachrome, even though the Kodachrome image would have to be enlarged to bring the subject to the same size.

Motor drives are extremely useful for photographing flying subjects. Their high speed of operation increases the number of shots that can be taken, improving the chances of success. The fastest that a camera can be operated manually is about two frames a second, whereas many motor drives offer rates of up to five frames a second.

Clear viewfinder screen.

Split-image viewfinder screen.

Focusing on fast moving birds can be difficult with a long-focus lens. use a clear viewfinder screen if possible –plain matt ground glass is best—rather than a split-image type. The latter are commonly supplied as standard on 35mm SLR cameras but are not really suited to photographing birds in flight. The bird may only fill the clear central area of the viewfinder and may appear to be in focus when it is not.

When large numbers of birds are feeding, such as these white ibis in the Florida Everglades, they will often take off in large groups, particularly when disturbed. At close range, with a long-focus lens, this gives the opportunity to fill the picture frame with movement. Inevitably, many of the birds in a shot like this will be out of focus, but as long as one or two individuals remain sharp, the effect is generally not objectionable.
Nikon with 400mm lens, Kodachrome 64, 1/250 sec at f5.6.

Stalking/birds in flight 2

The painted stork over a nesting colony at Bharatpur, India, is typical of those birds that are relatively easy to photograph in flight–large, slow flying, and with leisurely wing beats. This makes it possible to fill the frame at a reasonable working distance and to use a fine grained film with a moderate shutter speed. Small, fast flying birds, however, are much more difficult. Filling the frame means either being within a few metres, which may be impossible, or using a very long-focus lens, which increases the problems of focus, shutter speed and keeping the bird in frame. One answer, provided that a fine grained film such as Kodachrome is used, is to accept a smaller image of the bird by using a moderate telephoto lens, and then crop into the picture when it is printed or published.
Nikon with 500 mm lens, ASA 64, 1/250 sec at f8.

Focusing technique

As well as keeping the bird in frame, for which there are no special tricks, the crucial problem is focusing. With a bird in mid-air, there are no easy reference points and the distance will change as you follow the bird's flight. There are very few instances when the bird will be flying across your field of view at a constant distance. The most usual situation for effective shots is when the flight path is obliquely towards you. Anticipation and fast reactions are needed, but the results can be surprisingly good if correct framing and focusing are achieved.

There are three methods of focusing birds in flight–which is most suitable depends on individual preferences and skill. If a shot seems important, the fixed focus method is probably safest, despite the fact that only one picture is likely to be taken.
Follow-focus The most obvious focusing method is to attempt to keep the bird in focus for the whole time it is in view. This is extremely difficult, however. Even though the bird may be flying in a straight and predictable line, its rate of approach has to be matched by turning the focusing ring at exactly the right speed. Inevitably, the focusing either lags behind or moves too fast–then the problem is to recognize which way to compensate. One: special arrangement, the Novoflex system,

replaces the normal focusing ring with a sprung pistol grip. When the grip is released, the lens is focused at infinity. As the grip is squeezed, the lens focuses closer. This is intended to make precise and quick focus alteration easier, but the basic problem of drifting still remains.

Continuous re-focusing The normal method of focusing a lens on any subject is to move the focusing ring backwards and forwards around the approximate point of focus, with wide swings at first, the movements becoming smaller until the exact point is reached. For most people this is the most rapid technique, and by doing it continuously with a flying bird, you can expect to have the image sharply focused several times in a few seconds. No attempt should be made to keep the bird in focus the whole time. After each shot, the lens is deliberately thrown out of focus to start afresh.

Fixed focus For the greatest certainty of just one sharply focused shot, focus approximately on the approaching bird and then quickly re-focus closer. Leave the focus setting at this point, and continue panning with the bird in the centre of the frame, releasing the shutter as soon as the image is sharp, or fractionally before if the bird is moving quickly to allow for a slight delay in the shutter action.

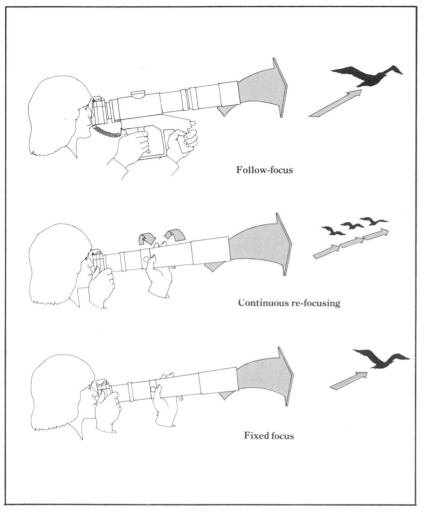

Follow-focus

Continuous re-focusing

Fixed focus

Three methods of overcoming the difficult problems of focusing birds in flight are shown above. Speed and sureness with the equipment you are using are essential. Follow-focus is a difficult technique with a normal telephoto lens—it is easy for the focus to drift and then to adjust the focusing ring in the wrong direction. Once the bird is out of focus, it can be impossible to correct the error in time with no points of reference available. The Novoflex system shown here has a pistol grip, with the lens focusing closer as you squeeze the trigger. This can be very effective, although it takes practice to be able to use it well.
Continuous re-focusing works adequately in normal circumstances, but with birds in flight it may be too slow, with the bird passing out of view before correct focus has been achieved even once.
Fixed focus is the safest and most efficient method. The focus is set for a point through which the bird is likely to pass and the shutter released just as the bird comes into sharp focus.

Exposure

Correct exposure is rarely straightforward with birds in flight, as the bird's image is usually small and set against the sky. The exposure setting should be based on the bird itself, but a through-the-lens meter reading will be overly affected by the sky background. A hand-held incident light reading is more accurate, but if you do not have time to make one, and must rely on the camera's internal meter, use the following rule of thumb:

Light, cloudy sky: increase exposure by two stops above the TTL reading.
Dark, cloudy or stormy sky: use the TTL reading or, if the clouds are very dark, decrease exposure by one stop.
Light blue sky, near horizon: increase exposure by one stop above the TTL reading.
Dark blue sky, directly overhead: reduce exposure by one stop from the TTL reading.

Another possibility is to use the TTL meter for a substitute reading. Here, the exposure is taken from an alternative, mid-toned subject (ideally an 18 per cent grey card) and this setting is maintained when photographing the bird.

This sequence of photographs shows how the image of an approaching bird appears in the camera viewer when the focus is pre-set using the fixed focus method. In a real situation, of course, there would be no point in shooting until the last frame shown here. First, the lens is focused substantially closer than the bird. On a regular flight path with a number of birds, you can judge the focus for the tightest framing. The bird is then kept in frame, and when the image reaches its sharpest, the shutter is released. A common problem is shooting a fraction of a second too late, usually because of uncertainty.

Hides

Stalking pits fieldcraft against the perception and alertness of the prey. The unpredictability of the chase is undoubtedly part of its fascination, but there are many situations where a more planned and considered approach would be better, ideally with the possibility of observing animal behaviour undetected over a period of time.

The best way of achieving this is to construct a hide–a concealed shelter overlooking a place where the subject animal makes regular appearances. When successful, the photographer can thus enter the most intimate area of an animal's territory without being noticed, becoming, in other words, an unseen observer.

Constructing a hide is not simply a matter of applying suitable camouflage to a shelter. Animals and birds often perceive their surroundings in quite different ways from human beings, relying on a different combination of senses. The slight flapping of a camouflaged canvas sheet, for example, may seem entirely insignificant to a human observer, for whom the hide seems to blend in perfectly with its surroundings. Yet this one small movement may cause violent alarm in a flock of ducks. We rely so much on our vision that we tend to think of concealment entirely in visual terms, and even then an overall appearance generally counts for more than movement. With other creatures, however, this is frequently not the case. When building and using a hide, the perception of the particular animal or bird that is the quarry must be fooled, not a human interpretation of it. A hide intended for photographing mammals, for example, must conceal scent more than anything else and have no noticeable scent of its own.

Natural hides

The simplest hides of all differ little from the natural cover used when stalking–undergrowth, bushes and rocks. First choose a natural site that offers a certain degree of concealment by itself. In particular, look for a confused background, perhaps tangled vegetation, that will conceal your out-

A portable canvas hide, like the one illustrated opposite, was used to approach the nest of this great bower bird in Northern Territory, Australia. The comfort and relative permanence of a well made hide can allow the use of quite elaborate equipment for good quality results–here including flash lighting (J-P. Ferrero).
Mamiya RB67 with 180 mm lens, ASA 64, 1/60 sec at f11 with two 200 Joule (watt-second) flash units at quarter power.

Natural hides can often be constructed from available natural materials. A pile of stones was positioned near the carcase of this young wild pony in the Pays Basque in south-western France to disguise the photographer's presence (J-P. Ferrero).
Nikon with 400 mm lens, ASA 125, 1/250 sec at f8.

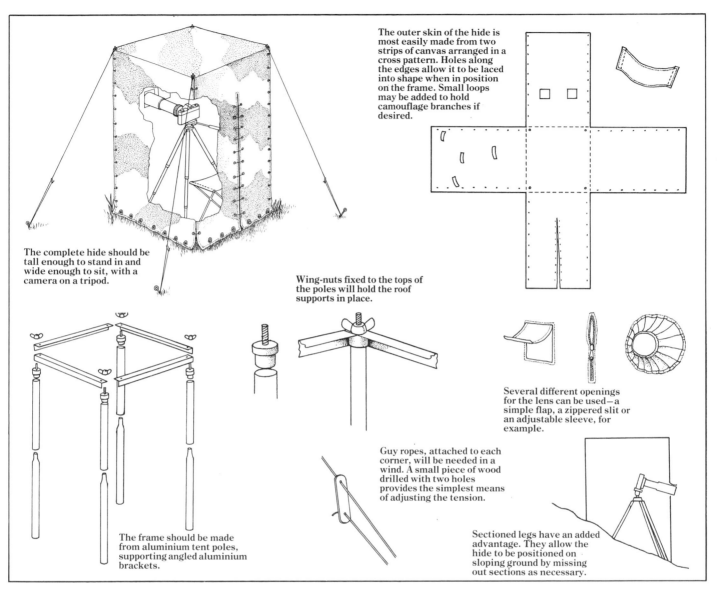

The complete hide should be tall enough to stand in and wide enough to sit, with a camera on a tripod.

The outer skin of the hide is most easily made from two strips of canvas arranged in a cross pattern. Holes along the edges allow it to be laced into shape when in position on the frame. Small loops may be added to hold camouflage branches if desired.

Wing-nuts fixed to the tops of the poles will hold the roof supports in place.

The frame should be made from aluminium tent poles, supporting angled aluminium brackets.

Guy ropes, attached to each corner, will be needed in a wind. A small piece of wood drilled with two holes provides the simplest means of adjusting the tension.

Several different openings for the lens can be used—a simple flap, a zippered slit or an adjustable sleeve, for example.

Sectioned legs have an added advantage. They allow the hide to be positioned on sloping ground by missing out sections as necessary.

line. Then construct a simple screen facing the direction you want to photograph, first with a basic frame made out of branches or whatever local materials are available, and then with a covering of brushwood, leaves or any other handy debris. The screen is unlikely to be completely efficient, and will not conceal your movements, but if you keep still it can be surprisingly effective. An additional sophistication is to drape a sheet of military camouflage netting over the makeshift frame.

Portable hides

The most common type of hide is portable, large enough for one person to sit or stand in comfortably for several hours, and adaptable to a number of ground-level uses. The design shown here is very versatile and it would be sensible to make one if you intend to undertake hide photography seriously. It consists of a lightweight, collapsible frame six feet high and three feet square in plan (two metres high by one metre square), covered with thick fabric, camouflaged either by paint or by

the addition of local materials. The frame is of aluminium and the uprights are in sections for portability. A wing-nut at each corner secures the uprights to the angled roof sections, locates the fabric covering in position, and provides a fastening for four guy lines that can be pegged into the ground and tightened to prevent movement. A row of eyelets around the base of the fabric enables more pegs to be driven in to prevent it from flapping in the wind. The choice of fabric is important. Above all it should be thick enough to be completely opaque, otherwise backlighting will reveal the photographer inside. Canvas, hessian and nylon tent material are all possibilities. The colour is not important, so long as it is not too bright, but a military camouflage pattern in drab green and brown is particularly effective. It is also useful that the hide should not be too conspicuous to humans, who will almost certainly investigate if they notice a hide and their presence will immediately scare away the animals the photographer has taken so much care to conceal himself from.

While portable hides can be ordered custom built, it is not difficult to make one for yourself. The materials should all be easily available from camping suppliers—the hide is, after all, a type of tent, consisting basically of canvas stretched over an aluminium frame. The underlying requirements are that it should be light and easily folded for transportation and that, once set up, it should be rigid and strong. It is particularly important that the material covering should not be loose, as movement—even the slightest flapping in a breeze—may scare away the animals.

Hides/choosing a location

The first priority in choosing a site for a hide is to have a clear view of a place that is inhabited or regularly visited by the animal or bird in question. Most creatures have patterns of activity that include specific locations for sleeping, feeding, drinking, bathing and rearing young. With a knowledge of these locations, and depending on which aspects of behaviour are considered to be most interesting, a location for the hide can be chosen.

Suitable places vary so much, from an East African watering hole to a marshland stopover on a waterfowl flyway, that few generalizations can be made about the best site for a hide. Nevertheless, it is usually a bad idea to position the hide in an exposed space such as a field or open grassland, where it will normally be too prominent and obvious for the animals to become accustomed to it. The edge of a clearing is a better choice, particularly where there is a hillside or a tall background of vegetation to help break up the lines of the hide. As when stalking, avoid creating a silhouette against the skyline.

The final choice will often compromise between a sufficiently close, unobstructed view and concealment. Make a careful reconnaissance of the proposed site with the lens you are most likely to use, making sure that the working distance is close enough and that there are no obvious obstructions visible from the height above the ground that you will be working from. Choose, if possible, a pleasing background, and check the view for man-made objects such as telegraph lines.

Anticipate the position of the sun, particularly at the times of day during which the animals are likely to make an appearance. If you expect your subjects to be visiting early or late in the day, when the sun is low, make sure that the hide itself will not cast a prominent shadow in the shot. The ideal lighting position is usually with the sun behind the camera and slightly to one side. Also consider the prevailing winds, making every effort to site the hide downwind from both the place you are photographing and the animal's approach path.

Moving the hide into position

If you are photographing nomadic or migrating animals or birds, it may be possible to arrive at the site, erect the hide in one session, sit down and wait for the animals to arrive. Creatures that have no regular and intimate links with a particular territory are not likely to be disturbed by the sudden appearance of a new object, provided of course that it appears to them to be natural. Geese, for example, may visit a stopping place perhaps only twice in a year when migrating. With most animals and birds, however, especially those whose clearly defined territory you are actually invading, it will take time to move the hide into position. Most creatures have strong fixed habits and routines, and anything that disrupts the normal daily pattern or looks unusual is quickly noticed. If the appearance of the hide is too sudden, your prey's activity may be disturbed. And if real alarm is caused, the animal may desert the territory for good and this may have the more serious consequence of young being abandoned.

Hides should be positioned near places it is known animals will visit. This sunbird had built its nest on the verandah of a house in Queensland, Australia. It was not necessary to search the forest for a suitable location – the hide (and in this case flash units) just had to be carefully placed to obtain a good view of the nest without disturbing the parent birds (J.-P. Ferrero).
Nikon with 400 mm lens, ASA 25, 1/60 sec at f11 with two 160 Joule (watt-second) flash units.

It would have taken impossibly good fortune to photograph this redstart with a recently caught caterpillar in any other location than near to its nest. A hide made the carefully planned approach and wait for the right moment possible. As here, variety can be introduced if the nest itself is not included in every shot (S. and D. Simon).
Canon with 200 mm lens, ASA 64, 1/60 sec at f16 with 160 Joule (watt-second) flash unit.

There are two methods of moving a hide into position. One involves erecting the complete hide at a sufficient distance for the prey not to become upset, and then moving it carefully forward over a period of time, perhaps a few yards at a time. In this way, the arrival of the foreign object at the site is gradual, and although the subject may be puzzled and a little wary, it is less likely to become seriously alarmed. In the second method, the photographer starts at the actual site of the hide, but begins with the foundations, adding just enough of the construction each day for the animal to become accustomed to it. A variation on this is to leave a small object on the first day – perhaps an upturned bucket painted the same tone and colour as the hide, replacing it each day with larger and larger objects, until the fully constructed hide can be brought into place.

Whichever method is used, the times you visit the area should be those least likely to disturb the inhabitants. With a watering place normally used by animals at sunrise and sunset, the middle of the day will be the safest time. Other sites can best be approached at night, depending on the particular circumstances. The period of time over which the hide is moved into place also varies according to how exposed the site is and the type of subject. With many birds, three or four days may be sufficient. With mammals, a longer time is usually required. Even with this guideline, particular circumstances may be atypical. As a rule, try to monitor the animal's general behaviour from a distance on each day that you move the hide. If you sense that it is becoming disturbed, halt the proceedings until its activity returns to normal.

When the hide is finally in position, there may be a few minor obstructions to the camera's view. A certain amount of 'gardening', as it is known, is possible, particularly close to the hide. Long grasses can be weeded out and even a branch or two can be cut down. This should be done with great care, however, and at times when the animal or bird is away from the location, otherwise all the stealth devoted to moving the hide onto the site will be wasted. Another important reason for being extremely careful when 'gardening' is the possible danger to the animals. In order to have a clear view of a nest, it may be tempting to cut away nearby leaves and branches, yet this will almost certainly expose the young to danger from predators. Remembering that a hawk has much better eyesight than humans, if an occupied nest presents a clear view to the camera, it will also be visible to birds of prey. In some cases, it may be possible to tie back branches or other foliage rather than permanently removing them.

Using the hide

If the hide has been efficiently constructed, and properly introduced to the animals or birds, you can experience a remarkable degree of freedom once inside. As long as the subject has accepted a new object into its territory, it will often show tolerance of noise from the hide. Nevertheless, it is wise to continue to take precautions. Keep noise down to a minimum, avoid touching any part of the hide that may move, such as the supports or fabric walls, and do not wear artificial scents. Camera operations should be as unobtrusive as possible, particularly movement of the visible lens front. Unless it is absolutely necessary, avoid using a motor drive. Because long-focus lenses are usually necessary, a sturdy tripod is an advantage. A cable release will further reduce camera vibrations.

Although hides usually have small viewing holes in addition to larger openings for camera lenses, placing the eye too close to the hole may make you noticeable from outside, and viewing through the camera is safer. Single lens reflex models (35 mm or medium format) are just about essential in hide photography. For the same reason, through-the-lens metering is preferable to a hand-held meter, which will have to be placed outside the hide for a reading. It may be necessary to replace the camera lens with a dummy, such as the end of an empty bottle, when the hide is not in use. In this way, the animals will become accustomed to the lens and will not be disturbed by its sudden appearance or disappearance.

Enter and leave the hide with as much care as possible. Although the hide may have been accepted as part of the surroundings, an active human will not be. Preferably, enter the hide when the animal or bird is not present. A waterfowl hide, for example, can be entered safely before first light. Otherwise, a useful trick is to take a friend or assistant inside with you, and then have him or her leave the hide alone. In normal circumstances, the subjects will assume that the hide is unoccupied again. Often, this 'showing in' technique is essential, even though the subjects may have accepted the presence of the unoccupied hide.

Hides/special types 1

There is no such thing as an all-purpose hide. As the hide has to blend in with particular surroundings, there is inevitably a need for a wide variety of designs. Quite apart from the individual preferences of photographers, every hide must to some extent be customized to a particular use. The models described here are among the most commonly used special hides, but the details of design are idiosyncratic–use them as a guide, but rely on different materials as and when necessary, improvising according to what is locally available.

Permanent hides

Some locations, such as wildfowl reserves, merit permanent hides. These can vary widely in design. Because the hide is intended to last for a number of years, it may be quite sophisticated. From the visiting photographer's point of view, this kind of hide is ideal because of the improved facilities and because the rangers or wardens responsible for its upkeep normally have long experience of what to expect from it and how to make the best use of it. Frequently, the areas in front of such hides are regularly baited with food or other lures to im-

prove the visitors' chances of seeing the wildlife on a single visit.

Tree hides

Elevated hides in trees are particularly useful for animals and birds that live in the trees, but they can also be employed when photographing large ground-dwelling animals. One of the greatest advantages of a tree hide is that it removes the photographer's scent from the trails–a valuable feature when photographing mammals. In addition, most ground-dwelling animals, such as deer or large cats, normally have no reason to look upwards. Provided you keep motionless, they may approach very close indeed. The construction depends on the form of the tree, but the ideal base is a trunk and two large limbs that allow a triangular platform to be laid on stout battens nailed between the branches and the trunk. Slats of wood nailed to the trunk provide an access ladder, and a simple roof frame gives support for fabric walls. A roof is important only as protection against rain. Note that in many areas there are laws preventing damage to trees, and nailing may not be possible.

This heron (below) was photographed from a well built permanent hide on North Dakota's Souris River. Such hides become accepted by the subjects because of their permanence. The location of the hide, on a small arm of the river, opposite a reed bed, gave good opportunities for photographing a wide variety of species.
Nikon with 500mm lens, ASA 64, 1/60 sec at f8.

A tree hide can produce good results (below far right). This Australian Nankeen kestrel was photographed by its nest as it returned with a lizard. Nikon with 200mm lens, ASA 64, 1/125 sec at f5.6, with fill-in flash.

Birds in trees (below right) can also be photographed from the ground. This toucan near its nest was taken from a natural hide constructed on the ground nearby (F. Gohier). Nikon with 400mm lens, ASA 64, 1/125 at f11.

Permanent hides can be well constructed to blend in with their surroundings over several years of use. Solid timber models like this are equivalent to garden sheds in construction, with permanent timber walls and roof. Camouflage may not prove necessary in the long term as the animals become accustomed to the presence of the hide.

Tree hides (below) can be easily constructed on a base supported on battens fixed between the trunk and stronger branches. The roof and sides can be made of canvas fixed over an additional roof frame.

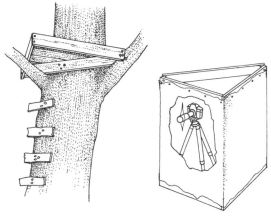

Hides/special types 2

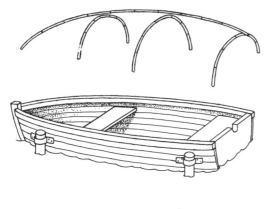

A floating hide is essentially a boat with a camouflaged covering. Some method of removing the covering when moving the boat into position is essential, as is an effective form of anchoring—here, poles pushed into the bottom through tubes fixed to the boat's sides.

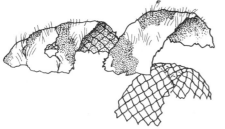

This whitebreasted waterhen (right) was photographed in India from a boat as it waded through the shallows. Birds can be surprisingly tolerant of boats if they are allowed to drift naturally.
Nikon with 400 mm lens, ASA 25, 1/125 sec at f5.6.

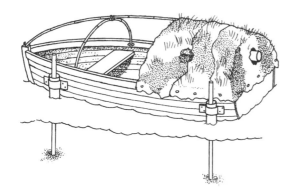

Pit hides (left) are simple to construct in the right terrain. Dig a hole on a suitable slope, with rising ground behind, and cover with a canvas roof. Be careful to establish some sort of drainage if rain is a possibility.

Natural hides can be effective, as long as too much disturbance is not created during the building process. Use available vegetation to build a temporary screen in front of a suitably confused background.

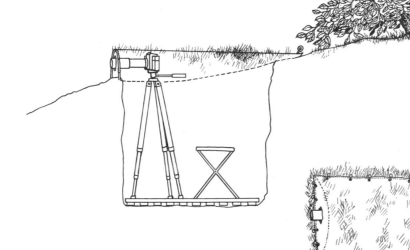

Floating hides

For marshland and river settings, the best location for a hide may be on the water itself. Most floating hides are built around boats, and so their construction is largely determined by the shape of the vessel. It is, however, possible to start from scratch with a purpose-built raft. Two considerations have to be kept in mind. First, it must be possible to anchor the hide in a fixed position. One solution, at least where the water is not too deep, is to fasten short lengths of tubing to the outside of the boat in vertical positions. Poles can then be passed through them and pushed into the bottom. The loose fitting between the poles and tubes allows the boat to adjust to changes in water level— important in tidal waters. The second consideration is that, as the floating hide must normally be propelled into postion, the camouflage must be easy to remove and fix in place from the inside. When moving, there must be enough room to use oars, and when stationary the covering must be complete. In the design shown here, the covering consists of a hooped frame nailed to the gunwales, and flexible sections of wire mesh covered with camouflaged fabric.

Pit hides

If the location is suitable, a good hide can be made from very few materials by sinking most of it below ground. An elevated natural background, prefer- ably a slope, is a prerequisite. The outline of photographer and camera are thus obscured. Be- cause drainage can be a problem, a duckboard plat- form inside is a worthwhile addition. Apart from this, little more is needed than a raised frame at the front, and a fabric covering that can be pegged tight so that it does not flap.

Photographed from the trees bordering a beach on Heron Island, Australia, with foliage constructed into a hide, this oystercatcher (top) remained unaware of the photographer's presence (J-P. Ferrero).
Nikon with 400 mm lens, ASA 25, 1/125 sec at f5.6.

One of the obvious advantages of a hide is that it allows time to choose the best moment to shoot. This Indian darter (above) was caught at the moment of take-off.
Nikon with 400 mm lens, ASA 64, 1/500 sec at f5.6.

Hides/baits and lures

Baits and lures, consisting of food, water, calls, scent or decoys, are an important element in hide photography. The aim is to provide an immediate attraction for the subjects so as to increase the photographer's control over the situation. Most baits and lures are very specific, relying on the particular tastes and reactions of individual species. Two general principles apply, however. The first rather obviously requires that the bait must be available in the right place—in the vicinity of the animals or birds it is intended to attract, and in a place where it can easily be found. As most animals must constantly consider their own safety from predators, baits are usually most successful when they are placed close to adequate cover, to give feeding animals an escape route in case of attack.

The second principle is that animals or birds should be baited when they are most receptive. If food is the bait, there is little point in using it when natural food is plentiful, normally in spring and early summer. In late winter, however, food is scarce, and animals are often extremely hungry. At this time of year, the animal's hunger will overcome fear and suspicion of the bait. Even so, it is not reasonable to expect an immediate response. You may have to persevere for days in succession before your subjects will accept it. Once the animals have responded, it helps to keep baiting regularly, so as to establish a predictable pattern of behaviour. Baiting should only be undertaken in a responsible way, however. Remember that animals may become dependent on this artificially introduced food, perhaps staying further north than they should in winter as a result. In these circumstances, they may starve when the photographer departs and baiting ceases.

For a particular animal or bird, especially in an unfamiliar area, local guides often have precise knowledge about the most effective baits or lures and the best places to use them.

Food and water

The most common bait is food, and although birds as a whole respond more readily than mammals, baiting with food can usually prove effective with most creatures. Remember that animals and birds tend to follow their normal patterns of searching for food, even when hungry. The majority of birds, for example, feed energetically early in the day.

Items from an animal's regular diet are an obvious bait. A live rabbit, for example, can be used as bait for a large hawk, a dead carcass for a vulture or other carrion eater, seeds for parrots and finches, and so on. As well as natural foods, substitutes can be used, and are often easier to obtain. A solution of sugar in water works for birds that feed on nectar, raisins are acceptable to fruit-eaters, and peanut butter to squirrels.

Fresh water as bait can be particularly effective in areas where it is naturally scarce. To make a small pool, a waterproof lining is needed. Heavy-duty plastic sheeting is effective and easily portable. It should be laid in a shallow pit and weighted at the edges. Mammals and reptiles locate water principally by smell, but birds tend to rely on vision. For this reason, a water drip over a small pool intro-

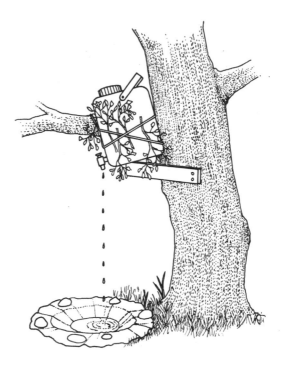

Where water is scarce, a water drip can attract birds. Form a pool with a small piece of plastic sheeting weighted with stones and place a drip-container, such as a picnic water bottle. Good camouflage of the equipment is essential.

An animal carcass makes excellent bait for raptors and carrion birds. These Andes condors in Peru were attracted by a dead lamb, positioned near a makeshift hide constructed from a pile of stones (F. Gohier). Nikon with 400 mm lens, Kodachrome 64, 1/250 sec at f8.

At this clearing on the Keoladeo Ghana sanctuary, Bharatpur, India, food was laid down late every afternoon so that a number of species, among them these chital, appeared predictably each day. When the ground is baited frequently, as here, there are normally no problems, but when it is planned for a limited period of time, the animals or birds may become dependent on it, and consequently suffer if this extra food supply suddenly disappears. Nikon with 180 mm lens, Kodachrome 64, 1/125 sec at f11.

duces some movement and is more obvious to birds. A picnic water jug with a tap fitted is ideal, provided it is camouflaged.

Calls

Sound can also be used to attract animals and birds. Calls are used to elicit any of four kinds of response. The first, which can be expected only during the start of the breeding cycle, is a mating response. For this, the female's mating call is reproduced in the hope of attracting a male ready for courtship. The second type of reaction is a territorial response, exhibited most strongly by males throughout the breeding season and also sometimes when the young are being reared. In this case, the male call is reproduced, attracting an indignant male ready to fight off the intruder. The third kind of response is a social one. Wolves and coyotes, for example, like to keep track of each other by howling, and ducks or geese can be attracted easily because they tend to feed in large numbers. The fourth response is the mobbing instinct, particularly common among small birds when faced with a threatening intruder. By reproducing the call of a well known enemy, or even the distress call of the same species, large numbers may be attracted to drive off the predator.

Calls can be made by many different techniques. Depending on your skill, you may be able to reproduce the call of, say, a coyote or an owl with no artificial aids. Alternatively, there are various commercially made whistles, particularly for game bird species. Other mechanical calls may be available through local guides. In Brazil, for example, the call of a jaguar is mimicked by drawing a waxed string through a gourd. Perhaps the easiest and most reliable method is to use a portable tape recorder. Calls can be recorded in advance, either from life or from existing recordings, and played back at will.

As with food baiting, a responsible approach is essential, particularly during breeding and when the young are being reared. Artificial calls can be so disruptive to the normal behaviour of birds or animals that serious harm may be caused: parents may be distracted from protecting or feeding their young, and repeated distress calls can overexcite some species.

Decoys

Decoys, whether live or artificial, can be used in a similar way to calls. With social animals and birds, such as ducks, a decoy in a suitable place can be an attraction, but for the majority of birds, a decoy of the same species, particularly if it is a male, will be seen as an intruder and will encourage threatening displays. Similarly, a decoy in the form of a common predator will tend to arouse mobbing behaviour. With some subjects, a mirror will serve as a decoy, the reflection playing the part of the intruding male. Precautions are needed in the use of decoys similar to those with calls.

Scent

Mammals can occasionally be attracted by scent, although there is still uncertainty about how effective it can be. Sexual scents offer the best opportunity, and commercial products are available that fulfil this function for game animals such as deer. Another kind of scent attraction, which works for reasons not yet understood, is anise oil. This attracts bears and horses, and perhaps deer.

Hides/remote control

Another approach using the hide principle employs remote control to trigger the camera. Here, the camera is placed in position for photographing the subject, but the photographer then retires some distance away to operate it by remote control. One of the advantages of this method is that the photographer's hide can be sited at a distance. The camera needs much less camouflage than the photographer, and it may be much easier to introduce it close to the subject. With inaccessible sites, such as cliffs and tree-tops, placing the camera on its own may be the only practical solution.

There are a number of different remote control systems. Radio transmission can be operated over considerable distances—up to 800 yards (700 metres) under good conditions and 350 yards (300 metres) in cities. Unfortunately, there is sometimes a risk of interference from other transmitters, and the remote control unit's transmission may also interfere with air traffic control and other broadcasts. As a result, their use is illegal in come countries such as the United Kingdom. Another cordless system uses modulated infrared pulses, and is less expensive than radio. Its range, however, is limited to about 70 yards (60 metres) and it requires line of sight operation as the remote control hand set has to be pointed directly at the triggering device on the camera. For closer working distances, cable extensions can be used. In all remote control work, a motor drive or automatic winder is recommended. With a manual shutter release, the camera must be approached after each shot so that the shutter can be cocked and the film advanced. In addition, pneumatic cable extensions, which are the normal method of non-motorized remote release, are slow to react to pressure on the bulb.

When using a motor-driven camera by remote control, you can reduce the noise by fitting a blimp, or silencer. A purpose built blimp for Hasselblad medium format cameras is made by the manufacturer. Otherwise, you can make one yourself out of padded quilt.

If the lighting conditions are likely to change while the camera is in position, a system with automatic exposure control is invaluable. If not, some cameras can be fitted with a servo control that mechanically alters the aperture ring.

A 250 exposure back can sometimes be fitted to 35mm cameras. This considerably extends the periods between having to approach a remotely-controlled camera. If you are some distance from the camera, a pair of binoculars will help you capture the best moment to trigger the shot. With practice you will have a good idea of what your distant camera is seeing at any moment.

For this night-time photograph of an Indian tiger (above), a pressure plate, similar to that shown was buried on the carefully located approach to a bait. The camera was pre-focused, and a single electronic flash unit positioned a few feet to the right (C. McDougal/ Ardea).

Two examples of remote-control devices that can be home-built without difficulty are a pressure-plate (above) and trip-wire (below). Both work on the principle of two electrical contacts separated by a spring; physical pressure by the animal brings the contacts together and completes an electrical circuit that includes battery, camera and flash.

This tawny owl, after a successful strike at a vole, was photographed in flight with its prey by installing a photoelectric beam close to its nest. As the bird breaks the beam, it triggers the camera and electronic flash (W. Curth/Ardea).

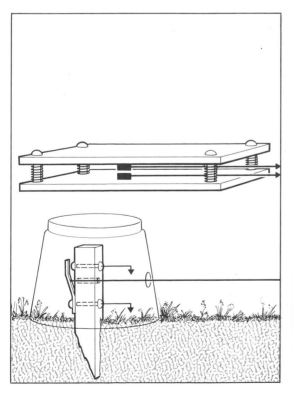

Having baited for this sparrow hawk (left), the photographer positioned camera and flash close to the tree stump, but waited 20 feet (6 metres) away in a hide, triggering the motor drive with an extension cable when he saw the bird land (I. Beams/Ardea).

Close-up/technique 1

The natural world exists for the photographer on many different scales. While most animals and birds need no special optical or lighting equipment, at scales of reproduction greater than one tenth life-size–that is, when the image on the film is greater than one tenth of the size of the subject itself–different techniques are needed. This scale can also be described as $0.1\times$ magnification. Photography of this type involves fresh problems of exposure, depth of field and resolution. The special equipment is of several different types, and not all of it is difficult to use.

Supplementary lenses

The simplest close-up attachments for modest reproduction scales are supplementary lenses, which are low powered magnifying lenses fitted to the front of the camera's normal lens. They are available in different strengths and add to the magnifying power of the basic lens, allowing a closer working distance between the lens and the subject. No adjustment to exposure is necessary, and they are quick to attach.

The strength of supplementary close-up lenses is measured in diopters. A +1 diopter lens focuses at one metre (just over three feet), a +2 diopter lens at half a metre, and a +3 diopter lens at one third of a metre. By bringing the focusing distance closer like this, the image is enlarged. For example, a standard lens (50mm on a 35mm camera) will reproduce subjects one metre distant at about one-twentieth life-size $(0.05\times)$. By adding a +1 diopter lens, the image is enlarged to about one-tenth life-size $(0.1\times)$.

Supplementary lenses can be added together for even greater magnifications, but at more than +4 or +5 diopters image quality begins to suffer noticeably. Even with low diopter lenses, a small aperture should be used to preserve sharpness.

Extension rings and bellows

Optically, extending the lens away from the camera body is the best procedure for close-ups. No new aberrations are introduced to degrade the image, and the only limits to the amount of magnification possible in this way are caused by loss of light and diffraction. Both these limits are not normally reached until the magnification is several times life-size, at which point a microscope provides a better optical system. Moving the lens further from the film and closer to the subject magnifies the image–the greater the distance over which the lens is moved, the greater the magnification.

There is essentially little difference between extension rings and bellows, beyond flexibility. Both perform the same function of extending the lens forward, and they can be combined to increase the distance. Extension rings are available in fixed lengths, providing a rigid extension that can be fitted rapidly between the camera body and lens. Bellows can be set at any intermediate position but are less sturdy than rings and slightly more cumbersome to attach and use. Some models have a front panel that can be swung or tilted to give the same control over the plane of sharp focus that is possible with a large format view camera.

View cameras and some medium format cameras such as the Mamiya RB67 in any case use a bellows for normal focusing, so that extending the lens for close-up work involves no more than a further adjustment to the regular focusing controls.

When a standard lens is extended with extension rings or bellows, the image quality may deteriorate slightly at magnification greater than life-size $(1.0\times)$. This is because a standard lens is deliberately designed to perform at its best when the lens-to-film distance is shorter than the lens-

If a flower is the close-up subject, the setting of an individual bloom is the first and most important factor. When there are several, it pays to choose carefully. Here, the flower of a South American Victoria Regia lily, presented such a clear, unobstructed view that the composition fell naturally into place, striking a balance between the shape and details of the flower itself and the background of its characteristically large leaves. The cross-lighting from a late afternoon sun was ideal for revealing texture, while the shadows were not so deep as to obscure detail. Nikon with 180mm lens, Ektachrome 64, 1/125 sec at f8.

With many close-up subjects, there may be a choice of several scales if you have the right equipment, and each may work in its own way. A tall, slender plant like this foxglove, for example, does not fit a normal film or print format conveniently, posing a problem of what to show – the entire stem or the individual flowers. Which of these three scales is the most satisfactory depends partly on personal taste and partly on which aspect of the plant is considered to be the most important.

Close-up/technique 2

to-subject distance. To overcome this problem, some lenses can be reversed with a special mount so that the rear of the lens points towards the subject. The lens is thus used with the ratios for which it was designed.

Macro lenses

A macro lens has its elements so arranged that the optimum focusing distance is very much closer than for a standard lens—within the range of close-up photography. Also, by building in a long range of movement inside the lens housing, the focusing range of a 50 mm lens may be extended down to about 9 inches (230 mm).

Exposure increase with lens extensions

Unlike supplementary lenses, achieving close magnification by extending the lens causes a fall-off in the light reaching the film. The greater the distance from the lens to the film, the less light there is to form an image. As a result, extra exposure is needed, either by opening the lens aperture to allow more light through, by using a slower shutter speed, or by increasing the amount of light falling on the subject.

The exact amount of light loss, and therefore the actual increase in exposure needed, obeys a basic natural law—the inverse square law. This states that the amount of light reaching a subject decreases in inverse proportion to the square of the distance between the light source and subject. So, with a lens normally attached to the camera, a certain quality of light reaches the film from the lens, but if an extension ring is fitted so that the film becomes twice as far away from the lens, four times less light will reach it. For example, if a 50 mm lens is extended by 50 mm from its normal position, the total lens-to-film distance will be 100 mm. Dividing this by the focal length of the lens (50 mm) gives the increase in extension of 2×. However, as the light falls off according to the square of the distance, this figure of 2 must be multiplied by itself to give the light loss: that is, 4× less. Therefore the exposure must be increased by four times to restore the correct amount of light reaching the film: by a longer exposure time or by opening up the aperture by two stops.

Portable flash at close distances

When a flash unit is used in close-up photography, perhaps to compensate for the light loss resulting from the use of a bellows extension, critical measurements are necessary. Because the light source is used at very short distances from the subject, movements of just a centimetre or two can make considerable differences to the exposure. Moreover, the appearance of lighting on the subject can only be judged by testing or through experience. It is extremely useful (especially in the field) to devise a constant lighting set-up with the flash unit or units in known positions. Even then, the initial flash distance and output must be calculated.

There are two stages to the operation. The first is to set up the lens and bellows extension, according to the magnification required. From this the

required increase in exposure can be calculated. The second stage is to work out the flash to subject distance and the aperture setting. To some extent these two are interchangeable, as the exposure can be altered either by moving the flash closer or further away, or altering the lens aperture.

The simplest and most accurate measurement of flash output can be made with a flash meter, and several pocket-sized models are now available. The flash unit's own guide number, which is a measure of its power, also gives a close indication, although some manufacturers tend to be over-optimistic about the output of their units. Careful testing should always be made before fieldwork.

If the flash unit is automatic, either the sensor should be taped over or the unit switched to manual, so that the full charge is used each time. In most close-up photography, the problem is usually to obtain sufficient depth of field, and small apertures are nearly always desirable. These need high light output, and therefore flash units are best used at full or 'manual' power.

One of the opportunities of photographing flowers or other close-up subjects in their natural setting rather than in the studio is to show them in relation to their habitat. Here, a wide angle lens, with its broad field of view and great depth of field, comes into its own. Although the small details of this Venezuelan flower are sacrificed, the sense of place —tropical savannah and distant plateaux—is established.
Nikon with 20 mm lens, Kodachrome 64, 1/30 sec at f 16.

By moving in very close, so that a flower's petals fill the frame completely and focusing on one small detail, such as a stamen, extreme close-ups can reveal extraordinary qualities. The restricted depth of field at this magnification prevents sharpness over the whole image, but this, in any case is not necessarily desirable – the blurred petals in the background simplify the picture.
Nikon with 55 mm macro lens, Kodachrome 64, 1/60 sec at f11.

For most flowers or static small animals photographed on location, a camera and lighting arrangement like this will give quite adequate control. A macro lens is a great convenience and the 200 mm lens shown here on a 35 mm SLR has the advantage of a good working distance and compressed perspective. Even when relying on daylight for illumination, a small adjustable reflector, such as a hand mirror, makes refinements possible, while a card clamped to a stand can act as a windbreak. Copper wire loosely bent around the stem can hold the flower in place.

One of the most straightforward approaches in flower photography is to isolate an individual bloom, blurring the background by restricting the depth of field to the flower itself, and framing tightly to remove other distracting elements. A macro lens is ideal for this scale of photograph (N. Freeman).
Nikon with 55 mm macro lens, Kodachrome 64, 1/125 sec at f11.

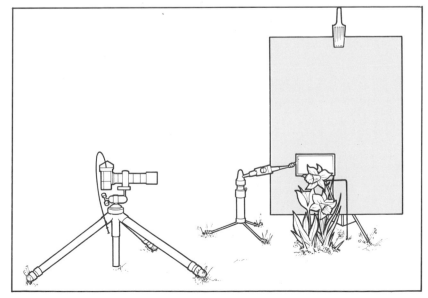

Close-up/flowers 1

Flowers generally occupy the scale of reproduction from one-tenth life-size (0.1×) for large plants to slightly greater than life-size for details of stamens and petals. Working in the field with flowers is usually more difficult than photographing them in the studio, where there is greater control. To a considerable extent the photographer is at the mercy of natural conditions and has little opportunity to influence the setting, background or lighting. Nevertheless, there are a number of techniques that can be used to give some measure of control, especially with advance knowledge of the likely conditions.

Composition and setting

In its natural setting, a flower, no matter how perfect a specimen, may not always be in the best position for photography. The camera viewpoint will be dictated by where the flower is growing, usually close to the ground. Grasses, leaves or other obstructions may be in the way, and the background may be distracting. Before setting up the camera, decide first on the general composition. Filling the frame with the whole flower is a commonly used approach, but you may prefer to show the flower in its natural surroundings, including as much of its background as possible. Alternatively, you may decide to close in on one detail, such as the stamen or the veins on a petal.

The composition will determine your technique and how much you have to alter the background, surroundings and position of the flower. If you choose an extreme close-up, the background will be irrelevant–the flower itself will become the background. If you show the flower in its broader setting, you avoid some of the technical problems of close-up photography, although you will have to consider depth of field and angle of view. Wide-angle lenses are often helpful for this kind of shot. Most flower photography, however, falls between these two scales, and the ideal is usually a bloom filling a large part of the picture frame, with a complementary background.

Background control is important with this kind of photograph. It will normally be out of focus, particularly if it is some distance behind the flower. A plain, uncluttered background is nearly always the best, and for most flowers a dark background is usually more effective than a light one. Shooting against the sky is rarely satisfactory.

The choice of lens can alter the relationship of the flower to its background. With a long focal length there is a narrow angle of view, and there is more opportunity to be selective. An additional advantage of a longer lens is that the background will be thrown more out of focus and will therefore be even less obtrusive. A good all-round lens for flower photography is one with a moderately long focal length and the ability to focus closely. The 105mm Micro-Nikkor and the Hasselblad 135mm S-Planar are two fine examples.

The camera position, high or low, gives some control, although the position of the flower itself can restrict the choice. Some adjustment to the plant can be made, however. If, for example, the background looks best from very low, but the

flower tilts upwards too much, the stem can be clamped gently and twisted into a better position. For this, one of the simplest arrangements is a length of thick copper wire with a clip attached to one end. It can be pressed into the ground and bent into any shape.

If the background is unsuitable from any angle, one solution is to use an artificial background. A sheet of black velvet, which reflects even less light than black card, can be suspended behind the flower. Different coloured backgrounds are also possible, although there is a danger that they will appear unnatural.

Finally, with the camera in position, the flower's immediate surroundings can be 'gardened'–foliage can be bent aside and distracting litter removed.

Depth of field and movement

At close distances, depth of field is limited, and it may not always be possible to have the whole

If the background is totally unsuitable, you can, with some trouble, provide one yourself. Use a plain sheet of material, in either a neutral or natural colour. Velvet is best, as it shows creases less than ordinary cloth or paper, and black is in most cases the most acceptable colour. Erect the sheet as far behind the flower as possible, to minimize the danger of the material's texture showing. This distance affects the size of the sheet that you need, as does the lens focal length and size of the flower. A one metre square sheet is satisfactory for most situations. Two small, collapsable stands make good supports, although it may be necessary to use tent pegs to secure them against movement. Attach the sheet with clips.

One way of simplifying a cluttered background is to throw it out of focus (left), here a Common Mallow against roadside grasses. With the preview lever depressed, the aperture can be adjusted until the right balance between sharp petals and blurred background is reached.
Nikon with 200 mm macro lens, Kodachrome 64, 1/15 sec at f11.

Of the several camera positions that may be possible, one may be preferable simply because it places the flower against an uncluttered background. In most cases, it will be a low position, close to the height of the flower itself. Otherwise the surrounding carpet of vegetation will be visible. These summer bluebells growing by a woodland path looked their best when photographed against the dark interior of the forest. The camera was just four inches (10 cm) above the ground.
Nikon with 200 mm macro lens, Kodachrome 64, 1/4 sec at f16.

Close-up/flowers 2

flower sharply focused. Most flowers are deep in relation to their width, and it may be necessary to pull back slightly and accept a lower magnification to achieve sharpness of both the front and back of the subject. Stopping the lens down to a small aperture gives the greatest depth of field, but a slow shutter speed will then be needed. Even a slight breeze is sufficient to cause movement, so that for shutter speeds slower than about 1/30 sec it is often necessary to provide some form of windbreak. An effective shelter can be made from a large piece of card or sheet of plastic, supported by two portable stands. The wire clamp already described can also help to hold the plant still.

A more radical alternative is to ignore the need for sharpness throughout and make the best use of an impressionistic effect. By concentrating on one detail, the remaining parts of the flower can be used as a softly blurred background.

Lighting

Natural lighting is difficult to control, and in general the best that can be done is to modify it slightly by using reflectors and diffusers to fill in shadows or accentuate poorly lit details. There is no guarantee that a good specimen will remain in perfect condition if you choose to wait for better weather or a different angle of sunlight.

In close-up photography, however, it is possible to work with a surprisingly wide range of natural lighting. Bright sunlight is by no means necessary. Even a dull, cloudy day can be used to advantage,

with the soft, diffused light bringing out the full saturation of the colours.

For the most complete lighting control, a flash unit can be used. If aimed at the flower it can mimic direct sunlight. Unfortunately, the result will appear highly artificial if a large amount of background is included in the shot as the lighting will not extend evenly over the whole picture. A better method is to diffuse the light from the flash with a photographic umbrella or a sheet of translucent white cloth. This not only spreads the light over a larger area, but also gives a softer and more enveloping style of light. With this degree of control, flower photography in the field begins to resemble studio work, where even greater manipulation is possible.

Camera supports for low-level work

Many plants can only be photographed from ground level, yet the camera must be held as securely as on a normal tripod. Some tripods can be adapted, either by splaying out their legs, or by reversing the centre column. Alternatively, a base plate or pocket or table top tripod can be used. A base plate is simply a heavy round plate fitted with a ball and socket head to take the camera. Pocket and table top tripods should be used with caution as they are not particularly stable. This is a more important item of equipment than is often realized, and it will probably be worth spending a little extra for a good quality model. Another good possibility is a ground spike with a tripod head attached.

The quality of natural light varies greatly, and normally you will have to make the best of available conditions. Although there are many exceptions, direct sunlight is, as a general rule, best when the angle of lighting is low, and is more effective at showing texture and shape rather than colour. The delicacy of this clump of exotic grasses is enhanced by backlighting, which gives each seed head a luminous fringe. Colour precision is less important here. Hasselblad with 250 mm lens, Ektachrome 64, 1/60 sec at f11.

In some situations it is possible to use a portable flash unit to mimic sunlight, either because the natural lighting is not satisfactory, or because a breeze creates a risk of blurring at slow shutter speeds. Because the illumination from a small flash unit falls off rapidly, lighting from the front always looks unnatural, and the most effective method is the one shown here, where the flash is used to introduce a certain amount of backlighting as well as overhead illumination. In the photograph (left) a shaft of midday sunlight isolates the head of a dandelion in a forest clearing. In the right-hand photograph, a flash unit held above and slightly behind the same flower gives a passable imitation.
Nikon with 200 mm macro lens, Kodachrome 64, sunlight: 1/60 sec at f11/ flash: f27 with guide number 80 (ASA) and flash at 3 ft (1 m).

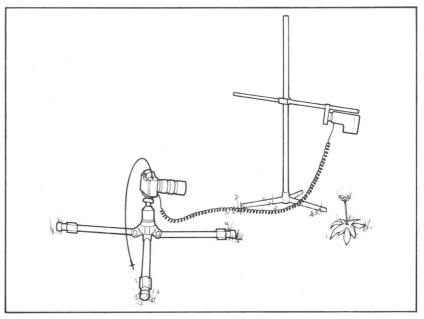

Dull weather or a shaded position is excellent for showing clear colours. The simple colours of this herb robert would have been lost in direct sunlight. Add a colour balancing filter if the light reaching a flower in the shade comes from a blue sky— an 81C, 81D or 81EF is usual. Nikon with 200 mm macro lens, Kodachrome 64, 1/4 sec at f11.

For an imitation of sunlight, as used in the dandelion picture (above), place the flash unit above and perhaps slightly behind the flower to achieve a degree of backlighting. A stand can be used as shown, or an assistant can hold the flash unit in place for you. Another method is to use the camera's delayed action timer and hold the flash unit yourself.

Close-up/insects and small animals 1

The practical problems of photographing flowers in close-up, such as depth of field and movement, are minor compared to those experienced with insects in the field. Given the size of most insects, depth of field is severely limited, and subject movement has to be expected. All of this makes natural light photography more difficult, although not impossible. Large insects that have predictable motionless periods, such as butterflies feeding, can be photographed in daylight, but to allow a fast enough shutter speed for hand-held shooting, the price is a wide aperture and shallow depth of field. The alternative is to use portable flash.

To find insects, you may rely on luck, or plan a search for a particular species whose habits you already know. If you have a specific subject in mind, research its habitat, seasonal cycle and diurnal activity beforehand. Otherwise, you may decide simply to set off on a nature walk and see what you can find. In either case, consider insect and small animal photography as a form of stalking, and be prepared to react quickly to short-lived opportunities. For this type of work, photographic techniques need very careful attention, as focusing, composition and lighting are all more critical than at normal scales. The basic rule is to have all the camera and flash adjustments pre-set.

Close-up equipment

The size of the insect or animal dictates the close-up accessories that you will need. Small lizards and large insects such as butterflies and dragonflies will fill most of a 35mm picture frame at magnifications of around 0.3×, and most of a 6 × 6cm frame when magnified to about 0.5×. Other insects may need to be photographed life-size (1.0×) or at even greater magnifications. The more the subject is magnified, the greater is the reduction in the depth of field, and very small insects are normally too difficult to work with in their natural habitats. They are better collected and photographed later in the studio or other controlled conditions.

Supplementary close-up lenses offer such weak magnifications that they are rarely useful, even with large insects. The best accessories are extension rings. Some now have couplings that allow viewing at full aperture even at a stopped-down setting. This feature is important, as focusing is extremely difficult through a small aperture, and working quickly in the field usually makes the use of a tripod and careful composition impossible. For the same reason, reversing the lens for better resolution at greater than life size magnifications is not normally practical, as it requires the aperture to be stopped down manually.

Because changes in magnification alter the focusing distance and exposure settings, you can easily lose valuable time in making calculations and adjustments. It is much simpler to choose an extension and focusing position before setting off,

Although the practical problems can be severe, many insects and small animals can be photographed using daylight alone. The two conditions are that the camera position and the aperture can be set so that the subject is covered by the depth of field, and that the creature remains reasonably still. This damsel fly was a good subject. Relatively inactive in the cool early morning, it could be approached to within less than a metre with a 200mm lens, and positioning the camera side-on to the long, thin body meant that very little depth of field was required.
Nikon with 200mm macro lens, Kodachrome 64, 1/4 sec at f16.

and work with these as much as possible. At close distances, the easiest way of focusing is not to adjust the focusing ring on the lens, but to move the whole camera towards the subject. To make the most of what depth of field there is, position the camera so that the insect presents the least depth–for example, side-on to a stick insect rather than head-on.

Standard lenses can be used, but as these are designed to give their optimum performance at normal scales of reproduction, picture quality suffers at close distances. Macro lenses are a much better choice–not only is resolution high, but the extended focusing range allows magnification up to about 0.5× without having to add an extension ring.

Choosing focal length involves compromise. Greater magnification is possible with any given extension when the focal length of the lens is short, but there are disadvantages. For life-size magnification (1.0×), a standard 50 mm lens needs only a 50 mm extension, which is not at all cumbersome, but the working distance becomes quite small–it can be little more than 50 mm from the lens to the subject. Apart from the danger of the lens casting a shadow, many insects will not tolerate so close an approach. For active or shy creatures, therefore, a longer focal length–100 mm or even up to 200 mm–is better, but high magnifications then demand unwieldy extensions. For the same life-size magnification, a 200 mm lens needs to be extended from the camera by 200 mm. Although extension rings can be added together to reach this length, a bellows is more usual. This can be difficult to use hand-held, however, especially if a double cable release is used for full-aperture viewing.

Using flash in the field

For the greatest sharpness and depth of field, portable flash is essential, and much of the success of insect photography depends on a reliable, simply used lighting arrangement. Because portability is important, the flash unit has to be small. This is not really a problem, for although a small flash tube gives harsh lighting with high contrast for large subjects, at the scale of insect life it is itself a relatively large light source. Even so, some method of filling in the shadow areas–whether with reflectors or secondary flash units–generally improves the photograph.

Because the flash unit is used at close distances, the output is usually high enough to allow very small apertures. Another advantage of small units is their ability to freeze the fast movement of insects and other small animals. With electronic flash, increased light output is achieved by extending the duration of the flash discharge, so that the larger the unit, the slower its speed. it follows that small units are particularly effective for freezing movement.

By far the greatest problems with flash in the field are the need to make sure that the head is directed exactly towards the subject and calculating the correct exposure. Without the modelling light used with studio flash units, there is no way of

Large insects such as this Australian spectacular grasshopper pose fewer problems. A lower magnification is needed, with greater depth of field and a smaller loss of light than when the lens is greatly extended. A longer focal length is better as it avoids frightening the insect with a close approach (J-P. Ferrero). Nikon with 55 mm macro lens, ASA 64, 1/60 sec at f11.

Insects are not the only subjects that can be found for this type of close-up photography. Small amphibians and reptiles are common in some parts of the world. This strikingly patterned, but tiny, arrow poison tree frog was photographed in Colombia. Nikon with 55 mm macro lens, ASA 64, 1/60 sec at f22 with portable flash unit.

Even with relatively large close-up subjects, such as this green lizard, depth of field can be a major problem. A side-on camera position achieved sharp focus for most of the creature, but the foreground and part of the tail nearest the camera were inevitably out of focus (J-P. Ferrero). Mamiya RB67 with 90 mm lens, ASA 64, 1/125 sec at f22 with two 200 Joule (watt-second) flash units at quarter power.

Close-up/insects and small animals 2

pre-viewing the lighting. The problem with exposure is to combine the calculations of flash to subject distance with the extra exposure needed for the lens extension. The inverse square law affects both of these—as the flash unit is moved closer, it gives stronger illumination, but as extensions are added between the lens and camera, more light is needed to give the same exposure to the film.

The only practical answer is to design a standard lighting set-up, checked in advance so that you are completely certain of the exposure and general quality of the lighting. A main flash unit combined with a small unit to fill in the shadows makes a good basic system, but to be really effective the flash units should be mounted firmly on a bracket attached to the camera. Then, the whole apparatus —camera, lens, extensions and lights—can be moved around the subject to focus and compose. The essential feature of a standard set-up like this is that it gives predictable lighting that can be reproduced under a variety of conditions.

To calibrate the lighting arrangement beforehand, run a test roll through the camera at different

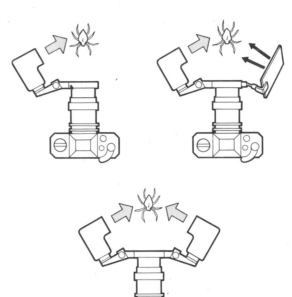

Flash positions are critical for close-up shots of small creatures. A bracket attached to the front of the lens can be used to obtain several different effective arrangements. The simplest is a single flash head but, although this type of light is easy to use, hard shadows may result. A reflector card fitted opposite the flash can provide useful fill-in. A more elaborate system uses two flash heads. Here, the effect is a more even illumination, closer in effect to a ringflash.

This leech (below) was photographed with the simplest of all flash arrangements—a single unit placed directly above the subject. This provides an acceptable quality of lighting with the least complication. An extension bracket, attached either to the camera body or to the front of the lens, as shown (above), gives the greatest consistency (J-P. Ferrero).

settings of the flash output, magnification and aperture. Over such critically short distances, guide number calculations are rarely very accurate, so bracketing is important when testing. A flash meter is invaluable, and as there are now many lightweight portable models available, it is a wise investment. Few photographers would consider working in natural light without an exposure meter, and a meter is just as essential for accurate flash work.

Ideally, the power and position of the flash unit should allow the use of the smallest aperture setting on the lens, in order to give the maximum depth of field. If the unit is too powerful, tape a neutral density filter or some diffusing material over the head, or alternatively use a slower film. Automatic units are usually better used on their manual settings, giving full output. On an automatic setting, the sensor drastically reduces the flash duration at close distances, and cannot make allowances for the lens extension. Neutral density filters can be taped over the sensor to fool it, but in the field there still remains the danger of the sensor reacting to a twig or leaf that is closer than the subject, so causing under-exposure.

Although a standard set-up is the key to accurate lighting, take the opportunity to experiment where possible. With a subject likely to remain in position–a spider on its web, for example–take the flash off its bracket and aim it from different directions. Cross-lighting, and even backlighting, may reveal interesting textures and outlines.

An alternative to standard portable flash units is a ringflash. Designed originally for medical use, it gives almost shadowless lighting by completely surrounding the lens, and is ideal for awkward, enclosed spaces. Even at extremely short working distances, the subject can be fully and evenly lit. Ringlights are normally available as separate units, but one interesting lens–the 200mm Medical Nikkor–has a circular tube actually built into the lens housing. Although highly specialized and limited in its applications, there is no more convenient piece of equipment for insect fieldwork. Coming almost from the lens itself, the light from a ringflash is flat which does not suit all subjects. In addition, any shiny surface, such as the carapace of some beetles, will give bright reflections.

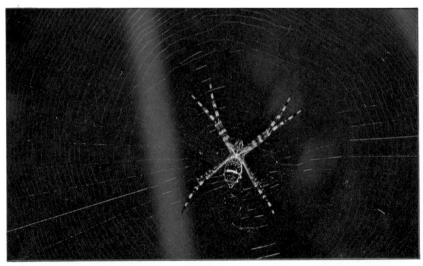

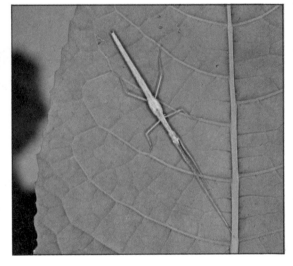

In close-up photography, the flash head is never more than a few inches from the subject, so that the background, unless extremely close, will be hardly illuminated at all. With subjects like a spider on its web (above left), this can be turned to advantage as it leaves fussy background details obscure (S. Peltz).

A medical lens is a compact combination of long-focus macro lens and ringflash. Less cumbersome than an added ringflash system, and containing its own tungsten modelling light, this specialized lens is ideal for small subjects hidden in confined spaces, such as this large spider (left) in its burrow. Because of the shorter working distance at greater magnifications, the depth of field is deeper than when the lens is used at moderate magnification.

An alternative to the small standard flash unit is a ringflash, fitted to the front of the lens and powered by a separate battery pack that can be slung over the shoulder or fitted to a belt. As the light comes from the same direction as the lens, there are virtually no shadows. This shows the shape of the subject poorly in some circumstances, but when the colour or tone of the insect is distinct from the background it can be very effective, as in this photograph of a tiny insect on the underside of a leaf in a South American rainforest (above).

THE ENVIRONMENT

Much nature and wildlife photography is concerned with individual plants and animals, and the treatment of these subjects inevitably tends towards a desire to reproduce an accurate appearance. Broaden the scope to include the landscapes and climate that provide the platform for life, and there is greater possibility of using the camera expressively. In fact, natural landscapes have a particularly strong emotional impact that can be used by the photographer, not least because of the contrast with our urban way of life.

With these large subjects, the aim is not simply to give a literal description, but to convey something of the variety of impressions made by, for example, a sweeping landscape, a forest, or an approaching storm. The environment is, by definition, the sum of many interlocking parts, and a successful photograph usually embraces more than a single quality. Frequently, we take our surroundings for granted, but one of the gifts of photography is that it forces us to take a closer look, to discover exactly which elements give a particular setting its special character. There is always the opportunity to find fresh and stimulating images, and nowhere is this more true than in the natural environment.

Landscape

Landscapes are the most accessible of all natural subjects. They are always available, they exist in infinite variety, and they change only in details of weather, season and the play of light. Nevertheless, they are among the most difficult of subjects to photograph, and probably cause more disappointment to photographers than any other type of subject matter.

The basic challenge of landscape photography is to evoke the experience of being a part of it. Because landscapes are such familiar subjects, we naturally expect no difficulties in being able to capture them on film, yet so many photographs are pale reflections of the scenes we remember. A casual shot, in the style of most postcards, conveys very little–to bring out a strong sense of place needs great care and skill.

A landscape combines many impressions, but the camera can record only a limited part of this. It is not simply the view that creates the sensation of beauty, drama or tranquility, but the interplay between elements: the wind in high trees, the chill of early morning mist over a meadow, the roll of thunder over a distant range of mountains, the fresh smell of grass after a shower. None of these things in itself can be captured in a single picture,

Whether the subject is familiar or exotic, a landscape photograph should be capable of provoking a fresh interest, either through the qualities inherent in the scene or through an individual treatment. Perched on the rim of a sandstone bowl, this landmark of eastern Utah has a natural grace that requires just two photographic qualities: a clear, uncluttered approach, and precise timing to capture the most effective lighting. Cambo 4 × 5 in (9 × 12 cm) view camera, Ektachrome 64, 1/60 sec at f16.

An accurate impression of the great emptiness of the desert is here expressed by the use of a panoramic format. The low lighting angle of evening gives enhanced contrast and sharp detail to the wind patterns in the sand, and overcomes the problems presented by the huge size and uniform tone of the sand-dunes. A low viewpoint emphasizes the scale of the subject. Panoramic camera, ASA 64, 1/30 sec at f16.

and the photographer must look for other ways to evoke the same feeling. When faced with a spectacular landscape, most people are content to enjoy it as a subjective experience rather than analyse its components. Yet this is what the landscape photographer must do–define exactly what it is in the landscape that is impressive, and translate this into imagery. The skill of landscape photography is in producing a picture that is equivalent to the photographer's experience.

With wildlife photography, however technically difficult it may be or whatever problems there are in finding your subject, you have one outstanding advantage–the animal itself is the obvious focus of interest. With landscape photography, on the other hand, you have to construct an interesting image from the raw materials of rocks, trees and sky. It may be overstating the case to say that landscapes need a more creative approach than wildlife, but they certainly do need a greater degree of interpretation, simply because there is such a wide choice of images in any one place.

Because landscapes are such flexible subjects they can be treated in many different ways. A photograph can be 'literal', using a representational treatment that conveys an instantly recognizable view and expresses the detail, texture and range of tones in the scene. Alternatively, it might be impressionistic, using graphic or textural elements for an unusual, subjective effect. The scale of landscapes can also be handled quite differently: the grandeur of a panoramic view is often the most immediate impression, but the compressed perspectives of a telephoto shot produce another treatment of large scale.

Above all, the essential element in landscape photography is lighting. This is the one quality that brings the greatest variety. It is often uncertain, always beyond the influence of the photographer, and occasionally, as with the approach of a summer storm, can create such unusual effects that the view is completely transformed from its normal appearance. By choosing the time of day or season of the year, and with patience and luck, the photographer can create a picture that stands apart from the expected. Many landscape photographers try to anticipate the way that a certain light will behave over a scene, and return, sometimes several times, until the angle and intensity of the sun and the form of the clouds are all just right. The low raking light shortly after dawn and before dusk is often the most interesting, emphasizing form and texture, while the rapid changes as the sun moves close to the horizon bring an exciting degree of unpredictability.

The individual approach: high-speed infrared film, which distorts the tones of the vegetation, is used here to create a weird and stormy effect. Landscape is the ideal subject for such highly personal interpretation. Nikon with 180mm lens, ASA 50 with Wratten 25 filter, 1/30 sec at f16.

Landscape/the panoramic view 1

The first reaction to an interesting landscape is often to take it in as a whole. It will be most immediately absorbed as a wide vista, stretching to the horizon. The eyes sweep across the scene, taking in the sense of scale, the mass of detail, the relationship between the foreground and the background. These are the appealing qualities of a panoramic view–expansive yet full of hidden interest.

To convey this impression on film takes care. Human perception views the scene quite differently to a photograph taken from the same viewpoint. With the real landscape, our eyes build up a composite impression by scanning, lingering over details one at a time. The difficulty with a photograph is the size it is reproduced. With a wide-angle lens there is no problem in capturing the full sweep of the view, but the end product is usually a small print or transparency that can be seen in just one glance. At a normal viewing distance, a picture that occupies half a page of this book can be taken in without moving the eyes. Pictures reproduced at this scale tend to diminish expansive views.

Lens and composition

Even with the limitations of picture size, there are several techniques that can help. A wide-angle lens is essential for this kind of work. A 24 mm lens on a 35 mm camera covers 74° horizontally, much wider than the 40 to 50° that we would consider to be our 'normal' angle of view.

With this kind of lens, which reproduces nearby objects large in comparison with those in the distance, you have an infinite choice of composition. By altering your viewpoint only slightly, the structure of the scene through the lens can change quite radically. Explore the way that the elements close to you appear in relation to the distant view. One of the fascinations of this kind of landscape picture is that the smallest details–grains of sand or blades of grass–can be juxtaposed against the massive scale of a range of mountains or an ocean horizon.

As such panoramic views rely heavily on the

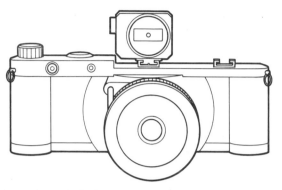

interplay of all the details in a scene, sharpness across the whole field of view is usually very important. A wide-angle lens has great depth of field–even at maximum aperture, a typical 28 mm lens for a 35 mm camera can render everything in focus from about 20 feet (6 metres) to infinity. But you will normally need to stop the aperture diaphragm down to its smallest opening, usually f22, if you want to bring the very near foreground into view at the same time as the horizon. At this setting, the shutter speed will often have to be quite slow, particularly close to sunrise or sunset when there is less light, and you will need a tripod or other support. A tripod with legs that can be angled for a low position is very useful, but otherwise you can press the camera down firmly onto a folded jacket placed on the ground or on a rock.

Film

According to the required effect, the choice of film is important. For the same reason that the lens is normally stopped down for greater depth of field– the need for sharpness–fine grain films are usually a better choice for this kind of shot than fast, grainy emulsions. Whether to work in black-and-white or colour is largely a matter of personal choice and style, but if you are in any doubt, think of the elements that compose the scene in front of you. Colour is such an integral part of some landscapes

The most effective way of obtaining panoramic views is to use a special camera. The Linhof Technorama shown here produces an image with three-to-one proportions on roll film. Unlike some other models which have rotating lenses, such as the Widelux, it has a fixed lens.

With normal cameras, wide-angle and fish-eye lenses produce the broad coverage needed for sweeping views of landscape. The angles obtained with the most commonly available short focal length lenses for 35 mm cameras are shown here.

The majority of landscapes, as we experience them, are essentially horizontal. The natural lines reinforce the eye's innate tendency to scan from side to side rather than up and down. The three-to-one proportions of a panoramic camera do much to reproduce this way of seeing–cropping off most of the sky and the foreground– without introducing noticeable distortion, as in this view of a valley in the central Andes of Colombia. Panoramic camera, Ektachrome 64, 1/30 sec at f19.

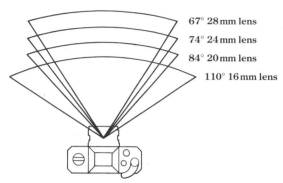

67° 28 mm lens
74° 24 mm lens
84° 20 mm lens
110° 16 mm lens

that colour film is a natural choice, but for others a strong graphic treatment can often be achieved more successfully with black-and-white film, which focuses attention closely on composition, tones and texture.

Framing

Although framing is inextricably linked to composition, it has a special importance in the panoramic view. Because the normal way of looking at things is horizontal, and our eyes scan more easily from side to side than up and down, most panoramic landscape views need a horizontal frame. The frame of the 35 mm format is ideal when used horizontally, being slightly longer than the 'classical' rectangular proportion. If you are using the square format of a 6 × 6 cm camera, however, you will have to crop the picture mentally as you take it, ignoring the wasted space at the top or bottom of the frame. A 6 × 7 cm medium format camera may be better in this respect.

One intriguing answer is a panoramic camera, which has an elongated frame. Although only certain views have the right distribution of interesting elements, this piece of equipment can be very effective in approaching the sensation of a wide, expansive view. Even without large reproduction, the stretched frame forces the eye to flick from side to side, just as in viewing a real landscape.

Very wide angle lenses can distort the image in two ways – by stretching towards the edges of the frame or, in the case of fish-eyes, by causing straight lines to bow out away from the centre. They can be used to create an abstract view as shown here by the unusual lines of this sand dune.
Nikon with 16 mm lens, Kodachrome 64, 1/60 sec at f16.

This photograph of the escarpment of the South Downs in England uses two methods of conveying a wide field of view: the first is to place the sun at the far left of the frame, contrasting with the storm clouds stretched across the remainder of the picture; secondly the very low viewpoint establishes a relationship between the close foreground and the distance.
Nikon with 20 mm lens with neutral graduated filter, Kodachrome 64, 1/30 sec at f14.

Landscape/the panoramic view 2

The effect of a wide-angle landscape photograph depends to a great extent on the size at which it is reproduced. Spread over two full pages and viewed at normal reading distance, this evening view of Monument Valley retains a sense of the scale of the original scene. Nikon with 20mm lens, Kodachrome 64, 1/15 sec at f8.

Landscape/the view camera

Although a specialized instrument, slow and cumbersome by comparison with modern 35mm equipment, the view camera has a special place in landscape photography. Its heritage is almost as old as the history of photography, and it is a tribute to its basically simple yet adaptable construction that its design has changed very little in over a century. Modern monorail cameras, widely used in studio and architectural photography, are refined pieces of engineering, yet they still comprise just four basic parts: a lens at the front, film holder at the back, a flexible light-tight container that connects them both, and a base that holds everything in place.

The view camera's large film size –4 × 5in (9 × 12cm) is the most popular format, but some models accept film measuring up to 11 × 14ins (28 × 35.5cms)–allows superb definition, and some of the world's most famous landscape photographers, such as Ansel Adams and Edward Weston, have made use of this to convey rich detail, fine textures and subtle tonal gradations. But perhaps even more important is the great optical control that the view camera makes possible. By being able to move the lens panel and film back in relation to each other, shapes can be altered and different parts of the image can be brought into focus simultaneously. Both the lens panel and the film back can be moved up and down. They can also be tilted forwards and backwards, and rotated from side to side. The bellows, which form the view camera's body, are flexible enough

Rather than simply narrowing the aperture to increase depth of field in order to bring sharpness to the whole image, the movements of a view camera offer a more elegant solution. By tilting the lens panel forwards, according to the principles described opposite, the stone in the foreground, less than two feet (60 cm) from the camera, and the horizon can be focused at the same time. In this way, a fairly wide lens aperture can be used, and consequently an acceptably fast shutter speed.
Cambo 4 × 5in (9 × 12cm) view camera with 90mm lens, Ektachrome 64, 1/15 sec at f11.

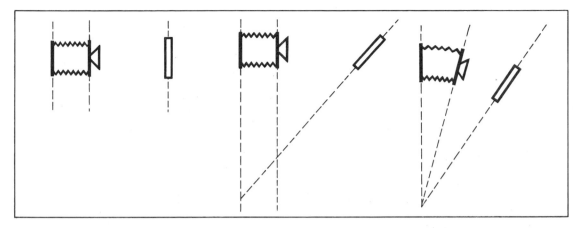

The principles by which the movements of a view camera are used to control focus are known as the Scheimpflug rule. When the subject, lens panel and film plane are precisely parallel (left), the whole subject will be in focus. When the subject is at an angle to the lens panel and film plane (centre), only part will be in focus. However, when subject, lens panel and film plane are all angled so that lines projected from them will intersect at the same point (right), the whole subject will once again be in focus.

to allow all of these movements to be combined and, provided that the lens has a sufficient covering power, these adjustments can solve otherwise insurmountable photographic difficulties.

A common problem, particularly when photographing trees, is the convergence of verticals in the shot. Pointing the camera even slightly upwards, which is often necessary if you want to frame a whole tree from ground-level, causes the perspective affect whereby parallel trees appear to lean towards each other. The view camera can solve this. With the camera level, the tree-trunks stay parallel to each other, but by either raising the lens panel or lowering the film back, the whole image area is shifted upwards so that the tops of the trees can be included in the frame.

A second, more frequent problem, is achieving sufficient depth of field to keep a close foreground and a distant background in focus at the same time. Stopping down the lens aperture is one solution, but a more effective method is to tilt either the lens panel or the film back. Doing this alters the actual plane of focus. With a normal, fixed-body camera, the plane of focus is parallel to the film plane – with the view camera you can choose exactly where it will lie. The basis of this remarkable property is the impressively named Scheimpflug Principle. According to this rule, if the planes of the film, the lens and the subject all meet at a common point, then the whole image will be sharply focused.

Take for example a scene with a stone in the foreground less than two feet from the camera and the horizon several miles away. Ordinarily, there is no way of increasing the depth of field to bring both into focus, even at the smallest aperture. By tilting the lens panel of a view camera forward slightly, however, the whole plane of focus can be moved from a vertical to an almost horizontal position, bringing the entire subject into focus. In almost every scene, there is one plane that will bring most components into sharpest focus. See the plane in your mind's eye, and swing or tilt the view camera's front or back to intersect it.

The view camera loses these advantages to some extent when faced with a distant view. Long-focus lenses for large format cameras can be heavy and bulky, and to use them requires a long bellows extension, which is extremely sensitive to movement from wind. A long-focus photograph has little need of an unusual plane of focus, however, and converging verticals are in any case less of a problem.

A view camera's movements can also be used to control the perspective of the image. Parallel lines, such as these pine trees, may converge unattractively if the camera is tilted upwards. By raising the front panel of the view camera, the lines are rendered parallel because the higher part of the subject can be kept in the frame even though the camera is kept horizontal.
Cambo 4 × 5 in (9 × 12 cm) view camera with 90 mm lens, ASA 25, 1/2 sec at f32.

Landscape/the distant view

A completely different approach to landscapes is to use a long-focus lens. Whereas a wide-angle lens is all embracing, drawing the viewer into the picture, the long-focus lens reaches out and selects parts of the scene. In a sense, it gives a more objective and dispassionate image, and is especially effective for strong, graphic compositions.

This kind of landscape picture is entirely the product of photography. Landscape painting developed many of the techniques of the panoramic view to a fine degree, but only the special optics of a long-focus lens could suggest this type of view. The two most important properties of the lens are magnification and the compression of perspective. Magnification makes it possible to select views that are not always apparent to the eye, cutting out the surrounding details. The compressed perspective flattens the planes of the picture, and actually restores a truer sense of scale. Distant mountains appear to loom over nearer hills, and the effect can be a more two-dimensional, graphic image.

In practice, one of the great advantages of this approach is that several quite different photographs may be possible from one viewpoint. A very powerful lens, such as 600mm on a 35mm

camera, covers only four degrees, a fraction of the complete panoramic view. It is unlikely that there will be equally interesting views in every direction, but a considerable choice can be expected.

Using a long-focus lens

Because the majority of landscape shots are static, there is usually time to use a tripod, and this gives the opportunity to stop the lens right down for maximum depth of field by using extremely slow shutter speeds—1/4 sec or longer. Although wildlife subjects often benefit from shallow depth of field, which throws foreground and background out of focus, landscapes tend to look best when everything is sharply focused. To some extent it could be argued that this is a question of style, but familiarity with landscape pictures that have a wide depth of field has certainly made it conventional.

When buying a tripod, select it for rigidity as well as for being easy to carry. You will probably have to compromise between these two qualities as the lightest tripods are rarely solid. Nevertheless, great weight alone does not make a tripod secure. Test the firmness of a tripod and tripod head by mounting a long lens on it and tapping the

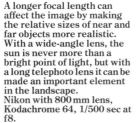

A longer focal length can affect the image by making the relative sizes of near and far objects more realistic. With a wide-angle lens, the sun is never more than a bright point of light, but with a long telephoto lens it can be made an important element in the landscape.
Nikon with 800 mm lens, Kodachrome 64, 1/500 sec at f8.

end of the lens. If there is any significant movement, the tripod will probably be of little use on a windy day.

When setting up the camera outside, find a sheltered location whenever possible. Wind vibration is one of the chief causes of camera shake. With a single lens reflex camera, reduce the risk of vibration even further by locking up the instant return mirror before releasing the shutter. And always use a cable release.

Because of the distances over which long-focus lenses are usually used, atmospheric haze can soften the image, weakening the colours. In mountains, it can contribute to an overall blue cast with colour film. Ultraviolet filters will partly correct this—they are available in different strengths, and with a very long focal length, such as 600mm or more on a 35mm camera, a strong ultraviolet filter is very useful. Even greater haze penetration is possible with a polarizing filter, and this can dramatically improve colour saturation. A polarizing filter is even more valuable for this property than for its more common use in deepening blue skies. Its only real disadvantage is that it needs nearly two stops additional exposure.

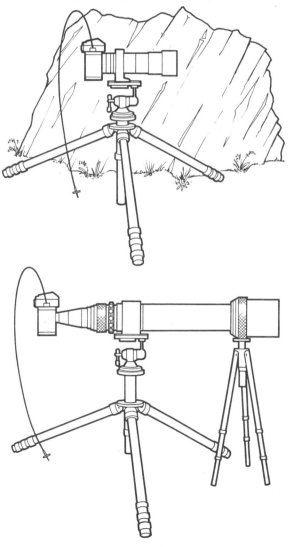

The longer the focal length of lens, the more susceptible it is to movement, even from a slight breeze. It is important to take precautions. First of all, use the tripod in its most stable position, with legs spread wide if this is possible or with the tripod set low with its legs retracted. Choose a site protected from the wind—such as behind a rock.'With a very long lens, it may be necessary to add a second smaller tripod to support the lens (left).

A long-focus lens renders perspective with a different appearance to wide-angle lenses. The foreshortened effect of the long lens gives the impression that the landscape is layered. This is most obvious when the viewpoint is high and the scene contains strong vertical components, such as these Andean foothills rising above the valley clouds. Hasselblad with 500 mm lens, Ektachrome 64, 1/250 sec at f 11.

Landscape/searching for the unusual

The shape and proportions of this long span of rock in Utah's Arches National Park are arresting enough under conventional lighting conditions, but by positioning the camera on the edge of the arch's shadow and underexposing, the lines are strongly abstracted. Using backlighting to create a silhouette is a useful way of eliminating most elements of an image other than shape. Nikon with 20 mm lens, ASA 64, 1/1,000 sec at f22.

More than anything else, photography is concerned with producing fresh images—different ways of looking at our surroundings. Landscapes are good subjects for experimentation as the basic elements are constant, unlike wildlife, which can be elusive and skittish, tending to demand quick reactions rather than individual interpretation.

In trying to produce new landscape images, two routes are open. You can search out unusual locations that are inherently interesting because of their strangeness, and you can deliberately look for original treatments of familiar scenes. In landscape, as in most other forms of photography, the unexpected image is highly prized.

Unusual locations

Searching for exotic locations can be arduous and time-consuming, but the results can also be extremely rewarding. Much of the world is already familiar, either through personal travel or through television, magazines and so on, but there are still some surprisingly accessible places that are quite unknown to the majority of people. In North America, there are many spectacular scenes within easy reach of good highways—Arches National Park, or Death Valley, for example. The well populated parts of Europe have, by definition, few really unknown landscapes, but Iceland and northern Scandinavia are two examples of areas rich in exciting views. Every part of the world has pockets of the unusual, and popular travel guides and television travelogues have by no means exhausted them all.

Unusual treatments

Creating the unusual with your own style and approach enables you to work with more familiar and easily available scenes, but there is a considerable challenge in attempting to find a fresh image of a well known view. One worthwhile approach is to reduce a landscape to basic graphic elements, creating a view that is more abstract than naturalistic. Essentially, this relies on your being able to find graphic possibilities to begin with, but there are a number of helpful techniques.

1. Careful choice of lighting is the most important control over a landscape that there is. Silhouettes at dusk, dawn, or against a low sun can reduce rocks, trees and other objects to simple shapes.
2. Lenses with either very short or very long focal lengths can introduce unfamiliar perspectives.
3. Altering the tonal range, particularly by using high contrast printing, tends to emphasize shape and pattern. This is easier to achieve in black-and-white, either by choosing a high contrast film, such as graphic arts line film or high speed infrared, or by using a hard grade of printing paper. Black-and-

The strange lighting effects of twilight are enormously varied. Here, the wisps of cloud are lit from below as the last glow of the sun disappears. Nikon with 180 mm lens, ASA 64, 1/125 sec at f11.

white infrared film can produce very striking images – most vegetation appears white, clear sky reproduces as black, and virtually all atmospheric haze is eliminated, making distant scenes appear sharp and detailed.

4. Altering colours with specialized darkroom techniques, such as solarization or the selective alteration of filters in colour printing, can allow an almost unlimited control over colours. Two relatively simple methods that do not require expert technique are to use colour infrared film and to process a normal transparency film as a negative. In both cases, unusual colours result, quite unlike those seen in the natural world.

5. Deliberate over- or under-exposure can be effective, particularly when combined with high-contrast lighting conditions, such as shots into the sun. Here, the graphic possibilities of silhouettes and reflections off shiny surfaces can be exploited.

Different items of photographic equipment can also introduce distortion of one kind or another – shape, colour or tone – but effects that rely completely on technical tricks should be handled sparingly, as their frequent use quickly becomes a cliché. True fish-eye lenses, for example, produce such a strong distortion that their very use completely dominates the image, whatever the subject or whoever is taking the picture. In addition, most so-called 'special effects' filters, particularly the multi-coloured ones, produce gimmicky results. Nevertheless, any photographic process is a potentially useful tool in creative hands.

The extraordinary shapes of natural phenomena such as these mineral deposits at Mammoth Hot Springs, Yellowstone National Park, Wyoming, can provide the photographer with striking opportunities.
Nikon with 105 mm lens, ASA 64, 1/125 sec at f16.

A little less than half an hour before sunset, the combination of deep blue sky and orange-red sunlight was at its strongest, and ideal for a treatment of this sandstone tower (far left) that concentrated on the colour of the rock. Frontal lighting reduced distracting shadows.
Nikon with 400 mm lens, Kodachrome 64, 1/60 sec at f8.

Colour infrared film, developed originally for camouflage detection and forestry surveys from the air, is made to respond to infrared, green and red light, rather than blue, green and red like normal colour emulsions. The infrared sensitivity causes the film to react strongly to the chlorophyl in healthy vegetation, which appears as a distinctive red, rather than green. Using different coloured filters over the lens can have unexpected results, rarely predictable. Here, a green filter was used.
Nikon with 180 mm lens, Ektachrome Infrared, 1/125 sec at f8.

95

Trees 1

More often than not, surrounding trees and vegetation make it difficult to obtain a clear view of a chosen specimen, and the choice of subject may be determined almost entirely by its location. In this forest in the northern Everglades, a long walk produced the possibilities of only two or three satisfactory views of the cabbage palm typical of the area. The clearing in front of this small stand was just large enough to work with a moderately wide-angle lens. Using surrounding leaves as a frame, and waiting until the late afternoon sunlight emphasized the palms also helped to clarify the view. Sinar 4 × 5 in (9 × 12 cm) view camera with 90 mm lens, Ektachrome 64, 1/30 sec at f22.

Single trees, particularly when set against a background that contrasts in either colour or tone, are among the easiest of subjects. The pale leaves and trunk of this birch in autumn, at the foot of a wooded hillside, make it stand out clearly against the darker trees behind even in the flat lighting of an overcast day. The focus was set soft to enhance the chiaroscuro appearance of the leaves, and a long-focus lens isolated the image.
Nikon with 180 mm lens, Kodachrome 64, 1/60 sec at f2.8.

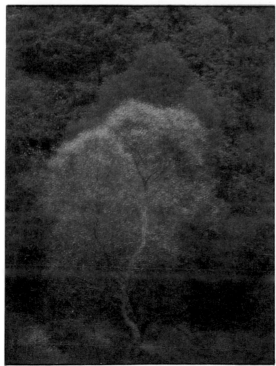

Although trees feature in many landscape photographs as part of the scene, and provide the setting for a variety of wildlife shots, they are also rewarding subjects in their own right. The apparent simplicity of good photographs of trees belies the care and selectivity they require. Most trees have complicated outlines, and they also frequently occur in stands, making it difficult to isolate individual specimens pictorially. As a result, the main preoccupation of tree photography is clarity. In order to show a single tree, you must find ways of making it stand out from its background—often a mass of other trees of the same species. Even when isolating individual trees is not the intention, photographing a stand or forest involves the problem of avoiding a cluttered and confusing picture.

Selecting a specimen

The first, crucial step is to find the right location, particularly if you are looking for a single tree. It should be representative of its type and in healthy condition. A degree of isolation and an attractive background will also help. There is no short cut to finding good specimens, and making your own reconnaissance is the only effective way. Other people's glowing descriptions usually ignore the details that ruin a photograph—telegraph wires in

The strong shapes of old, weatherbeaten trees such as these, high on the slopes of a Costa Rican volcano, can produce strong images. Here the conditions were extreme, with heavy rain and a driving wind. The distortion of an ultra wide-angle lens added to the mysterious effect. Nikon with 18mm lens, ASA 64, 1/125 sec at f3.5.

These Monterey cypresses in California show the graphic impact that can be found in the twisted branches of dead trees. The low lighting angle of evening and the vegetation behind combined with the use of a long-focus lens to emphasize the two dimensional qualities of the subject. Nikon with 180mm lens, ASA 64, 1/250 sec at f8.

view, an unsuitable background, or no one view-point that includes the whole tree.

Viewpoint and choice of lens

Having found the best specimen available, look for the best camera angle. Walk right around the tree, at different distances. If the light appears wrong, it may be better at another time of day. If the tree is surrounded closely by obstructions or other trees, a wide-angle lens may provide the solution as it can be used from a short distance, but perspective distortion may be a problem—wide-angle distortion, where objects near to the camera appear relatively large, is particularly unacceptable with trees, simply because the crowns tend to disappear from view.

In many cases, a long-focus lens gives the best proportions, reducing perspective distortion, and also helps to give an isolated view. In order to find a clear distant viewpoint, stand by the tree itself and look for a clearly visible hillside or stretch of open ground. These places will probably offer an unrestricted view back to the tree.

Lighting

Though there is very little that can be done to control lighting conditions when photographing

Trees 2

Low-angled sunlight often picks out individual trees while leaving the remainder in shadow. On a Colorado mountainside, these brilliantly coloured aspens stand out clearly in the backlighting from an afternoon sun.
Nikon with 180 mm lens, ASA 64, 1/250 sec at f8.

Although details are often obscured and colours muted, fog and mist can be useful weather conditions for separating individual trees from their backgrounds. The mist before dawn in South America's Guiana Highlands clearly reveals the shape of this rainforest tree by masking its surroundings. Less than an hour later, it was virtually indistinguishable from the mass of vegetation on the hillside behind.
Hasselblad with 500 mm lens, ASA 400, 1/8 sec at f8.

trees, they are an essential element. Here too, the ideal is a clear view. With most trees, the mass of detail in leaves and branches can make the scene confusing in bright overhead sunlight. The complex appearance of highlights and deep shadows overwhelms the shapes. Three kinds of natural light are useful for overcoming this difficulty:

Low, raking sunlight The low angle and warm colours of early morning and late afternoon are attractive for landscapes in general and also for trees in particular. The special advantage of a low sun in tree photography is that, under the right conditions, it can highlight individual trees while leaving the background in shadow. Unfortunately, the precise effect is difficult to predict in advance, even if you carefully work out the sun's path earlier in the day. With this kind of lighting, it is best simply to take advantage of it as you find it.

Flat, overcast lighting Dull, cloudy days are rarely ideal for photographic subjects, but for trees and plants, particularly those with complex detail, they can provide the perfect lighting. With the minimum of shadow and low contrast, shapes, patterns and colours of leaves and branches can be recorded more faithfully than at any other time. Problems to avoid are silhouetting a tree against a

dull white sky, which will weaken the image of smaller branches with flare, and uninteresting backgrounds. Generally speaking, flat lighting is best for detail shots and views where a mass of trees fills the frame.

Fog and mist Early morning mist, banks of fog, or shifting clouds at high altitude can produce atmospheric, impressionistic effects. They also tend to isolate individual trees by separating them from their background. As with low sunlight, these conditions are frequently unpredictable, and the choice of lens depends largely on how thick the mist or fog is—if it is dense, you may need to move closer and use a wide-angle lens in order to be able to achieve any detail in a photograph of an individual tree.

Details

Bark, leaves, or the contorted shapes of limbs are sometimes more interesting than the whole tree. For example, the bark of a silver birch is its most arresting characteristic, and it may be possible to use it more effectively in close-up than in an overall shot. Selecting details can also add visual variety to a collection of several tree photographs if they are presented for viewing together.

The intricacy of these giant ferns in the undergrowth of a gully in the northern Andes would have suffered from confusing shadows and highlights in direct sunlight. The strongly diffused, shadowless lighting of an overcast day was ideal for keeping the image simple. Hasselblad with 38 mm lens, ASA 64, 1/30 sec at f9.

Particularly when combined with larger scale views, details such as these close-ups of bark and lichen broaden any photographic coverage of trees by varying the scale.
Nikon with 55 mm macro lens, ASA 64, 1/2 sec at f16.

Volcanoes and geysers

On an acidic volcano that experiences occasional moderate activity, such as Purace in central Colombia, the upper slopes of the cone are typically strewn with ash, varying from granules and cinders to fine dust. There are also likely to be a few boulders, all ejected from the last eruption. Mild activity often continues in the form of acidic steam and sulphurous clouds pouring from vents in the slope. Vegetation is usually absent. Panoramic camera with 90 mm lens, ASA 64, 1/4 sec at f32.

Even without the forecast of a major eruption, many craters still give the impression of activity and make good subjects for photography, although there may be considerable danger. In the centre of the large crater of Poas, in Costa Rica, fumaroles cluster at the edge of a lake of hot sulphurous acid, and frequent gas eruptions blow rocks into the air. Conditions like this are extremely corrosive to equipment. Hasselblad with 38 mm lens, ASA 64, 1/125 sec at f5.6.

For those who have stood beside a molten lava flow, or walked on the thin echoing shell of a volcano's crater floor, the earth will never again seem such a solid, immutable foundation. Volcanoes, and all their associated features–geysers, hot springs, fumaroles and mud pots–are in one sense landscape curiosities, but in another way they are the core of the natural environment, as close as it is possible to get to the origins of the earth. Just as with the most active and skittish animals, volcanic activity is unpredictable enough to be an exciting photographic subject.

Volcanoes

The most violent volcanic activity involves pyroclastic or lava eruptions. Volcanoes are complex and highly individual landforms, not easily classified, but the composition of lava makes a big difference to their behaviour and appearance. Some lava volcanoes, such as Halemaumau and Kilauea in Hawaii, contain very little silica. Their eruptions are relatively quiet, with copious streams of molten lava. Volcanoes with very acidic lava, however, such as Vesuvius, are rich in silica and produce lava that is thick and solidifies quickly. Their lava tends to plug the vent, like a cork in a bottle, and eruptions tend to be violent and destructive. This kind of volcano conforms to the popular image of a steep cone, whereas basic volcanoes are usually flatter and cover much larger areas.

Eruptions are obviously dangerous, and you should always seek informed local advice before approaching an active volcano. However, even in relatively quiescent stages, volcanoes can be full of

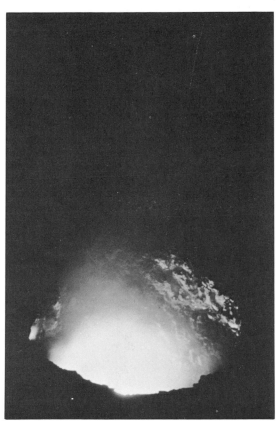

interesting activity. For millenia after an eruption, the crater and flanks can emit clouds of corrosive steam from vents known as fumaroles.

Hot springs and geysers

Water in contact with volcanic rocks produces some fascinating features. Hot springs are characteristic of recent volcanic activity. These upwellings of lukewarm to boiling water, heated by molten subterranean materials, are rich in disolved minerals, particularly silica, and are often brightly coloured, both from the minerals and from strains of algae that thrive in the heated water. The Grand Prismatic Spring in Yellowstone National Park contains colours that range from the deep indigo of the central pool to the reds and oranges of the algae-covered margins. In some instances, the dissolved silica precipitates as a hard deposit, which can form either a surrounding crust or whole terraces.

Geysers are very similar to hot springs, save for one important quality – they spout violent bursts of boiling water at more or less regular intervals. The mechanism of a geyser is in theory relatively straightforward, but the necessary conditions involve a delicate balance of several factors. Below ground is a column of water, in contact at the bottom with hot volcanic rocks. At great pressure, this water cannot boil. Instead, being very hot, it rises by convection. As it nears the surface the pressure is relaxed, and the water boils rapidly. A large pocket of steam then pushes the topmost column of water up into the air in a dramatic gush. Old Faithful, perhaps the world's most famous

geyser, regularly spouts 100 to 200 feet (30 to 60 metres) into the air, but even this is not the highest. The world record is held by Waimangu Geyser in New Zealand, which in 1909 reached more than 1,000 feet (300 metres).

The behaviour of geysers is finely tuned – only the right blend of temperature and pressure distinguishes them from hot springs. Most geysers can, in fact, be 'tickled' into life by pouring soapy water into their throats, reducing surface tension and causing foaming, or even by stirring with a stick. Apart from being potentially dangerous, these practices are normally forbidden in regulated areas of geyser activity.

Care of equipment

For photographic equipment, volcanoes are as extreme a condition as any that exist. Heat is an obvious problem, but as sheer discomfort discourages the photographer from staying too long near its source, it is not normally the greatest risk. Airborne grit and dirt are more serious, and continuous cleaning is usually necessary. Sulphur dioxide is a major component of volcanic gases, and when combined with steam produces sulphurous acid, much more damaging than water. A Hasselblad belonging to the author exposed for half an hour to fumarole gases in the crater of a Costa Rican volcano was corroded so badly that it had to be thrown away. Close to an eruption site, the vibration transmitted through the ground can be an unexpected difficulty, particularly at night when a tripod and long exposures are needed.

As a shot to establish the main elements of a scene, the cone of an acidic lava volcano is so typical that it often merits a treatment that emphasizes its familiar shape. A silhouette, at sunrise or sunset, is often effective, as in this view across Guatemala's Lake Atitlan (above left). Hasselblad with 38 mm lens, ASA 64, 1/60 sec at f5.6.

Although molten lava is popularly associated with eruptions, there are a number of volcanoes where lava activity is normal and relatively quiet. Under the crater floor of Santiago volcano in Nicaragua, a lava lake is easily visible through the main vent. With molten lava, night is the most interesting time to shoot, but the long exposures necessary may be difficult to make without camera shake as a tripod can transmit vibrations from the earth. Nikon with 500 mm lens, ASA 64, 1/2 sec at f8.

Weather 1

Capturing the shape and texture of clouds on a heavily overcast day, without direct sunlight, is usually difficult, and depends on finding a bank of clouds with a definite structure, such as this large mass over a curve of the River Amazon. The thin horizon line at the bottom of the picture gives a sense of scale and a base to the composition.
Hasselblad with 80 mm lens, ASA 64, 1/125 sec at f4.

The most changeable and active aspect of the natural environment is the weather. It not only controls the quality of lighting, but it can also produce powerful images in its own right. Inevitably, strong cloud formations are the easiest subjects, but there is no practical method of anticipating them. Even when armed with a weather forecast, there is no certainty that, say, a passing cold front will actually look distinct or interesting. Good photographs of weather are almost exclusively a product of luck and the fast reactions of a photographer.

Viewpoint

Almost a cardinal rule of weather photography is the inclusion of at least a small part of the ground in the shot. An edge to edge picture of sky, no matter how interesting the clouds are, gives the viewer no reference point and no sense of scale. A thin horizon line at the bottom of the frame, however, establishes a relationship between sky and land, and gives a measure of how the weather affects the rest of the environment.

Choice of focal length depends entirely on the area of interest. Rain falling in a curved sheet over a distant hillside calls for a long-focus lens, but a weather panorama that includes both the horizon and the sky overhead needs a very wide-angle lens, probably 20 mm for a 35 mm camera. Interestingly, the original use of circular image fish-eye lenses was to record weather conditions across the whole area of the sky.

One exception to the need for a horizon line is an aerial view of weather. In a horizontal shot at cloud-level, the perspectives are more recognizable, and well defined cumulus, for example, can take on the appearance of a mountainous landscape.

Lightning

One weather curiosity that is often gratifyingly easy to photograph, at least at night, is lightning. In a sense, lightning takes its own picture, for the only practical way of photographing it is to place the camera on a tripod, aim it in the general direction of where the next flash is likely to occur, and leave the shutter open until the lightning strikes. A moderately wide aperture—perhaps f2—and even a moderately slow ASA 64 film will be sufficient. In

Climbing above the clouds can give a very different view of the weather. Lower down the slopes of these Andes foothills, the landscape would be shrouded in thick cloud. Above, the light is stronger and the clouds themselves provide effective surroundings for the distant hill.
Hasselblad with 80 mm lens, ASA 64, 1/125 sec at f8.

If conditions are right, the backlighting from a rising or setting sun can heighten contrast and show up heavy storm clouds well. By the nature of storms, these conditions usually change rapidly, and quick camera work is usually needed. Where the clouds, rain and horizon are silhouetted, as here, it is normally better to expose for the highlights rather than risk overexposure, with bleached out highlights and weak silhouettes.
Nikon with 400 mm lens, Kodachrome 64, 1/125 sec at f5.6.

These clouds were silhouetted against the twilight sky and also reflected in the still waters of the Venezuelan lake to give a moody, sombre shot.
Nikon with 24 mm lens, ASA 64, 1/30 sec at f3.5.

Weather 2

Although an overcast sky may be almost featureless, composing the photograph so that a dark sky dominates the picture area heightens the importance of the weather. In this desert storm on the Rio Grande in Texas, the visible details of the horizon benefit from the contrast.
Cambo 4 × 5 in (9 × 12 cm) view camera with 150 mm lens, ASA 64, 1/4 sec at f11.

Lightning is not as difficult to photograph as might be expected, as long as it is night-time or at least dim twilight. The camera is placed on a tripod, pointing in the direction of the last flash, with the shutter left open. The lightning then photographs itself (M. P. Kahl/Bruce Coleman). Nikon with 28 mm lens, ASA 64, time exposure at f2.

practice, there is a wide range of acceptable exposure for lightning.

Fortunately, lightning flashes usually occur in a series, and are normally close to each other. Having seen one, you can reasonably expect more to occur in the same direction. A wide-angle lens improves the chances of catching the next flash in frame. The shutter can even be left open for subsequent bolts of lightning, although if there is a strong wind, the cloud edges illuminated by each flash will appear as a series of ghost images as the clouds move across the frame.

The best time to photograph lightning, although there is usually little choice, is when there is just enough natural light to show the horizon. The most difficult time is during the day, when the light levels are so high that the shutter cannot be left open for long. In this case, a certain amount of luck and a lot of film are the only answers.

The powerful shapes of massed clouds make a perfectly adequate subject in themselves—particularly when backlit, as here. Hasselblad with 250 mm lens, ASA 64, 1/125 sec at f5.6.

Here, a panoramic view, including only a limited area of sky, gives a strong impression of the low clouds scurrying across the landscape. Panoramic camera, ASA 64, 1/125 sec at f11.

SPECIAL LOCATIONS

The basic techniques of stalking, working from hides, close-ups in the field and landscape photography are perfectly adequate for most conditions and suit a variety of woodland and grassland environments. In detail, each photographic area has its own peculiarities, but there are principles which remain constant. Within the specialized discipline of wildlife photography, for example, patterns of animal behaviour respond ultimately to the type of climate, terrain and food supply, and so long as these remain within certain broad limits, the same techniques can be used.

At the same time, life on Earth inhabits a very wide range of conditions. There are few places so hostile that they do not support some living thing—and some of these are sufficiently extreme or unusual that they need special consideration. Extremes of temperature, humidity and altitude test the limits of organisms to adapt, and also pose severe difficulties for the photographer, together with his film and equipment. Cameras and emulsions are designed for temperate conditions and need special protection when exposed to a sub-zero Arctic day, the baking heat of a tropical desert, or air so saturated with moisture that it permeates and corrodes equipment. Even the apparently benign environment of the seashore demands special precautions—salt water can destroy a camera as quickly and effectively as any hazard.

Although some of the extreme locations that follow may seem a little adventurous and beyond the experience of most photographers, they hold the fascination of some of the most interesting and unusual landscape and wildlife subjects. Extreme conditions encourage ingenious adaptations, such as the pigmentation changes of polar animals or the talented mimicry of some tropical insects. Not surprisingly the special conditions that are described in this section include the least explored and least photographed habitats—they are so full of new opportunities that the difficulties of working in them are, in most cases, amply rewarded by the wealth of interesting subject matter.

As camera and film technology improves continuously, more of these special conditions come within reach of the non-specialist. Underwater photography, once the preserve of a few professional divers, is now a popular amateur sport, and catered for by a wide range of simple commercial camera housings and waterproof equipment. Aerial photography, which can give a completely different perspective to the natural environment, has followed the boom in light aircraft—an hour's flying time with a professional pilot is, in most countries, not prohibitively expensive and with a careful choice of location and weather conditions, can yield pictures of striking beauty.

Grotto Geyser erupting in
late afternoon sunlight,
Yellowstone National Park.

Polar conditions 1

One of the most severe limits on life is imposed by cold. In the high latitudes of the Arctic and Antarctic, low temperatures dominate the environment. Virtually all the evolutionary adaptions of living things are devoted to withstanding the extreme conditions, underlining the fact that it is climate more than anything else that marks the boundaries for survival.

Conserving heat is the chief preoccupation of most Arctic and Antarctic dwellers, and most have evolved specialized physiologies. Air pockets in the fibres of fur or feathers are a common form of insulation, as are loose folds of skin and 'undercoats' of down. Because the intensity of cold varies from summer to winter, these adaptations are often seasonal. Many Arctic animals have two and sometimes three distinct phases, growing winter coats for the worst conditions of the year.

The snow that comes with the lower temperatures brings another danger, clearly exposing animals and birds to the attention of predators. The winter coat for many is a well camouflaged white. At the onset of winter, the arctic fox, ptarmigan and others stop producing melanin, the dark pigment responsible for skin and pelt tone. The result is a winter appearance in striking contrast to the creature's summertime coat. These distinct phases are of obvious photographic interest.

One of the most extreme adaptations to a cold life is found among plants. The undistinguished looking lichens are probably better suited to the rigours of the Polar winter than any other form of life. Actually a partnership between a fungus and a type of algae, lichens combine resilience with an ability to function chemically at sub-zero temperatures. The fungus partner provides a tough, spongy physical protection, while the algae can continue to produce energy by photosynthesis in extreme cold. When the temperature drops below even the lichen's limits, the plant simply goes into suspended animation.

Switching off like this is one of two ways in which life survives the very worst of the Polar winter. The threshold of activity differs from creature to creature, but once it is reached, a solution for many animals is to go into hibernation, retiring with a large food supply and reduced metabolism until the spring thaw.

The second answer to winter is to avoid its worst effects altogether by moving to a milder climatic zone. At the end of summer, the migrations begin, following the sun to warmer latitudes. As many migrating animals and birds prefer the safety of numbers on what is often a hazardous and arduous journey, migrations can be an exciting subject for photography.

Photographic problems

Snow is an unusual condition for wildlife and nature photography, partly because of the way it affects the quality of light, and partly because it makes concealment very difficult. Stalking in a completely snow-covered landscape taxes the skills of field-craft and demands special camouflage techniques.

This polar bear (top) was photographed from an eskimo boat in Hudson Bay, with a twin lens reflex camera (F. Bruemmer). Rolleiflex, ASA 400, 1/250 sec at f16.

Studying the behaviour of the Kodiak bears for some days (above) made it possible to anticipate their actions—resulting in this striking shot (F. Bruemmer). Nikon with 200 mm lens, ASA 125, 1/250 sec at f8.

At 40 C below freezing (right), reacting to photographic opportunities can be difficult. Seconds after this shot in the Arctic snow, the musk oxen turned and fled (F. Bruemmer). Nikon with 200 mm lens, ASA 125, 1/500 sec at f11.

Polar conditions 2

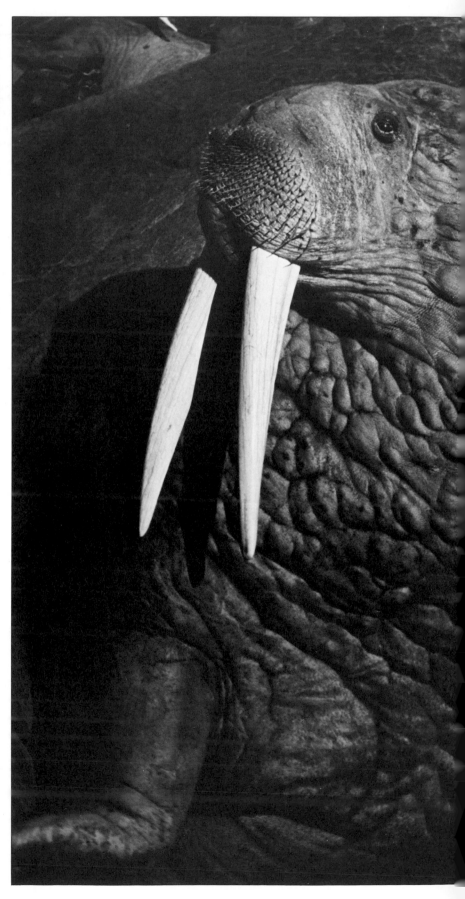

A spectacular Arctic sight (above)—hundreds of walruses sleep together on the beach of a remote Alaskan island (F. Bruemmer). Nikon with 55 mm lens, ASA 25, 1/125 sec at f8.

Approached closely, this walrus bull (right) reared up to display its size and strength—a convincing display to warn off intruders (F. Bruemmer). Mamiyaflex with 180 mm lens, ASA 400, 1/250 sec at f11.

Because snow and ice have such bright, reflective surfaces, they increase the amount of illumination from the sun, often by about one aperture stop. The response of a light meter, however, can be confusing. Direct exposure readings are nearly always too high, simply because they measure a white surface rather than one with average tones, and the result is frequently an under-exposed image. Automatic cameras suffer particularly in this respect.

The secret of accurate exposure measurement in snow is not complicated. It is merely a question of deciding in advance how you want the tonal levels to appear in the photograph. Light meters do not interpret – they simply indicate the exposure that will record the scene in front of them as an average tone. Sunlit snow should ideally appear luminous and bright, at the same time retaining a hint of detail and sparkle. If you use the camera's through-the-lens meter or some other direct reading, increase the exposure from that indicated. How much you adjust the exposure depends on how bright you want the snow to appear–two or three stops increase will make it appear white. Snow that is in shadow or lit by a low sun can be treated more as an average subject, although at least an extra stop will usually be needed even here.

Exposure readings in the snow

1. A direct exposure measurement of an average scene in bright sunlight will give an average reading. In a typical example, this would be 1/125 sec at f11 with ASA 64 film.
2. Under similar lighting, and with film of the same speed, a snow-bound scene may be four times brighter overall, and the light meter will indicate an exposure of 1/125 sec at f22. This will produce an

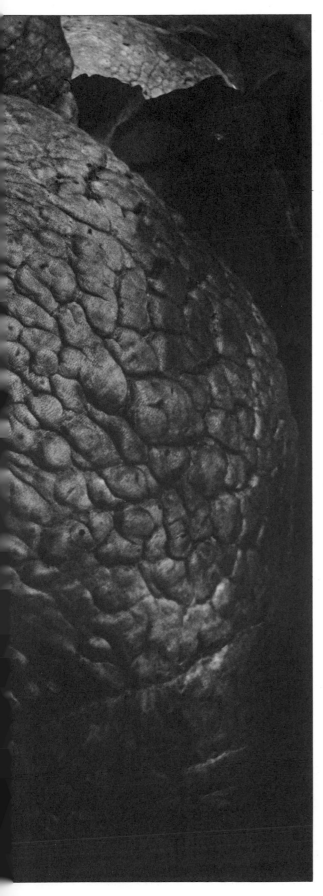

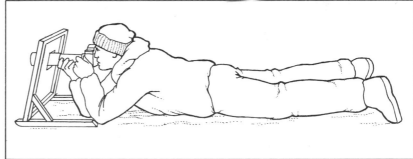

image with the same average tones as before—the snow appearing grey, not at all how we think of it.

3. To appear white and luminous in the photograph, snow should be given an exposure several times greater than a direct exposure reading indicates—in other words, two or three stops more. Typically, the exposure might be 1/125 sec at f11 or f8. The exact amount will depend on the range of tones in the scene. As a rule of thumb, sunlit patches of snow will be three stops brighter than an average subject.

4. An alternative and generally safer method of measuring exposure is to take an incident light reading, which measures the light source and so is unaffected by the reflective properties of snow and ice. Many light meters can be fitted with a translucent plastic dome for this type of reading.

Wildlife in snow

Stalking in snow gives rise to the same problems for the photographer as for any predator. It creates a stark, even background with little opportunity for concealment. White clothing is an obvious precaution, but this camouflage may not be effective if the snow includes areas of rock or vegetation. Often, the only natural cover is the unevenness of the terrain, so that one of the best stalking techniques is to crawl flat on the stomach. For close approach this is essential, and here an Eskimo trick using a simple type of mobile hide can be useful. A small white cloth screen on a light

Caribou cross the shallows of a tundra lake in northern Canada (top). The high viewpoint was gained from a helicopter carrying out a count of the animal population for conservation purposes (F. Bruemmer). Nikon with 135 mm lens, ASA 64, 1/500 sec at f4.

A special ploy used by eskimos for hunting can be borrowed for photographing animals in the snow-covered landscapes of the polar regions (above). A small screen is covered with white material to blend in with the surroundings and is used as a mobile hide, with a flap for the camera lens.

Polar conditions 3

This polar bear (right) was photographed from the roof of an all terrain vehicle on the ice near the coast of Hudson Bay, Canada. The animal approached of its own accord, apparently unafraid (F. Bruemmer).
Nikon with 135 mm lens, ASA 64, 1/500 sec at f8.

Another animal with white protective colouring in the snow (far right)—a harp seal pup on the ice of the Gulf of St. Lawrence, Canada. Although such subjects are cooperative, the photographer's knowledge of their habitat was an advantage (F. Bruemmer).
Nikon with 135 mm lens, ASA 125, 1/500 sec at f11.

frame acts as a screen, which the photographer can push ahead while crawling. A small flap cut in the centre of the cloth allows the camera's lens to be poked through.

Care of film and equipment

Low temperatures can have a considerable effect on the mechanical operation of cameras. Normal lubricants become more thick and viscous, and some moving parts may either slow down or lock completely. With modern silicate lubricants this is less of a problem than it used to be, but the safest approach is still to test your equipment in advance by placing it in a refrigerator or freezer at approximately the temperatures you are likely to experience. Check particularly that the shutter continues to work accurately–the blade or blind movements may have slowed, which would cause over-exposure.

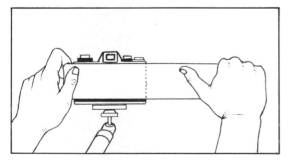

Use camera tape to seal equipment against icing in extreme cold. White tape also makes the camera less conspicuous.

A second problem is condensation. Bringing a camera into a warm room from sub-zero conditions will cause moisture to condense inside the body, which can ruin the mechanisms. The answer is to carry plastic bags that can be effectively sealed, put the equipment in the bags while you are still out in the cold, preferably with a sachet of silica gel

desiccant which will absorb moisture. In this way, the condensation will occur on the surface of the plastic rather than the camera. Use this procedure when you are testing the camera in a freezer.

When going out into the cold from warmer conditions, moisture can be a problem in a different way. Wind blown snow can easily find its way into gaps in the camera body, where it will melt on contact with the still warm metal, and then freeze again. Your breath can have the same effect. The best insurance against icing up the camera in this way is to seal over most of the openings and crevices with camera tape. This has the added benefit of protecting you from contact with the cold metal, which can stick to the skin and cause painful injury.

Batteries are very susceptible to low temperatures, and drain much more quickly than usual. Do not rely on battery powered equipment, unless you can keep the batteries warm in a separate pack under your clothing. A hand-held selenium cell light meter, which generates its own power without batteries, is the most reliable type.

Film also suffers in the cold, in three ways. Most seriously, it becomes brittle as the temperature drops, and sharp winding movements can snap it. Cock the film advance lever gently, regularly holding the camera to your ear when using a 35mm camera to listen for ripped sprocket holes. Motor drives are particularly unsuited to these conditions. The second kind of damage that film can suffer is electrostatic discharge. The movement of the film against the sides of a cassette opening or the camera causes a build-up of electricity, which frequently discharges as a small spark, exposing the emulsion. This is another good reason for winding gently. Finally, condensation is as much a problem for film emulsions as for the camera, causing drying marks. Take the same precautions, avoiding extreme changes of temperature and sealing the film in containers with a desiccant.

The hooded seal with her calf (above) is agressive and dangerous than the harp seal and must be approached cautiously (F. Bruemmer). Mamiyaflex with 180 mm lens, ASA 400, 1/500 sec at f11.

An adult harp seal emerges through the ice—merely curious about the photographer's presence (F. Bruemmer). Nikon with 135 mm lens, ASA 64, 1/250 sec at f8.

113

Mountains 1

The great and spectacular mountain ranges of the world–the Rockies, Andes, Himalayas and Alps– appear massive, solid and enduring. But on the scale of geological events, they are mere new-comers–transient phenomena with a limited future. Mountains are created by uplift, typically being squeezed up between two of the plates which form the earth's crust moving against each other. As soon as the crust begins to buckle upwards, the new mountains fall prey to the forces of erosion. They attract higher rainfall by compelling winds to rise and unload their moisture, and young moun-tains thus have a dense and intricate pattern of rivers and streams covering their surfaces. The steep slopes give the running water more power to erode, and the rivers vigorously attack the rock, cutting back towards their headwaters. Even in an arid climate, erosion continues, for the lack of a protective vegetation cover partly compensates for the irregularity of the rains.

A second powerful shaper of mountain land-scapes is ice. The higher the elevation, the colder the climate, and nearer to the poles–and even at great elevations within the tropics–snow can lie without melting, gradually compacting to ice with each successive season. At a certain point, when a sufficiently massive body of ice has accumulated, the conditions may be right for the birth of a glacier. Glacial action has been responsible for much of the steep and rugged scenery often considered typical of high mountain areas. Smooth sided U-shaped valleys have been ground out by deep rivers of ice, excavated as if by a large ice-cream scoop, and sharp peaks, like the Matterhorn or Grand Tetons, owe their dramatic shapes to scalloping by the heads of glaciers. Although glacial erosion reached its peak about 200,000 years ago, it is still active in the highest and most northerly and southerly of the world's mountains.

Ecological zones

Nature and wildlife in the mountains is profoundly affected by relief and elevation. One of the most immediately noticeable feature is horizontal zoning –of climate, vegetation and animals. The simple difference in temperature that altitude causes is sufficient on its own to create a stack of different ecologies, layer upon layer. Nowhere is this zon-ing more evident than in the tropics, where high sea-level temperatures can support a habitat lushly different from that around the mountain peaks. The northernmost slopes of the Andes, where they meet the Caribbean, show this to per-fection. Standing in the surf, facing the palms and rainforest that reach the edge of the beach, one can, on a clear day, look straight up to permanent ice-fields at 17,000 feet (5,000 metres) only 12 miles (20 kilometres) away. In between, the bands of different vegetation are clearly visible, one above the other.

Mountain weather is frequently unpredictable, particularly when a range interrupts the passage of rain bearing winds. As the air is forced to rise, it is cooled and can no longer hold all its moisture. The rain or snow then falls heavily on the windward slopes, leaving the other side of the mountains

As the temperature and other climatic conditions change with altitude, all mountains exhibit some kind of vertical zoning—with different environmental layers stacked one on top of the other (far left). The snow line is the most prominent division of all, but its height depends on the season and the location of the mountain range. Rising from the hot Caribbean lowlands of Colombia, the Sierra Nevada de Santa Marta experience snow only above about 5,000 feet (1,500 metres). Pentax with 50 mm lens, Kodachrome 25, 1/500 sec at f4.

Even quite large animals sometimes live above the snowline. The Canada lynx (far left below) is one such animal, here photographed in Alaska with a dead caribou (C. Ott/Bruce Coleman). Nikon with 400 mm lens, Kodachrome 64, 1/250 sec at f5.6.

By forcing approaching air masses to rise to altitudes where the lower temperatures cause moisture to condense and precipitate, most mountains experience high rainfall. This, combined with the cold and wind, encourages a number of plant adaptations, and one of the commonest types of mountain vegetation is boggy moorland. On the slopes of a central Andean peak, these Espeletias are the largest plants in a habitat made up of grasses, sedges and mosses. They avoid heat loss by growing compact and close to the ground, and by exposing as many leaves as possible to the sun. Nikon with 20 mm lens, Kodachrome 64, 1/125 sec at f11.

Mountains 2

relatively dry. Frequently, the opposite sides of a mountain thus support quite different ecologies.

Steep slopes and rock faces have encouraged some obvious adaptations among mountain wildlife. Agility and surefootedness are common skills –animals such as the mountain goat, bighorn sheep and Dall sheep all rely heavily on their mountaineering abilities for protection. The mountain goat even has a non-slip pad protruding from between the blades of its hooves for a better grip. Eyesight among mountain animals is usually better developed than any other sense. In difficult, craggy terrain, the great advantages of flight are exploited by some of the world's largest birds of prey–the golden eagle, condor and lammergeier are all essentially mountain dwellers.

At great heights, another adaptation becomes important–living with less oxygen. At 18,000 feet (5,500 metres) there is half the pressure of oxygen that exists at sea-level, and even at lower altitudes life would be uncomfortable for creatures lacking special techniques for rapidly and efficiently absorbing oxygen. Greater lung capacity is one solution. Another is a higher concentration of red corpuscles in the blood. The Andean llama has more the 12 million red corpuscles in each cubic millimetre, and the vicuña more than 14 million. By comparison, the average count for a human at sea level is only four and a half million. As a result, even at heights of 12,000 feet (3,500 metres), vicuñas can run at about 30 miles per hour for several miles.

Photography in the mountains

On balance, although mountain areas can be physically tiring and difficult, there are more good opportunities for photography than there are problems. High relief gives endless possibilities for interesting compositions, backdrops and view-

The marmot (above), here in Yellowstone National Park, Wyoming, thrives in the mountains. It nests in long burrows with chambers, lined with grass for warmth, some ten feet (three metres) underground. It does not hoard food but builds up a considerable layer of fat in the summer to survive hibernation through the winter months.
Nikon with 400 mm lens, Kodachrome 64, 1/125 sec at f5.6.

The ibex (left), photographed in December at an altitude of 8,000 feet (2,400 metres) in the Gran Paradiso National Park, Italy, shows the ability of a few large animals to cope with the harshest mountain conditions. With a thick coat to ward off the cold, it can dig through the snow with its hooves and horns to reach the fodder beneath
(J.-P. Ferrero).
Nikon with 105 mm lens, Kodachrome 64, 1/60 sec at f5.6.

The Rocky Mountain goat (far left) is found in apparently uninhabitable mountains locations. A fine example of adaptation, it has short stocky legs and small feet for its size, enabling it to scramble energetically over the wild crags of its habitat. Its thick white coat and a layer of fat help it to withstand extreme cold.
Hasselblad with 250 mm lens, Ektachrome 64, 1/60 sec at f5.6.

Mountains 3

Inhabiting the high slopes of the Andes, generally above 12,000 feet (3,600 metres), the vicuña, a member of the camel family, protects itself from the often intense cold with its famous wool, which traps an insulating layer of air among the extremely fine hairs. To be able to avoid predators on the plateaux, it also needs to be a strong runner, and to be able to reach and maintain speeds of around 30 mph (50 kph) it has evolved an extremely high concentration of red corpuscles in its blood. This compensates for the reduced oxygen pressure at these high altitudes (F. Gohier).

points. A very long-focus lens is particularly useful for isolating a variety of images, and is usually necessary when stalking animals in conditions that frequently offer great visibility. Access to mountain wildlife may sometimes be arduous, but the settings are anything but monotonous.

Because great distances are common in mountain photography, and because there is less atmospheric screening at altitude, ultraviolet scattering is greater and more obvious than normal. To avoid a strong blue cast to colour photographs, use an ultraviolet filter, even on wide-angle lenses. Pronounced backlighting reveals ultraviolet scattering very prominently, so that shots aimed towards the sun will render any distance blue, even with a filter, except close to sunrise and sunset. A polarizing filter will improve colour saturation even more.

Care of film and equipment

As mountain photography usually involves backpacking, the amount of film and equipment should be pared down to the minimum. When hiking up steep slopes or clambering over rock scree, every pound counts, and loading up with lenses or gad-

gets that may not be strictly necessary can reduce your ability to reach good picture opportunities. Under these conditions, small, lightweight cameras have the edge.

The chief hazard for cameras in mountains is physical damage—knocks and bangs are common. All equipment should be packed securely, with plenty of padding. A shoulder bag may be ideal under normal conditions, but if there is any climbing or rough scrambling to be done, a backpack will be better. Ease of access to the cameras may have to be sacrificed in favour of safe carriage, and in some circumstances, a simple camera bag may actually be dangerous, swinging off the shoulder or upsetting your balance. The ideal is a camera bag that can also be used as a secure backpack when necessary.

As the weather can be so uncertain, always be prepared for the worst, and carry waterproof covering for the equipment as well as for yourself. One special mountain condition damaging to cameras is to be enveloped in cloud, and in this situation, which is normal in cloud forest habitats, water droplets can enter equipment more efficiently than rain itself can.

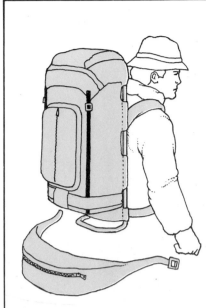

Commercial backpacks are convenient for large amounts of equipment, but do not allow rapid access.

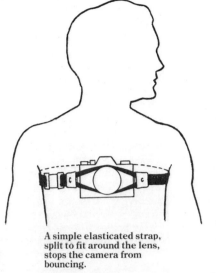

For smaller amounts of equipment, kidney shaped bags that can be slung around the hips on a belt are useful.

A simple elasticated strap, split to fit around the lens, stops the camera from bouncing.

Climbing, and even plain scrambling, can subject cameras and lenses to damaging knocks. As a precaution, either pack equipment securely in a backpack or hip bag, or use elasticated straps to hold a camera firmly against the body.

The lower atmospheric pressure in mountains causes a special problem for birds, as there is less lift. The condor's answer to this, which enables it to fly at heights up to about 18,000 feet (5,500 metres) is a larger wing surface—it is, in fact, the world's largest bird of prey, with a wingspan of up to ten feet.

Another view of the remarkable vicuña, a creature perfectly adapted to life at the extreme altitudes of the Andes Mountains (F. Gohier).

Deserts 1

The simplest definition of a desert includes any area that receives less than 10 inches (25cm) of rain in a year. Deserts are not always hot, although high temperatures increase the rate of evaporation and most of the world's arid regions are found in the tropics. For the definition to apply, however, the rainfall must be uneven. Even as little as 10 inches of rain can support quite lush vegetation if it falls regularly throughout the year. For this reason, one feature of desert life is its ability to cope with the sudden arrival and departure of moisture. Many dry areas receive their annual quota of precipitation in a few sudden storms. This completely dominates the way such desert ecologies function, and although the usual appearance is barren and inactive, it is the unpredictable and rare bursts of rainfall that sustain life and shape the landscape, each followed by a rapid period of plant growth and animal activity.

Although some deserts, such as those on the Peruvian and Chilean coasts, almost never receive rain–their total moisture is supplied by sea-mists–life in most arid conditions depends on being able to make the maximum use of water at a moment's notice. The spadefoot toad in the south west of the United States, for example, has adapted to a largely underground existence. It remains cool beneath the surface during the heat of the day and hunts only at night. With the onset of rain, however, it launches into a rapid mating and breeding cycle, laying its eggs in the short-lived pools of water. Tadpoles hatch within two or three days, becoming toads in little over a month. Many other desert dwellers share the brief opportunities that rain brings. The fairy shrimp, hatching from an egg that may have lain dormant for years, has to complete most of its life cycle, including mating and laying new eggs, before the temporary pools dry up.

Still other creatures have been able to reduce their need for surface water to the bare minimum. The kangaroo rat, whilst as dependent on moisture as any animal, has adapted so that it loses very little of its body fluids. It does not sweat, and its kidneys are five time more efficient than man's,

Another distinctive feature of arid regions is the rapid evaporation of moisture on the surface. When the rains fall, the water is quickly gone, absorbed by the dry earth and evaporated by the heat. Various salts that are dissolved in the short-lived streams and small lakes remain in crusty deposits, like these ribbons of salt in Death Valley, California (below).
Nikon with 180mm lens, Kodachrome 64, 1/500 sec at f2.8.

Sparse and infrequent desert rainfall means that, for most of the year at least, there is very little cover of vegetation. Indeed, in some desert areas such as this part of Monument Valley in Arizona (right) there is virtually no plant life at all. Although the barren dunes and rock are an extreme example, the dominant feature of most deserts for photography is that the underlying structure of the landscape is more visible without the softening effect of vegetation. This gives the opportunity to make use of clean, simple lines and definite shapes.
Nikon with 20mm lens, Kodachrome 64, 1/60 sec at f11.

Deserts 2

so conserving most of its meagre water intake. By these and other methods, the rat can make do with the very little moisture contained in its diet of dry seeds, and has no need actually to drink water.

Photographic problems

As the daily life of most desert animals is dominated by temperature, photography of active creatures is normally limited to the early morning and late afternoon when it is cooler. Some species lead nocturnal lives – here night photography techniques can be used, but the lack of good cover often makes it impossible for a hide to be built. Desert fauna is never very abundant, even under the best conditions, and there is little activity in the middle of the day – fortunately so, as high temperatures can be damaging to film, equipment and also to the photographer!

Desert lighting can sometimes cause difficulties. The generally open skies, together with bright sand and rock, give high levels of illumination, and visually this can be confusing. Use a light meter frequently and with care. Incident readings (measuring the light falling on the subject) are often more useful than the direct readings of a through-the-lens meter which, as in snow covered landscapes, can cause under-exposure if followed too faithfully.

Over distances, heat haze can lower contrast, producing evenly toned and dull images. In extreme cases, there can be visible distortion of the

Insects (above right) **are a central element in the ecology of the desert. Their great efficiency at surviving in great extremes of temperature with a limited food supply enables them to inhabit these inhospitable regions – in turn providing a food supply for small mammals and reptiles. Here, two stenocara phalangium beetles mate in the relative cool of early morning in the Namib desert,**(D. Hughes/ Bruce Coleman).
Nikon with 55 mm macro lens, ASA 64, 1/30 sec at f5.6.

The moloch lizard of Australia (right) **is a remarkable species, covered with sharp spines and with a frightening appearance to warn off would-be predators. Able to withstand the direct heat of the sun, it moves about very slowly in its search for the ants which provide its food** (J-P. Ferrero).
Nikon with 55 mm macro lens, Kodachrome 64, 1/60 sec at f11.

Before the immense heat of the day, insects such as this onymacris beetle are relatively active—here gathering fog moisture in a pendulous drop under its body. The fog is virtually the only source of moisture in this part of south-western Africa (D. Hughes/Bruce Coleman).
Nikon with 55 mm macro lens, ASA 64, 1/60 sec at f8.

After a rare experience of rainfall, the desert rapidly springs to life (below). Flowers bloom almost immediately and a compressed cycle of life begins before the moisture is once again baked from the soil. Here, a woma python in Australia's Northern Territory was spotted during the evening of an overcast day—a form of lighting that enhanced the colour saturation of the desert flora (J.-P. Ferrero).
Nikon with 180 mm lens, Kodachrome 64, 1/60 sec at f8.

Deserts 3

air over hot sand. When using a long-focus lens, a strong ultraviolet filter, or even a polarizing filter, will greatly improve colour saturation and increase the tonal range. Haze is more of a nuisance in the middle of the day, and this is also the time when the lighting is least attractive. With the sun directly overhead, textures and shapes are poorly rendered, and the desert may appear formless. Few animals are active at midday, so there is usually little reason for working at this time.

At sunrise and sunset, on the other hand, deserts can take on a spectacular beauty. Raking sunlight accentuates the shapes and surfaces of sand and bare rock. Sand dunes in particular can appear strong and dramatic when their crests divide the shadowed and sunlit slopes. When the sun just grazes the surface, ripples and even individual grains are emphasized.

Care of film and equipment

Although free of the excessive humidity that makes rainforest photography so ruinous to equipment, deserts have problems associated with extreme dryness. Without moisture, dust particles, grit and sand become airborne in the least breeze, causing abrasive damage to the mechanical parts of cameras. Inside the camera body, particles can adhere to the film's surface before exposure, and ruin the image, and if trapped between the emulsion and any other surface, can cause horizontal scratches.

Photograhers used to working in dry, dusty conditions usually tape over all joints and gaps on the camera to keep out dust. Cameras are also best left in a sealed case whenever they are not being used. Blown grains of sand can etch and grind very efficiently—as is proved by the wind-carved rock formations common in deserts. The front surface of a lens is particularly vulnerable. The answer is to use a clear ultraviolet filter at all times. When finally worn beyond usefulness, it can be replaced inexpensively, with the lens itself unharmed. Using the camera in a dust storm or sand storm courts disaster, but if there is really no alternative, use a plastic bag in the same way as described for sea and shore photography.

Many deserts experience extremely high daytime temperatures. The thermometer regularly exceeds 100°F (39°C) in the shade in the Sonora,

Mojave and other south-western deserts of the United States, and the July record for Death Valley is 134°F (56°C). At these temperatures, quite apart from considerations of personal welfare, lens cement can craze, weaken or even melt, and lubricants can run. Colour film can acquire a distinct colour cast, and with formats larger than 35mm, the film base may buckle as it heats, throwing parts of the image out of focus.

Most of the precautions against heat involve nothing more than common sense—avoiding direct sunlight and storing equipment in the coolest areas available. Black objects absorb heat quickly, making it particularly important to protect the black surfaces of cameras and lenses from the sun. Camera cases should have white or reflective metal surfaces, never black. Polystyrene (styrofoam) lined cool boxes of the kind sold as picnic hampers can be a great help, and the evaporation from a moistened cloth draped over a camera case will cool it down slightly. Good ventilation is also important, and both film and equipment should be raised above the ground whenever possible—temperatures on the ground and in the sun are not uncommonly 30°F (17°C) higher than those in the air and in shade at the same location. As a final precautionary warning, consider the results of measurements made by the United States National Park Service in Death Valley. On one day in 1972 they recorded a ground temperature in the sun of 201°F (94°C), practically the boiling point of water!

The heat in deserts can be extreme and it is vital to keep equipment cool. Even simple precautions, such as never leaving film or equipment exposed to direct sunlight in the middle of the day, are crucial in desert conditions. Containers should be either of reflective metal or painted white—never black—and always kept in the shade if possible.

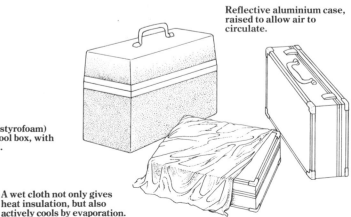

Reflective aluminium case, raised to allow air to circulate.

Polystyrene (styrofoam) lined picnic cool box, with frozen sachet.

A wet cloth not only gives heat insulation, but also actively cools by evaporation.

Cross-lighting can be very useful to reveal the textures of sand in an otherwise featureless desert floor. Here, it effectively shows up the sidewinder's distinctive tracks. This snake of the deserts of South-western Africa uses this method of locomotion to traverse soft sand (D. Hughes/Bruce Coleman).

In many deserts there is a double reason for avoiding the middle of the day in favour of early morning and late afternoon. The height of the midday sun in these tropical latitudes casts very small areas of hard shadow in an otherwise uniform glare, often producing unsuccessful results in a photograph. In the early morning and late afternoon the shadows are longer and, in addition, the warm colours of sand and rock are enhanced, as in the sandstone environment of this brush-tailed rock wallaby in Australia (J-P. Ferrero).
Nikon with 105mm lens, Kodachrome 64, polarizing filter, 1/30th at f22.

Rainforest and swamp 1

The rainforests of the world are concentrated in an irregular belt straddling the equator, including the Congo basin and its surroundings, large parts of south-east Asia, and the largest natural living environment remaining in the world–the Amazon basin. Although most rainforest is tropical, some isolated temperate areas do exist, such as the Olympic rainforest in north-west America, and swamplands are found in most latitudes. The characteristic they all have in common, of course, is a world of water and vegetation, a habitat that normally encourages an extraordinarily rich variety of wildlife as well as producing some specific photographic problems.

In tropical rainforest, which is the most extreme and fecund example of a high-rainfall environment, the two most important elements for plant life are available in abundance–sunlight and moisture. Photosynthesis is possible on a grand scale, and results in an exuberance of vegetation unmatched anywhere else in the world. Most of the conditions for life are ideal in this natural hothouse. There is no winter, no drought, none of the harsh conditions that have to be faced by the animal inhabitants of deserts or ice-bound landscapes. Temperatures are high but not excessive, varying little either through the day and night or through the year. Water is regularly available, and the humidity is close to saturation point most of the time.

On the other hand, most rainforest grows on extremely impoverished soil–partly because of the geological conditions that have left these regions undisturbed for a long time and partly because the heavy rainfall quickly leaches out the nutrients from the soil. A typical rainforest sub-soil is not far from being infertile, and in a more temperate climate would be barren. The luxuriant growth so typical of rainforest is, in fact, an ingenious solution to the problem of poor soil–by rapidly converting forest debris into usable nutrients (complex associations between fungi and

trees play an important part in this) the energy budget of the whole system is recycled quickly, without entering the soil beneath. Most tropical rainforest soils are little more than a horizontal support for the ecosystem.

Rainforest wildlife

The variety and quantity of plant life, together with the hothouse conditions, favour a complex variety of coexisting wildlife, occupying all kinds of specialized niches. Unlike most other natural environments, the rainforest is three dimensional, with very definite layers that house quite distinct groups of animals. The water areas–rivers, swamps, streams–are one separate region. The forest floor is another. Most characteristic of all, perhaps, is the canopy layer–the dense, interlocking pattern of treetops raised one or two hundred feet above the ground. In each of these layers, and in all the other niches and microenvironments, some of the earth's most highly specialized creatures have adapted to very distinct ways of life. Around the water margins practically everything can swim, even jaguars and snakes–including the giant anaconda which frequently

Typical of tropical forest areas, the Amazon Basin is dominated by two elements–thick high forest and rivers (far left). There is virtually no open ground, except at the margins of waterways.
Hasselblad with 80 mm lens, Agfachrome 50, 1/500 sec at f4.5.

In mangrove swamps such as this stretch of the Venezuelan coast (above), the tangle of elevated roots and thick mud restrict exploration to the margins, using a boat.
Nikon with 20 mm lens, Kodachrome 64, 1/30 sec at f3.5.

Marshland, can be surprisingly difficult to move around in, but this impenetrability is a protection for many species. Here, in India's Bharatpur reserve, painted storks use isolated acacia trees for nesting.
Hasselblad with 38 mm lens, Ektachrome 64, 1/125 sec at f3.5.

Rainforest and swamp 2

hunts from the water. In the upper canopy, all the inhabitants show great agility. The monkey-hunting harpy, for example, although the world's largest eagle, has such short stubby wings that it can fly through the canopy layer with the skill of a slalom ski champion.

The abundance of good living conditions has thus sponsored an incredibly diverse range of creatures, and some fascinatingly extreme forms – in appearance and habits. However, because of the inherent poverty of the soils, the total food supply is actually quite low, a feature that has not favoured large animals. The majority of rainforest wildlife is small, and there are few species of large mammals. Also, the largest animals, such as panthers, tapirs and jaguars, are relatively few and are widely dispersed – the poor food supply in the forest cannot support even moderate concentrations of these large eaters. This has obvious consequences for wildlife photography, for while tropical rainforest is virtually a cornucopia of insect and reptile subjects, its mammalian life is extremely difficult to find and photograph. Size is a definite disadvantage in the enclosed world of the rainforest – much more important qualities for survival are stealth, camouflage and a secretive lifestyle. This heavy reliance on concealment and avoidance means that the wildlife photographer must be more perceptive and knowledgeable in order to find the animals to be photographed.

The techniques used by rainforest wildlife to avoid being detected are many. Silent movement is a skill possessed by most of these creatures, even the largest. A full-grown tapir has a heavy and ungainly looking body that appears ill suited to silent movement among the trees, yet it can move with surprising agility and hardly any noise. To avoid cracking branches it makes a habit of keeping to well worn, narrow trails. The sloth has carried the art of gentle movement to an extreme, travelling with an almost excruciating slowness. It is so effective that it can rarely be noticed, and if you are not looking directly at the animal, its movement is usually too slow to draw attention.

Camouflage is also highly developed, particularly among the insects. In these ideally hot, moist surroundings, many diverse varieties have evolved. Some katydids and mantids have created almost perfect leaf imitations, so detailed in some species that not only are the veins and texture reproduced, but also the blights and imperfections. The means of camouflage vary greatly. The rosette spots of a jaguar make the animal's outline difficult to see against the dappling effect of shafts of sunlight filtering through the branches. The sloth's shaggy coat is made even less noticeable by the characteristic growth of greenish algae on the hairs. The gnarled and ragged carapace of the Amazon's matamata turtle closely resembles crinkled dead leaves commonly seen floating in streams.

The nocturnal or twilight habits of the majority of rainforest creatures is another method of concealment, and one that makes the photography of many creatures impossible without the use of flash. Tropical rainforest at midday gives the

Many rainforest animals have evolved to live in more than one of the different habitats. The South American anaconda (above left), **is equally at home in the water or in the trees, and hunts from both.**
Hasselblad with 80 mm lens, Ektachrome 64, 1/125 sec at f8.

The waterways of lowland rainforest contain a wide spectrum of life, including the South American black cayman (left).
Hasselblad with 500 mm lens, Agfachrome 50, 1/125 sec at f8.

The Amazonian squirrel monkey (above) **is one of the commonest, noisiest and most active inhabitants of the canopy – the topmost layer of the rainforest.**
Hasselblad with 250 mm lens, Ektachrome 64, 1/250 sec at f5.6.

impression of being almost lifeless, apart from a few reptiles and insects. In the early morning or at dusk life emerges, and throughout the night the rustles, squeals and growls can at times be deafening.

Photographic techniques

Insects and reptiles are relatively abundant in tropical rainforest, principally because the heat and humidity represent almost ideal conditions. The techniques of insect photography in this environment are no different from those in less taxing conditions, but the abundance of species and individuals make field trips more immediately successful. Because there is normally no shortage of subjects, stalking is a good way of getting a general coverage of a particular area, and can be quite casual. It can also be a way of discovering unusual habits that would not be seen by attracting insects with an artificial lure. Leaf-cutter ants, for

example, can provide a fascinating series of pictures, including the process of selecting a tree or plant, the cutting techniques, the traffic flow of streams of workers, and the ingenuity often displayed in overcoming physical obstacles on the path as they carry the leaf portions back to the nest.

Lures such as rotting meat and overripe fruits can also attract creatures, while a light can be used to make a thorough collection. Bed sheets draped around a strong lamp will normally bring hordes of moths and other insects attracted to light. They can then be picked off the sheets and placed in containers for later, captive set photography.

Larger animals are more of a problem. Because of the lack of visibility in dense rainforest, often only a matter of yards, casual stalking is not usually very productive, and chance encounters with animals tend to happen at great speed. The forest floor is generally quite gloomy, and there is

Rainforest and swamp 3

Keeping out of sight is commonly a major priority of rainforest life and involves a considerable variety of techniques. The two-toed sloth moves with such deliberate slowness that it attracts little attention from predators tuned to respond to rapid, jerky movements. Hasselblad with 250 mm lens, Ektachrome 64, 1/125 sec at f6.3.

Some of the most advanced methods for avoiding detection are found among tropical insects. Their capacity for rapid evolution has enabled some to develop mimicry almost to perfection. When still, and in a suitable setting, leaf insects may be undetectable. Even the detailed structure of veins is faithfully reproduced, and some species have even the blotches and imperfections common in tropical forest leaves (J-P. Ferrero). Nikon with 55 mm macro lens, Kodachrome 25, 1/60 sec at f8.

generally insufficient light for action photography. The forest margins, in clearings and on river banks, are often the best locations. By choosing a good viewpoint, they can be used to wait for chance opportunities. Canoes can sometimes be useful as they are silent and provide a good view of both banks of small rivers. One of the best ways of using them is to travel downstream, allowing the canoe to drift as much as possible. Rounding a bend will occasionally give the chance of a single shot of a bank dwelling creature, although there is usually little opportunity for more.

With larger animals, a guide is almost always essential, as in most unfamiliar environments. With many creatures, the only way of having any chance at all of photographing them is to use local knowledge of their habits and territories. With large mammals, such as jaguars, the full paraphernalia of hides, flash units and remote control camera operation, at night, is needed.

Care of film and equipment

Rainforests and swamps, particularly in the tropics, deserve caution as adverse conditions for film

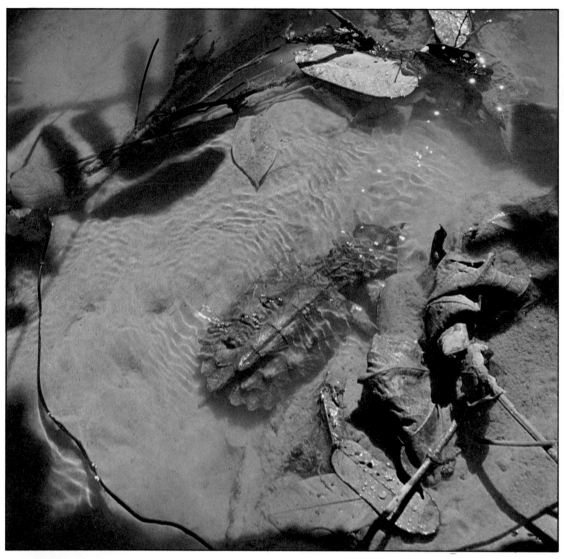

Although camouflage is not its only purpose, the rough, drab carapace of a matamata turtle in the Amazon makes it difficult to notice among the general litter of dead leaves. Hasselblad with 80 mm lens, Ektachrome 64, 1/125 sec at f8.

While the pattern of a boa constrictor's skin does not mimic any feature of its surroundings, it is highly effective at blending in with the characteristic dappling of sunlight filtering through leaves, confusing the reptile's outline in exactly the same way as military camouflage is used. Hasselblad with 80 mm lens, Ektachrome 64, 1/125 sec at f6.3.

Rainforest and swamp 4

One enormous group of subjects that are never difficult to find in the rainforest environment is the insects and spiders. Many interesting species can be spotted, even on a casual walk, and it usually pays to have close-up equipment at the ready. These massed homoptera were photographed clustering on a tree trunk in Khao Yai National Park in Thailand. Nikon with 200mm macro lens, Kodachrome 64, 1/60 sec at f8 with portable flash unit.

In the high humidity of the rainforest, a good camera case can be an essential piece of equipment. With a rubber gasket seal around the lid, and packed with a sachet of silica gel crystals to absorb moisture, it will keep cameras and lenses relatively free of ruinous condensation and fungus growth.

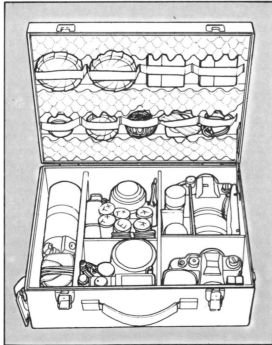

and equipment. Film is particularly susceptible to the combination of heat and humidity. Under these two conditions, film deteriorates fastest, particularly after exposure and before processing. Do not break the seal on any film container until you are ready to use it. The air inside the factory packing is much drier than that in the forest. Once the film has been exposed to humid conditions, re-pack it in sealed containers with a desiccant. The most common desiccant is silica gel, in the form of crystals which absorb water strongly. Sometimes it is available with a colour indicator that changes hue when the crystals have absorbed too much water to be effective. The silica gel can then be reactivated by drying in an oven or over an open fire. Another good precaution is to pack everything very tightly, so that very little air is included in the container. If silica gel is not available, or in an emergency, grains of rice can be used, although they are about ten times less effective. Condensation can also be a severe, immediate problem, making photography quite impossible as glass surfaces constantly attract a film of moisture. There is no choice but to allow the camera to warm up to the temperature of the surrounding air. But keep it out of the sun.

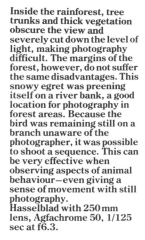

Inside the rainforest, tree trunks and thick vegetation obscure the view and severely cut down the level of light, making photography difficult. The margins of the forest, however, do not suffer the same disadvantages. This snowy egret was preening itself on a river bank, a good location for photography in forest areas. Because the bird was remaining still on a branch unaware of the photographer, it was possible to shoot a sequence. This can be very effective when observing aspects of animal behaviour—even giving a sense of movement with still photography.
Hasselblad with 250 mm lens, Agfachrome 50, 1/125 sec at f6.3.

To keep film cool, an ordinary picnic cool box provides quite good insulation, and if you are in one place for more than a day, burying it in the soil will lower the temperature by two or three degrees. In any event, always keep film containers in the shade, out of any direct sunlight. Refrigeration, even if it is available, is not always wise because it can cause condensation. It can be useful when combined with large quantities of desiccant, but otherwise it may cause additional damage. The best solution of all is to keep film in hot, humid conditions for the shortest possible time, and process it as soon as possible after exposure.

Equipment needs as much care as film, and should be kept both cool and dry as far as is possible. Equipment cases are best if they are highly reflective, ideally white or with a bright metallic finish, and should be gasket sealed so as to be moisture proof and watertight. Inspect the equipment regularly, and do not leave it out except when you are actually taking pictures. Danger signals are condensation forming on glass or other surfaces, mould on leather parts, faulty electrical operation, and, most insidious of all, fungal growth actually on lens surfaces, which will etch the glass and permanently ruin the lens.

Because the environment is so difficult to penetrate, a competent local guide is even more important in rainforest regions than in most others. Some animals, such as this giant otter in the upper Amazon (above left), are not necessarily difficult to photograph. This species, for example, is quite active by day and inquisitive rather than shy. But finding them involves knowing the likely locations.
Nikon with 400 mm lens, Ektachrome 64, 1/250 sec at f8.

Sea and shore 1

Where two natural regions meet, there is often an abundance of life, making these areas particularly good for observing wildlife. Not only are there two different wildlife societies within easy reach, but often there is a zone of transition, with specialized creatures inhabiting just these margins. This 'edge effect' is one of the great attractions of coastal regions, where not only are marine life and shore life accessible, but the tidal zone is an added bonus.

There are many kinds of coastline, from river estuaries where the land slowly encroaches on the sea to cliffs being eroded by the pounding of waves, but they all have one thing in common—they are unstable zones of transition, in a continual state of flux. There is nothing permanent about any coastline, either from day to day or across geological time.

Shoreline life

With few exceptions, the coast is the best place for watching marine life above water. Creatures that are completely aquatic allow only a few possibilities for surface photography. Whales, for example, normally offer only a few tantalizing glimpses, and great luck and quick reactions are needed to capture on film the sight of one breaking the surface.

Animals that spend only a part of their time in the sea are much better subjects. Seals and sea-lions, for example, are not only especially photogenic, but their range of activity between hunting and playing in the water and basking on rocks and beaches offers a wide range of photographic opportunities.

Most sea birds make good subjects, and are often quite easy to photograph. The shoreline is such a limited zone that the activity and flight paths of many birds are predictable. Also, the inaccessibility of many nesting sites—on offshore rocks or sheer cliffs, for example—makes many species relatively indifferent to human presence.

Because areas such as sea-lion colonies and gulls' nests are generally difficult to approach

Nowhere is the flux and activity that characterizes shoreline life more evident than on a rocky coast. Battered by waves and the surge of strong currents, the rocky islets of this headland at Point Lobos, California are undergoing rapid erosion, but support sea-lions, cormorants, sea otters and many other coastal dwellers living off the rich food supplies that are concentrated where the land and sea meet. Nikon with 400 mm lens, Kodachrome 64, 1/250 sec at f5.6.

Sea-bird colonies are among the most interesting—and often the most spectacular—subjects to be found along a coastline. Of course, they are almost always on inaccessible cliffs and islands, making it difficult to reach them and demanding planning. The creatures' reliance on inaccessibility for protection, however, means that, as with these king cormorants photographed on the coast of Patagonia, they can occasionally be approached closely enough to use a wide-angle lens, setting them in the context of the landscape (F. Gohier). Nikon with 24 mm lens, Kodachrome 64, 1/60 sec at f11 with polarizing filter.

Without actually going underwater, the opportunities for photographing wildlife at sea are limited mainly to creatures that surface occasionally to breathe or bask. However, when they do occur, the results can be spectacular, as in this close surface shot of a California grey whale photographed from a small boat during the annual migration at a point off Monterey where the whales come close to shore (F.Gohier). Nikon with 24 mm lens, Kodachrome 64, 1/125 sec at f5.6 with polarizing filter.

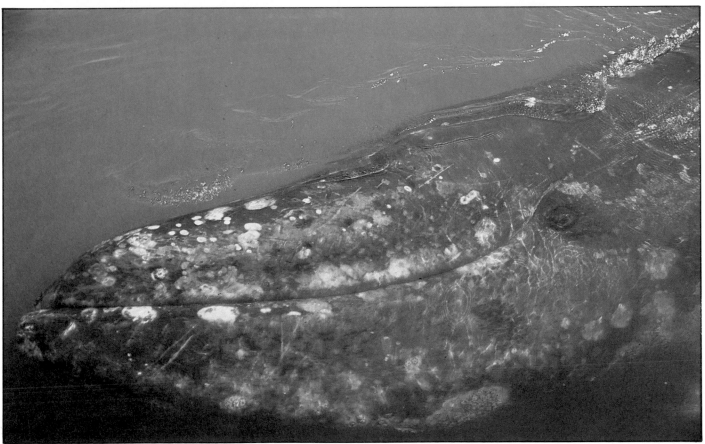

Sea and shore 2

closely, a very long-focus lens is valuable. Even a focal length of 1,000mm on a 35mm camera is desirable, and for once the natural light is favourable to the photographer. Because of the generally exposed conditions and the reflective surface of the sea, light levels in coastal areas are generally high. Using ASA 64 film, for example, on a bright sunny day, exposure settings of f11 at 1/125 sec are usually possible, virtually one stop more than would be found in an inland location.

Tidal pools

On a much smaller scale, crabs, molluscs and other creatures are left stranded temporarily by the retreat of the tide. Tidal pools offer in microcosm a fascinating and accessible glimpse of a marine environment. The pools that are richest in life are usually those closest to the low tide mark, as they are isolated from the sea for the shortest time. Depending on the location, a surprising variety of organisms can be found, from anemones to hermit crabs, limpets or small flounders. For the photographer, these pools are especially valuable as small, temporary aquaria. The shallow water makes photography from the surface possible, and a macro lens is ideal for the scale of subject usually found.

Reflections can be a problem. Using a polarizing filter is not necessarily the answer, because the required one and a half to two stops extra exposure can only be achieved at the expense of much

Sea-lions (far left above) normally choose specific rocks as a base for operations and for basking in the sun, and although these are usually inaccessible, a long-focus lens from a nearby headland can be perfectly satisfactory.
Nikon with 800 mm lens, Kodachrome 64, 1/125 sec at f11.

Birds such as this cormorant (far left) obtain most of their food by diving into the sea itself for fish.
Nikon with 400 mm lens, Kodachrome 64, 1/250 sec at f6.3.

The good lighting conditions along coastlines allow good opportunities for working with slow long-focus lenses —even with the light behind the subject, as with this young gull (above) with a small sea urchin.
Nikon with 400 mm lens, Kodachrome 64, 1/125 sec at f6.3.

Mammals are also adapted to shore life. This sea otter (left) feeds on shellfish in rocky tidal pools (J. Foott/Bruce Coleman).
Nikon with 180 mm lens, Kodachrome 64, 1/125 sec at f8.

Sea and shore 3

Anemones and a hermit crab in an abandoned shell are the main inhabitants of this temporary rock pool, a marine microcosm that survives the twice-daily retreat of the tide with just a few inches of water. Using the method shown opposite, with the sun low in the sky and a dark card used to cut down reflections from the surface, it is a straightforward matter to photograph tidal pools like this. The enclosed space and shallow water give them the advantages of natural aquaria. This pool was photographed by sunlight. Nikon with 55 mm macro lens, Kodachrome 64, 1/60 sec at f6.3.

needed depth of field. There is not normally any difficulty in holding the camera steady over a pool at 1/30 sec or even slower, but shrimps and crabs usually move too fast for this.

A better solution is to choose early morning or late afternoon sunlight, so that the oblique rays do not reflect from the water's surface. Then, photograph from a slight angle, so that neither you nor the camera are reflected back into the lens. If the sky is a fairly deep blue, its reflection will be dark enough not to interfere with the image, but otherwise a black card can be held over the pool by a friend or assistant to block the reflections of clouds.

Direct sunlight is usually necessary in order to bring out sufficient contrast in the pool, and on cloudy days a pocket flash can be substituted. Use the flash obliquely to avoid reflections from the surface of the water.

Care of equipment

Salt water can be surprisingly destructive to cameras and lenses, and is much more corrosive

than fresh water. A complete soaking is not the only danger to guard against, as even wind blown spray can be damaging. A basic precaution is to keep all equipment in a protective container, if only a shoulder bag, except when shooting. Another is to use a lens cap and an ultraviolet filter to cover the front element of the lens. Carry a rag and a small bottle of fresh water—or better still, alcohol—to wipe off the greasy film of salt from equipment that has been splashed.

In rough weather, when there is no way of avoiding spray, wrap the camera in a plastic bag, with just a small hole for the lens, sealed tight with a rubber band. An amphibious camera, such as the Nikonos, is ideal in such conditions.

In a real emergency, where a camera has actually been dropped in the sea, there is only one, drastic answer. Immerse the complete camera in fresh water, and deliver it to a camera repair shop as quickly as possible. Even so, there is no guarantee of successful salvage, but the alternative is to write off the equipment as a total loss.

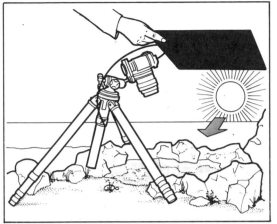

Small marine creatures are often abundant and can make good subjects (top right) – although rarely as spectacular as this Galapagos crab (F. Gohier). Nikon with 200 mm lens, Kodachrome 64, 1/250 sec at f8.

A moderately low sun or a portable flash gun similarly placed produce the best illumination for rock pool photography. Without reflections from the surface of the water, these so-called 'red crabs' in Baja, California are shown with good resolution and colour saturation (F. Gohier). Nikon with 55 mm macro lens, Kodachrome 64, 1/125 sec at f11.

The best precaution against salt-water spray is to cover the camera temporarily with a plastic bag (right), securing the opening around the end of the lens with a rubber band.

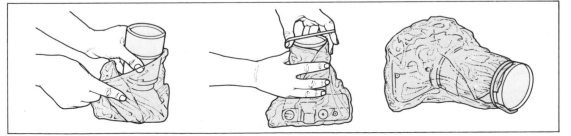

Underwater 1

Although a highly specialized area, underwater photography is rapidly becoming more accessible to the casual diver. A considerable range of equipment is now available, and most of it, even amphibious flash units, is completely reliable. If you already have basic diving skills, photography underwater need not be daunting. A certain amount of shallow water work can be done with face mask and snorkel alone, but serious photography calls for scuba equipment. Under no circumstances, however experienced you are, should you dive alone–using a camera underwater absorbs so much attention that you are likely to be less aware of danger.

Underwater optics

The altered behaviour of light in water is responsible for most of the photographer's technical problems. Because water is denser than air, rays of light passing from one to the other are bent, or refracted. Place a straight stick partly in the water, and this effect is immediately obvious. When seeing or photographing underwater, refraction has the following results:

> 1. Objects appear to be closer by one quarter.
> 2. They appear to be larger by one third, apparently magnified.
> 3. The angle of view of a lens is narrowed by one quarter.
> 4. Some optical aberration increases.

Some water contact lenses are now available which are designed to correct these problems. They are intended for use with amphibious cameras such as the Nikonos, and cannot be used out of water. When using ordinary surface cameras in watertight housings, the simplest way of overcoming most of these problems is by using a dome port. In effect, this becomes an additional front element for the lens, restoring the original angle of view, removing the magnification, and at least partly correcting such aberrations as pincushion distortion and blurred edges. The only thing that a dome port does not correct is the apparent distance. Acting as a negative lens, it actually requires closer focusing, and either a lens extension or a supplementary close-up lens is usually needed to be able to focus normally.

Equipment

The basic choice of equipment is between a truly

amphibious camera, which effectively means the Nikonos, its predecessor the Calypso or the 110 format Minolta Weathermatic, and a watertight housing for your existing surface camera. Neither approach has a complete advantage. For size, convenience and technical efficiency, an amphibious camera with water contact lenses is theoretically superior, but the considerable drawback with the Nikonos is that it is a viewfinder camera and not a single lens reflex. The Weathermatic is an automatic, with much more limited versatility. Inevitably, a complete range of equipment solely for underwater use is much more expensive than a single housing that can make use of an existing camera system. On the other hand, a housing is more unwieldy, changing film and lenses is slow, and there is a greater risk of ruining equipment through a water leak.

Although there is little choice of amphibious cameras, commercial housings are available from many manufacturers. The simplest is a soft vinyl case with a flat port and glove-shaped inset: it is reasonably safe down to about 30 feet (10 metres). For serious work, however, a better choice is from a range of moulded transparent plastic housings, available for most major makes of camera. Geared knobs and levers allow control of all the major camera functions. The most rugged and professional housing is of cast aluminium. Although expensive, this design is both safe and adaptable, allowing the use of a motor drive–a great advantage underwater.

Although a camera's internal light meter functions adequately underwater, the needle or LED (light emitting diode) indicators in the viewfinder are usually difficult to see through housings, and a separate amphibious light meter is the most commonly used exposure measurement system.

For underwater flash units, there is a choice between bulbs or electronic flash. Bulbs are more

Considerable changes in the operation of a camera result from the optical distortion experienced when working underwater. The image is considerably enlarged and subjects appear closer than in air. A single lens reflex camera allows the photographer to see the image as it will appear on the film–a great advantage in framing the shot correctly. Alternatively, specially corrected underwater lenses are available for the non-reflex amphibious Nikonos. In addition, domed ports can be fitted to underwater housings to restore the normal performance of the lens.

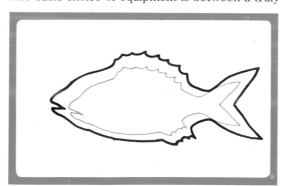

Separated from the remainder of the natural environment by the surface of the sea and by the quite different conditions of pressure, optics and ecology among others, the underwater world offers an enormous range of photographic possibilities. The strangeness of this habitat and the extraordinary character of the animals that inhabit it can provide images with surprising impact. Here, spiny lobsters march single file across the sandy sea bed during their mysterious migration activity (R. Schroeder/Bruce Coleman).

A great variety of underwater equipment is now available, not necessarily at great expense or requiring particular expertise of the photographer. Amphibious cameras and waterproof housings for standard equipment are the alternative starting points.

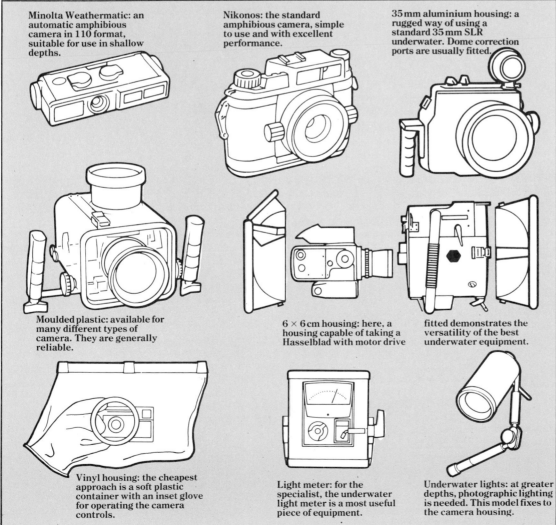

Minolta Weathermatic: an automatic amphibious camera in 110 format, suitable for use in shallow depths.

Nikonos: the standard amphibious camera, simple to use and with excellent performance.

35 mm aluminium housing: a rugged way of using a standard 35 mm SLR underwater. Dome correction ports are usually fitted.

Moulded plastic: available for many different types of camera. They are generally reliable.

6 × 6 cm housing: here, a housing capable of taking a Hasselblad with motor drive

fitted demonstrates the versatility of the best underwater equipment.

Vinyl housing: the cheapest approach is a soft plastic container with an inset glove for operating the camera controls.

Light meter: for the specialist, the underwater light meter is a most useful piece of equipment.

Underwater lights: at greater depths, photographic lighting is needed. This model fixes to the camera housing.

Underwater 2

Photographing moving subjects underwater can be difficult, particularly when working with natural light. Fortunately, these South American sea-lion were found in clear water, off Argentina's Valdes peninsula (J. and D. Bartlett/Bruce Coleman).

A major difficulty with using natural daylight as the only illumination underwater is that the water selectively absorbs light. This means that not only is the quantity of light reduced with increasing depth, but the longer wavelengths are affected first; at about 20 feet (6 metres) reds have been removed, at about 35 feet (10 metres) oranges have gone, and so on until at around 100 feet (30 metres) only a dull grey-blue remains. At the shallower depths, coloured filters can be fitted over the lens to compensate for the missing parts of the spectrum.

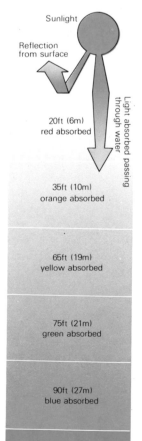

Sunlight

Reflection from surface

Light absorbed passing through water

20ft (6m) red absorbed

35ft (10m) orange absorbed

65ft (19m) yellow absorbed

75ft (21m) green absorbed

90ft (27m) blue absorbed

powerful, and the gun is relatively inexpensive, but changing bulbs underwater can be awkward and time consuming, and the cost of each flash is high. The latest electronic flash units, designed solely for amphibious operation, are greatly superior, although the initial cost is higher.

Care of equipment

Whether you use an amphibious camera or a housing, you will need to take the same rigorous precautions to maintain a watertight seal and to prevent the build-up of salt deposits that can both corrode and cause leaks.

1. Dive with a new housing before fitting a camera inside to test for defects that may cause leaks. The greater the depth, the greater the pressure, and the more likely a leak is to be caused.
2. O-rings, which are a form of rubber gasket, are the critical points in any housing or amphibious camera. Follow the manufacturer's instructions for their care, clean them thoroughly after each dive, and grease them when necessary.
3. Use O-ring grease on screws and other moveable metal parts to prevent corrosion.
4. After a dive, do not just rinse off the housing or waterproof camera. Soak it in a bucket of fresh water for at least half an hour, so that all the salt is dissolved.

5. Do not leave a sealed housing in the sun–the temperature can rise rapidly and damage camera and film.
6. Avoid moving a housing rapidly from cold to heat to avoid internal condensation.
7. Rinse and dry housings before changing film or lenses, having previously rinsed your hands in fresh water and dried them.
8. With a new housing, test it for negative or positive buoyancy underwater. Negative buoyancy is easier to handle, but there is a risk of losing the equipment in an accident and opinions vary as to which is better. Add weights to increase negative buoyancy or to balance the housing.

Without the correction of a dome port, the angle of view of surface lenses is reduced by 25 per cent. Although the effect is similar to using a lens of longer focal length, there is, of course, no actual change to the focal length.

Natural light underwater

Having checked the equipment, it is important to decide on the type of photography you will be doing on a particular dive. Although lenses and lighting equipment can be changed on dry land, they cannot underwater. As a result, moving quickly from close-up work to overall views is not possible without having more than one camera to hand. To

Lens focal length (on a 35mm camera)	Angle of view at the surface	Angle of view underwater
16mm	170°	127.5°
20mm	94°	70.5°
24mm	84°	63°
28mm	74°	55.5°
35mm	62°	46.5°
50mm	46°	34.5°
55mm	43°	32°

Depth	Filter to give approximate correction
5 feet (1.5 metres)	CC20 Red
15 feet (4.5 metres)	CC30 Red
20 feet (6.0 metres)	CC40 Red
25 feet (7.25 metres)	CC50 Red

this extent, underwater photography is controlled by technique and equipment.

Technically, the simplest form of underwater photography, shooting with sunlight, is an ideal starting point. It is, in fact, the only method of photographing views of large subjects. Although it may suffer from a lack of colour rendition and resolution, these faults are often more than compensated for in atmosphere and scope.

Weather and water conditions are of crucial importance. The ideal conditions are a bright sun well above the horizon, and calm, clear water. Any diffusion of bright sunlight worsens the problems of low contrast and colour saturation. Haze or cloud cover are particularly damaging, but so are surface waves, which scatter the light. Water clarity varies enormously, but conditions of minimum working visibility are generally considered to be those where details of objects can be seen at 30 feet (10 metres).

Currents and wave motion near the surface can make it difficult to maintain the position you want for shooting. A heavy glove on your free hand will let you hold on to rock or coral. You can anchor yourself further with your fins braced against solid objects. Just before you squeeze the camera release, hold your breath momentarily.

Selective absorption makes the available light increasingly blue at greater depths, so use a red colour compensating filter. As you cannot change the filter during a dive, you will have to anticipate the depth you expect to work at and accept the incorrect filtration for shots at other depths on the same dive.

For overall scenic shots, use a wide-angle lens, such as 28mm or 24mm on a 35mm camera, with a corrected port wherever possible. By enabling you to include a part of the foreground, a wide-angle lens makes the water appear clearer. The wide coverage of this type of lens also makes it easy to include at least a partial view of the surface. Generally speaking, shots that include the surface from below tend to have more contrast and graphic interest than those taken with the camera pointing downwards. Coral and fish, partly or completely silhouetted against the bright sky can be especially attractive. With this kind of shot in particular, it is sensible to use several different exposures.

Close-ups may be more disapointing in natural light. Except with a fast film, the shutter speeds you are likely to be working with may not be fast enough to stop the motion of a fast fleeing fish, and colour saturation at shallow depths is appreciably less than at the surface, even with the correct filter.

To achieve a sense of landscape underwater, a wide-angle lens can be used. Shooting from below, so that the subject is partly silhouetted against the surface, maximizes contrast, thus overcoming a major problem of underwater photography by natural light (T. O'Keefe/Bruce Coleman).

Underwater 3

Although a wide field of view is impossible with just one or two artificial lights, underwater flash removes at a stroke all the problems of insufficient illumination, low contrast and colour loss that beset natural light photography. An accurate idea of the colour of this elkhorn coral would have been impossible without the flash. At a depth of 20 feet (6 metres) reds and oranges lost by absorption, and therefore not visible either to the eye or film, are recovered (T. O'Keefe/Bruce Coleman).

With fish, shrimps and otl.er moving underwater subjects, flash is essential for a sharp image (right). As speed is independent of aperture in flash photography, the lens aperture can be stopped down for the greater depth of field needed with close-ups. Here, a colourful banded coral shrimp is seen among orange sponges (T. O'Keefe/Bruce Coleman).

At a depth of more than just a few feet, the intensity of sunlight is severely reduced, and colours are lost in the bluish cast caused by selective absorption. On a cloudy day, photography is not likely to be very successful using only natural light, even in shallow water. Most underwater photography, therefore, relies heavily on artificial light, particularly when shooting individual fish or corals. A properly balanced light restores the original colours to a subject, and gives sufficient illumination to allow the small aperture settings needed for good depth of field in close-up. Continuous lights, such as those used for movie filming, can be used for still photography, but are generally cumbersome in relation to the amount of illumination they give. Flash, whether bulb or electronic, is the normal choice.

Exposure

Judging the correct exposure is the first problem. Thyristor circuits, which on the surface quench an electronic flash unit's light output when the subject has received a predetermined quantity of illumination, are generally unsatisfactory underwater, where the subject may be small and where particles and small fish may interfere with the reading. The best method is to use the manufacturer's guide number as a starting point, and make a series of tests. If you are using a surface flash unit in a

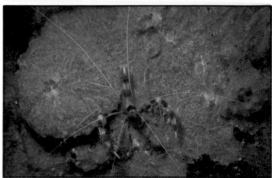

watertight housing, remember that most guide numbers are too optimistic and are calculated for room interiors where the reflections from ceiling and walls add to the light intensity. In water there is usually little reflection, and some of the light is absorbed. As a result, effective guide numbers for surface flash units used underwater are generally one third reduced from that stated. Experiment with different distance settings and with both dark and light subjects.

Colour

The greater the distance that the light has to travel through water, the more blue it will appear. Except for extreme close-ups, you will normally

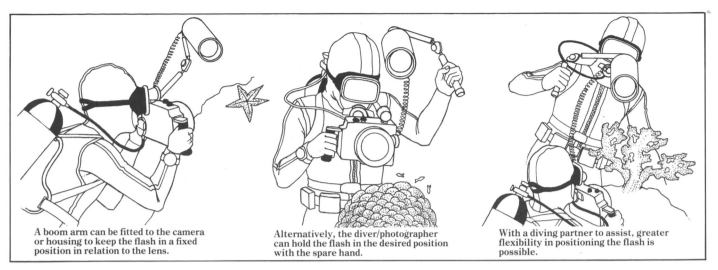

A boom arm can be fitted to the camera or housing to keep the flash in a fixed position in relation to the lens.

Alternatively, the diver/photographer can hold the flash in the desired position with the spare hand.

With a diving partner to assist, greater flexibility in positioning the flash is possible.

By positioning the flash away from the camera, the monotonous effect of flat, frontal lighting can be avoided. The flash unit should be placed above and to one side by one of the methods shown above. The tube sponges (left) have the appearance of being at great depth because of the strong directional lighting from a flash unit held above them (T. O'Keefe/Bruce Coleman).

need to add a red filter, either to the flash head or in front of the camera lens. A CC20 Red colour compensating filter gives moderate correction suitable for most situations.

Lighting positions

Although the simplest lighting technique is to aim the flash from the camera position, the result is not very natural, and can produce monotonous results if used without variation. An additional disadvantage is that suspended particles between the camera and subject are also lit. This phenomenon, known as back scattering, can be avoided by using the flash head at a distance from the camera, either with a jointed extension arm bolted to the camera

housing or bracket, by holding it at arm's length, or by having your diving partner aim it. As well as reducing back scattering, varying the lighting position generally provides better modelling and, when aimed from directly overhead, imitates direct sunlight for a natural effect. With the light at a considerable angle to the camera, there is some danger of sharp shadows, and a second light, either less powerful or at a greater distance from the subject, can be valuable to balance the illumination from the other side.

By adjusting flash intensity, shutter speed or aperture, the illumination from the flash unit can be balanced against the natural light so that both play a part in the photograph.

Underwater/rivers and lakes

Freshwater photography offers an interesting alternative to marine locations. The conditions are quite different, and although there is nothing that approaches the diversity and quantity of life surrounding coral reefs, some rivers contain fascinating phenomena, quite unlike anything found in the seas. The annual spawning of salmon, for example, creates concentrations of fish much denser than a marine underwater photographer could hope for. The shallow water offers no escape for fish that would otherwise disperse easily when faced with an intruder.

River conditions vary, with visibility ranging from excellent to almost non-existent, depending on the quantity of sediment suspended in the water. Visibility in the main stream of the Amazon can be measured in millimetres, whereas some Arctic rivers are almost as clear as distilled water. Often,

soil and decaying vegetation along the banks stain river water unexpected colours—so-called 'blackwater' tropical rivers, for example, are the colour of tea, and at more than a foot or two below the surface appear a pronounced red.

In cases like this, the filtration used with sea water is clearly inappropriate, but clear water rivers are rarely so deep that the selective absorption of light waves becomes a problem. Rivers with deep channels are usually in the mature stages of their lives, carrying so much sediment that underwater photography is not normally possible. The clearest water is usually found in shallow rivers flowing over rocky ground. Being shallow, there is often plenty of light, and flash units may not be necessary. In some circumstances only the camera need be lowered into the water—using a right-angled viewing screen instead of a prism head, the

Only occasionally are rivers and streams so clear and shallow that fish can be photographed from above the surface. Close to a natural spring, this small Amazonian stream had the additional advantage of a pale sandy bed, which showed up the young arapaima effectively. Even in ideal conditions like this, one small problem remains, wavelets on the surface distort the image slightly, like an uneven sheet of glass.
Hasselblad with 80 mm lens, Ektachrome 64, 1/125 sec at f8.

photographer can simply stand in the water, holding the camera just underneath the surface. This is possible even without special underwater equipment: the camera is placed in a small aquarium or other transparent watertight container, although in a flowing stream there is a risk of water splashing over the edges.

Unlike most marine locations, in rivers there is always a constant flow of water in one direction. Strong currents are common, and this can make swimming underwater difficult and even dangerous. It may be necessary to anchor yourself in position, preferably from a boat already moored or from the bank rather than directly to the river bottom. Dense vegetation below the surface is particularly dangerous in combination with a fast current. Remember too that there is less buoyancy in fresh water than salt.

Provided that the river is shallow enough and the water is not so turbulent that it splashes over the edges, an ordinary domestic fish tank can make it possible to use a standard camera beneath the surface of the water. A right angled viewing system is best—ideally down onto a plain ground glass viewing screen. This favours a 6 × 6 cm camera, although 35 mm SLRs with removeable pentaprism heads can also be used. If additional lighting is needed, place the flash on a stand above the camera and tank. If it is mounted on the camera's hot shoe, the light will be reflected from the glass, degrading the image.

The breeding cycle of the sockeye salmon in the Adams River, British Columbia, Canada, is a spectacular natural phenomenon that is quite accessible to the photographer. The water of the river is shallow and the natural light is sufficient for photography. Here, an amphibious Nikonos camera was used while the young fish shoaled close to the camera (J. Foott/Bruce Coleman).
Nikonos with 28 mm lens, Kodachrome 64, 1/125 sec at f3.5.

Returning to the river after years in the open sea, the sockeye salmon advance up the river in a dense mass to breed and then die. In these circumstances, they are not concerned by the presence of the camera and can be photographed at close range —in this case, with the Nikonos's standard lens (J. Foott/Bruce Coleman).
Nikonos with 35 mm lens, Kodachrome 64, 1/125 sec at f2.5.

147

Night photography

Many creatures are at their most active after dark, which creates obvious difficulties for the photographer. It is possible for some animals to become gradually accustomed to floodlights, but the level of illumination is necessarily low and as a result flash is a virtual necessity. Flash, however, can only be used with some method of sighting and focusing on the subject. An artificial light source is usually needed for observation, although steps can be taken to make the most of night vision. Allow about twenty minutes for your eyes to become adapted to the dark, and from then on avoid looking at any lights, as far as is possible. Tape around the rim of any flashlight and close your eyes briefly when firing a flash unit. Because less of the eye's night vision is taken from the central part of the retina, better night viewing can be achieved by looking slightly to one side of the subject.

Some animals will tolerate the beam of a flashlight, provided that it is not moved abruptly, and it can thus be useful for spotting creatures through the reflections from their eyes. Often, two small pin-points of light may be the first sign of a nocturnal animal. There is much less risk of disturbing the animal, however, if the light is covered with a piece of red acetate – virtually all nocturnal creatures are insensitive to red light. Nor is the human eye very sensitive to this wavelength, so that a fairly powerful flashlight will be necessary.

Stalking is difficult to accomplish effectively at night, as humans relying largely on vision are at a decided disadvantage to animals with superior senses. Vision and hearing are always acute among nocturnal creatures, so that concealment and stealth are paramount. If your skin is fair, then your face and hands can be surprisingly visible at night, even over a distance, and some blackening will help camouflage them.

Most night photography of wildlife is done from a hide, or uses remote control equipment, for which concealment is less of a problem. The most common sites are the animal's lair or other regular visiting place, sometimes with baits or lures employed. You will need knowledge of the behaviour of your subject, and this may mean several nights of observation before attempting photo-

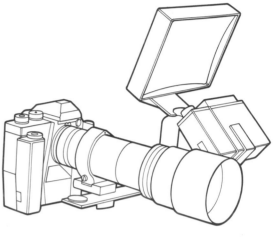

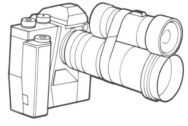

Two devices that may help with night-time photography of wildlife are a telephoto flash attachment (above right), which concentrates the flash into a beam with a parabolic mirror, and a battery torch attached to the lens (below right), providing sufficient light for focusing in the dark.

With larger animals, a long-focus lens may have to be used at a distance so that the photographer can avoid being noticed. Most portable flash units, however, are just not powerful enough for use above a few metres away. To be effective at, say, 100 feet (30 metres) with ASA 64 film and an aperture of f4, the guide number would have to be 400. Faster film is a partial answer, but a more effective solution is to focus the beam of light from the flash unit with a parabolic mirror, so increasing its effectiveness at a distance. This photograph of chital was taken at a distance of about 200 feet (60 metres) with this equipment and a standard portable flash unit. The bright reflections from the animals' retinas are an unavoidable result of using a light from very close to the lens position.
Nikon with 300 mm lens, Ektachrome 400, 1/60 sec at f4.

graphy. With animals that have underground lairs, such as badgers or foxes, you can identify whether an entrance is in use by carefully arranging a few sticks at its mouth and noting if they have been disturbed by the following day.

Flash units at night

When using a flash unit, be prepared for only one picture opportunity, as the sudden burst of light will probably alarm the animal. The guide numbers given for flash units by manufacturers are often unreliable outdoors, where there are few bright reflective surfaces to increase the illumination. Make an exposure test under similar conditions to those you will be working in. You will probably find that an extra stop is needed over the recommended setting. The 'ready' light on most portable flash units begins to glow before there is a full charge. For maximum power, wait a few more seconds before firing.

At distances of more than a few yards, a single portable flash unit may not be powerful enough with film of average speed. In addition, greater distances will require lenses of longer focal lengths to fill the frame with the subject, and this usually means a small maximum aperture. With ASA 64 colour film, an f5.6 telephoto lens and a flash unit with an effective guide number of 120, the greatest realistic working distance is 21 feet (7 metres). To calculate the maximum distance, take the guide number for the film speed you are using, and divide by the maximum aperture of the lens. The result will be given in feet if you have used the ASA rating, or metres with the DIN rating.

Using high speed film will increase the working distance, as the guide number will naturally be higher. Another method is a tele-flash attachment. This is a device for directing the light output from the flash by means of a lens or mirror, and can give up to two, or even three times greater efficiency.

Camera operation in the dark

Viewing and focusing are particularly difficult at night—even more so when using a tele-flash at a distance. Even when fully adapted to the dark, the human eye has poor acuity compared to its daytime performance, and single lens reflex viewing is usually unsatisfactory. A sports finder, or even a home-made wire frame, is easier to use. Another aid is to mount the observation flashlight next to the camera on a bracket.

Even with a flashlight, accurate focusing is not easy unless there are sharp, definite shapes in the picture, such as the branches of a tree. One solution is to set the focusing ring of the lens in advance. A few lenses, such as the 500mm Tele-Tessar for a Hasselblad, have moveable knobs that can be positioned at any distance setting by touch. Otherwise, a plastic ring can be made to fit around the lens, with screws or projections attached to mark useful distances. This approach is not foolproof, as the distance of the animal still has to be judged visually, but it can help. Aperture changes can be made in the dark by feeling the clicks as the aperture ring is turned. The shutter speed, when using flash, needs no adjustment.

With careful preparation and advanced technique, some wildlife photographers achieve images of remarkable quality and precision using flash at night. Here, a barn owl returns to the nest with food for its young (S. Dalton/Bruce Coleman).

A torch was used to set the focus for this shot before the arrival of the animal itself as its movements could be anticipated. The Australian possum passed this spot regularly and the camera and flash unit were positioned in advance (J-P. Ferrero). Nikon with 105mm lens, Kodachrome 25, 1/60 sec at f8, with one 200 Joule (watt-second) flash unit.

Underground

The combination of flash and tungsten lighting in this photograph of a cave complex in Minas Gerais, Brazil, adds interest and depth through the variation of colour temperature. On daylight film, a fine exposure of the tungsten lights installed for visitors records as orange, while the photographer's own flash, held high above the camera, illuminates the foreground stalactites and roof (L. C. Harigo).

One specialized environment, quite unlike any other, is found in caves. Water, rock faces and unremitting darkness are the typical characteristics, creating problems that are by no means purely photographic. As with diving, the actual activity of caving is specialized and should never by approached casually. Some of the skills of diver and mountaineer are needed, and more besides. Caves can be dangerous places, and in deep caving photography is necessarily second to all-important safety procedures.

Cave life

There are three kinds of creatures that live in caves, classified according to how dependent they are on this special environment: troglodytes, troglophiles and trogloxenes. Only the first of these are the true, permanent inhabitants of darkness, usually lacking any colouring and totally sightless. Cave shrimps, fish and salamanders, together with certain fungi, are examples. Troglophiles are margin dwellers, including some beetles and spiders, living in the cave only as far from the entrance as there is some light. Trogloxenes are temporary visitors, using the cave as shelter or nesting place. Bats are the best known trogloxenes.

Equipment and lighting

In cave photography, confined spaces and the complete absence of light are the two main problems. For portability, small camera formats have a distinct advantage, and the tough conditions make demands on the ruggedness of all equipment. Single lens reflex cameras are not necessarily ideal, as focusing in dim torchlight is difficult–the eye is less able to resolve detail when it is dark adapted–and a simple, direct viewfinder camera is more likely to withstand hard knocks successfully.

Wide-angle lenses are the most useful for general views, and as most caves and passages are irregularly shaped, distortion, even with an extreme wide-angle lens, is not usually noticeable. One exception is the convergence of verticals when photographing stalactites or stalagmites without aiming the camera horizontally. Long-focus lenses can be used for isolating details, but a macro lens, which is essential for small cave life, can also be used in these conditions, if light weight is at a premium.

Except at cave entrances, all lighting must be artificial. Electronic flash is standard, and when photographing animals and fungi in close-up, there are no special difficulties. Lighting caves for overall views, on the other hand, involves some special considerations. First, most flash units are calibrated for use in interiors that have fairly strong reflective surfaces–manufacturers' guide numbers allow for this, as do the thyristor circuits of automatic flash units. In caves, the walls are not usually very reflective, and the recommended setting for the unit will normally give too dark an exposure, by about a half stop. Bracket exposures where possible.

Wide-angle views, with a 28mm lens on a 35mm camera, for example, or less, are normally impossible to light evenly with just one flash unit. And firing a flash from the camera position will only be satisfactory if the cave features that appear in the picture are all at approximately the same distance. In a large space, with both foreground and background features, the light will fall off sharply away from the camera. A better alternative is to mount the camera on a tripod or other secure support, open the shutter on the 'B' setting, and fire the flash from a number of different positions around the cave. It is even possible to light up the whole cave in this way. One important precaution is to conceal the flash unit itself from the camera's viewpoint–behind a pillar or outcrop, for example. Provided that the flashlit areas do not overlap, calculate the aperture setting on the basis of one flash exposure.

Care of equipment

Water and hard knocks are responsible for most camera damage underground. Secure packing is essential, preferably in padded, waterproof cases. Take extra care when handling all unpacked equipment in the dark. Take cameras and lenses out of their cases only when you are about to use them, as the air is frequently saturated with moisture and condensation is common. Pack desiccant, such as silica gel, in the cases to absorb moisture. Remember that even low voltage flash units can be dangerous when wet.

This Mouse-eared bat, in a typical hanging position, was photographed in a low-roofed cave, and was quite easily accessible for a moderate telephoto lens. The flash unit was hand-held to one side, away from the camera (U. Hirsch).

One of the rarer cave species is the oilbird, photographed here in a cave in Trinidad with a direct, camera-mounted flash. Focusing on birds and bats in flight is extremely difficult, even with a light attached to a helmet–the most successful method is to pre-focus on a nesting site, as here (C. Zuber).

Aerial photography 1

A single jacaranda tree in flower stands out against the uniform green of the canopy of rainforest trees in the northern Amazon Basin. Although not easily predictable when planning a flight, contrasting colours like these often make good subjects. It helped to know that this was the season for flowering and that rainforest species rarely occur in groups but normally as isolated specimens. Hasselblad with 80 mm lens, Agfachrome 50, 1/500 sec at f4.5.

Aerial photography offers the opportunity of a really new view of the natural world. Aeroplanes, helicopters and even balloons all make suitable camera platforms, and although in some countries hiring them can be expensive, a well planned flight can be very rewarding to the photographer. The viewpoint is so completely different from that at ground level, especially when the shots are taken directly downwards towards the ground, that aerial photography has its own language—a distinct range of subjects and very specific pictorial styles. Patterns, for example, that cannot possibly be seen from the ground can dominate the aerial view, and large landforms such as mountains and lakes can often be visualized more completely from above than from ground level.

Subjects

Viewed from the air, there are fewer large definite shapes than from the ground, and most subjects are in the same plane. Because of this, many aerial views show a confusing mass of detail, and casual shooting is not likely to be very successful. It is better to plan flights in advance, consulting the

pilot and developing a good idea of the likely subjects, rather than wandering aimlessly. Flying time costs money – a good reason for making the best use of every minute.

Definite, graphic shapes and lines Strong, obvious features usually work best in aerial photographs, and you can anticipate many of them from a large scale map. The boundaries of water and land – sea coasts, lake shorelines, rivers and small islands – are always worth exploring, as are the edges of the snowline. In all these cases, there is usually a good tonal contrast. Heavy vegetation cover, on the other hand, tends to obscure strong lines and gives flatter pictures, with less contrast. Barren terrain is generally much more graphic. Desert, volcanic and rocky areas all have good possibilities, particularly when a low sun accentuates their surface shapes by casting long shadows.

Patterns A repetitive landscape that can seem dull and uninspiring from the ground can sometimes redeem itself by offering a distinct pattern to an aerial viewpoint. Repetitive patterns are fairly common, because the conditions that create one particular feature – a sand-dune or a clump of mangroves, for example – often exist over a wide area. Patterns like these are more obvious with high contrast, nearly always enhanced by the raking light from a rising or setting sun. Patterns that do not repeat themselves are particularly common around water-borne deposits, such as salt fans in a desert or the mud-flats of a river estuary.

The braided course of the Mazaruni River in Guyana, photographed here on false-colour infrared film to eliminate afternoon haze, adds interest to a view of thick forest. Non-repetitive patterns such as this are useful subjects.
Pentax with 50 mm lens, Ektachrome Infrared, 1/250 sec at f4.

The snow-covered inner wall of Crater Lake, Oregon, and the small Wizard Island opposite, contrast with the deep blue water to make a strong graphic composition which owes much to the distinct lines of the water's edge and snowdrifts. Shorelines nearly always have a definite appearance from the air, and shooting opportunities can often be identified from a map. Topographical and aeronautical maps, particularly those which use shading to emphasize relief, can be used to predict interesting subjects in advance. Islands, drainage patterns, shorelines, cliffs and canyons are all obvious.
Nikon with 20 mm lens, Kodachrome 64, 1/250 sec at f4 with polarizing filter.

Aerial photography 2

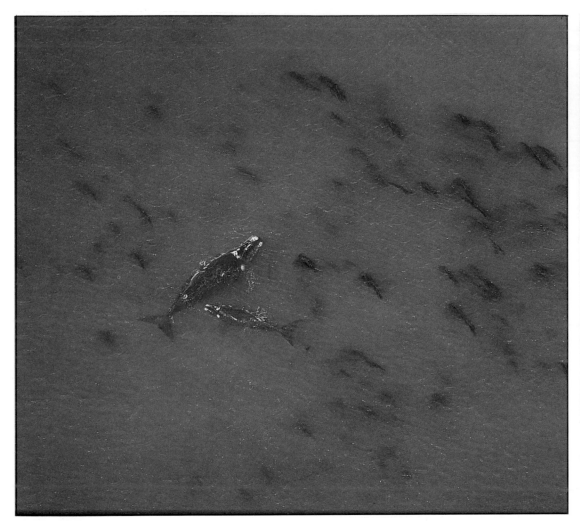

Whales can be more easily photographed from the air than by any other method. This southern right whale with her calf was clearly visible in the shallow seas off the Valdes Peninsula, Argentina (J. and D. Bartlett/ Bruce Coleman).
Nikon with 50 mm lens, Ektachrome 64, 1/500 sec at f5.6.

Contrasting colours Strong differences in colour are not a particularly common feature of the aerial view, but where they do occur they can make very interesting photographs. With vegetation, for example, the scale of aerial photography makes it difficult to distinguish individual flowers, but a whole tree in blossom can create a dramatic effect. In the fall, stands of aspen or red maple are another possibility. Geysers and hot springs sometimes produce vivid colours, particularly from algae that thrive in the warm water.

Lighting

Above all, make the maximum use of lighting. For any given subject, there is a tremendous difference between times of day and weather conditions, and choosing the right time for flying is an important skill. For most aerial views, the best lighting is a low sun—it gives the highest contrast, and the long shadows bring out details that would be hidden in cloudy weather or under a high, midday sun. The quality of lighting is crucial in aerial photography because of the large scale of most views. Trees, rocks and hills that would appear as obvious features of the landscape from ground level because of their height usually appear insignificant from an aircraft unless strongly angled sun-

light emphasizes their form with highlights to one side and prominent shadows to the other. Early morning and late afternoon are, however, unpredictable times for flying in many parts of the world, and there is often no certainty that the conditions will be clear. Familiarity with local weather conditions and a study of the immediate forecast will improve the chances of a successful trip.

Low sunlight will throw large areas of a landscape with pronounced relief—deep valleys and steep slopes—into shadow. This is useless for photography. If you have a specific subject that is likely to be in shadow during part of the day, you will need to time the flight more carefully, perhaps after exploring the area on ground level.

Wildlife from the air

Few wildlife subjects make promising material for aerial photography, once again because of the scale. Flying low enough for a close view, perhaps at 100 feet (30 metres), is not only dangerous but will also alarm most creatures. Herds and flocks are likely to be the most successful subjects for aerial photography, particularly when there is strong contrast in colour or tone between the birds or animals and their background. White pelicans against dark water, for example, or a herd of black

Photographing birds in flight demands faster reactions and a better sense of orientation than when dealing with a relatively static subject on the ground. A moderate telephoto lens is always necessary to give any reasonable image of individual birds, yet the varying relative motion of aircraft and flock needs frequent re-focusing, which is more difficult with a long focal length. This is one aerial situation where the lens cannot be left focused at infinity. Because the camera 'window' from a small aircraft is limited, the basic technique, used here with a small flock of spoonbills over the Florida Everglades, is to fly towards them at a close but safe shooting distance, and then bank away. This gives a few seconds of shooting time only.
Nikon with 180 mm lens, Kodachrome 64, 1/250 sec at f2.8.

The massing of animals makes a particularly good subject for aerial photography, particularly when they contrast against an uncomplicated background, such as the sea or open grassland. A fairly low pass may be necessary, as with this shot of Steller's sea-lion (J. Van Wormer/ Bruce Coleman).
Nikon with 180 mm lens, Ektachrome 64, 1/500 sec at f4.

Aerial photography 3

wildebeest against straw-coloured grassland, can make a powerful image—and will also fill the frame when photographed from a distance.

Because the noise and proximity of an aircraft will put most creatures to flight, flying over them at close range should not be undertaken casually. The welfare of the wildlife should be the first consideration, and if the aircraft does appear to cause alarm, restrict your photography to a single pass.

Flying technique

Whatever type of aircraft you use, it becomes, for the purposes of photography, an aerial platform for the camera. With this in mind, there are a number of things that can be done to make the platform more stable and convenient.

First, select the most suitable aircraft. This may seem obvious, but the needs of aerial photography are not necessarily the same as those for flying. Above all, you need a clear, unrestricted view, and in a fixed wing aircraft this requires two things: the ability to open a door or window as shooting through windows degrades the image, and a high wing. Sometimes, with larger, low wing aircraft, such as some Beechcraft models, it is possible to shoot from a rear luggage hatch. In any case, discuss the problem with the pilot well before flying. If you ask for a single engined, high wing Cessna, which are common aircraft at most airfields, you will be reasonably certain to have a good camera platform. At least one of the windows can be opened fully by unscrewing its retaining bar.

Flying with an open door or window can be difficult under some circumstances. If possible, keep the window closed except when actually taking photographs, and warn the pilot when you are about to open it. The choice between fixed wing aircraft and helicopters is usually determined by

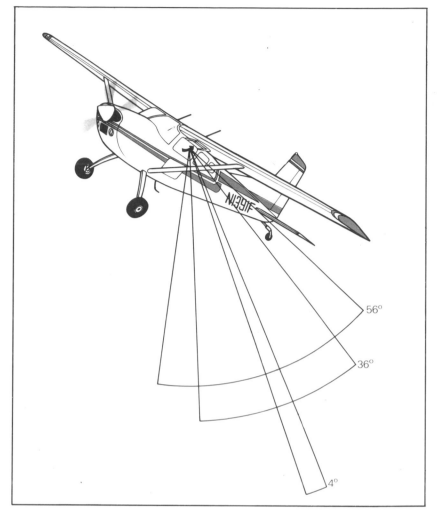

56°
36°
4°

Parts of the aircraft which may appear in the shot inevitably restrict photography, the more so when a wide-angle lens is used. In a high winged, single engined aircraft with non-retractable wheels—the type most commonly used for aerial photography—the available view is like this, with the wing tip and wheel marking the upper and lower limits of the frame. For vertical and near-vertical shots, this Cessna must be banked to port, which means putting it into a curved path over the target.

**Although haze is normally pronounced during the middle of the day, this photograph of Yosemite in California's Sierra Nevada retains clarity and high contrast through the use of a very wide-angle lens from a low altitude with a polarizing filter. A high sun, which is poor for most aerial photography, here gives a clearer view of the deeply etched relief.
Nikon with 20 mm lens, Kodachrome 64, 1/250 sec at f4 with polarizing filter.**

the particular assignment, but, as a general rule, helicopters need more experience to work from and are several times more expensive in flying time. Although one of the helicopter's great advantages is its ability to hover, this is generally a poor time to shoot as hovering sets up strong vibrations. Fixed wing aircraft are generally simpler to use, although they are not as manoeuvrable.

Balloons, by contrast, are quite free from vibration and flying them is a delightful experience. Longer lenses and slower shutter speeds are possible and there is more time to select subjects and compose shots. A balloon drifts according to the winds, however, and there is virtually no control over its movement. Once a subject has passed, there is no going back.

Camera technique

Most cameras can be used from the air, but some are more convenient than others. There is a restricted view from aircraft, and the conditions are usually difficult—engine noise, wind, cramped space, and often low temperatures. Because of this, it is generally better to use an uncomplicated camera with controls you are familiar with and which is simple to operate. Eye level viewing is indispensable and a single lens reflex design is preferable to a direct viewfinder camera, as struts, wheels and other obstructions will be clearly visible through the eyepiece. The noise inside a light aircraft is usually too high to be able to hear a camera shutter operating, and the release of tension on the winding lever is often the only indication that the camera has fired.

Judging exposure is easiest with through-the-lens metering. If you are using a hand held meter, remember to shield the receptor from the sky, which may cause serious under-exposure. As with ground level photography, consider the exposure that you want rather than the value indicated by the meter. If, for example, you are taking pictures of a flock of light coloured birds over a dark background, the direct meter reading will be incorrect. It will result in correct exposure for the background, which dominates the picture area, but the birds will be grossly over-exposed. Be aware of the problem, and give one or two stops less exposure than indicated.

Choice of lens is restricted by the problem of vibration and aerial haze. Although long-focus lenses are tempting to use because of the distance between plane and subject, they are the most difficult to use well. A long-focus lens magnifies not only the image, but also the effects of vibration. As even a lens of normal focal length used in an aircraft needs a shutter speed of about 1/500 sec to avoid camera shake, longer lenses must have even higher speeds. A further difficulty is that photographs taken with long-focus lenses suffer more from the effects of aerial haze, and as most aerial photographs are taken through at least 500 feet of air, this can weaken the image considerably. For the high contrast, a wide-angle lens used from a low altitude will give good results, although this will produce panoramic views rather than selected details. Ultraviolet or polarizing filters will reduce haze and improve the image of any lens.

Whatever lens is used, set the shutter speed to the highest setting possible. The low depth of field at minimum aperture is unimportant—at normal flying altitudes the ground is, to all intents and purposes, in a single plane. For the same reason, in most situations the focusing ring can be set at infinity. The only exception, where re-focusing might be necessary, is when extremely low passes are made or when birds in flight are the subject.

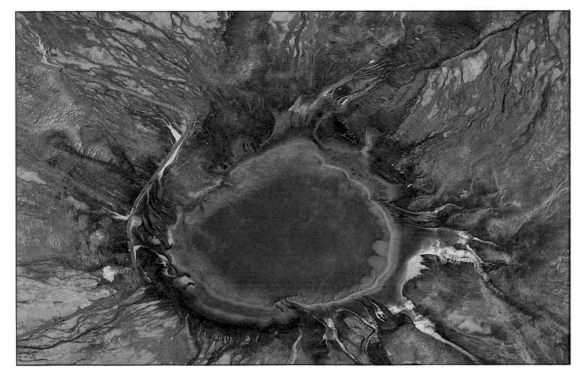

Although a telephoto lens is more difficult to use than a wide-angle, needing a higher shutter speed and more careful focusing, it has the dual advantage of magnifying small scale features and giving more choice of composition. It may not be possible to move a wide-angle lens more than a few degrees without part of the aircraft coming into shot, but a long-focus lens has a narrower angle of view and framing can be more precise. This near vertical photograph of the Grand Prismatic Spring in Yellowstone National Park, was a clear candidate for a long focal length. A wide maximum aperture, however, is a real advantage. Nikon with 180mm lens, Kodachrome 64, 1/500 sec at f2.8.

THE STUDIO

When photographing wildlife in the field, there is little opportunity to exercise photographic control. The photographer is, in a sense a hunter, and the moments for picture taking have to be seized when they occur. Even when working from a hide, the photographer is largely at the mercy of the animal's pattern of behaviour.

An alternative approach to fieldwork is to photograph captive creatures under controlled conditions. Although the excitement and accuracy of natural conditions are sacrificed, in their place you have the freedom to arrange your own photographic schedule, choosing camera angles, subjects, timing and virtually any other factor that may make a better photograph. With some shy, elusive animals, such as small mammals or small marine organisms, it may be the only practical method of working. Even with more straightforward subjects, it is worth considering the advantage of captive sets.

As a basic principle, controlled conditions should be used to improve the image through the greater control available. In practice, this simple rule is often ignored. There is little point in having the possibilities of composing lighting and planning composition only to treat the photograph casually. The haphazard image, unavoidable in many situations in the field, reflects a wasted opportunity in the studio, where a wealth of highly developed technique is available to be applied to wildlife photography. For example, the technical and aesthetic control of lighting is the single most important consideration in most normal studio work—with a wildlife subject, the same careful approach is needed. Studio management and the planning of a shooting session are other areas of expertise that can only be of benefit to wildlife photography.

In its own way, photographing wild creatures in the studio can be very demanding. The welfare of the subjects must always come first, and animal husbandry takes time, effort and skill. In addition, arranging the studio conditions so that they imitate or reproduce the animal's natural environment is not always easy. Apart from practical problems, such as controlling temperature or providing the right vegetation, experience is needed to avoid the glaring errors that are surprisingly common, such as the inclusion of unnatural elements in the picture.

Most controlled wildlife photography is of small creatures, for practical reasons large enclosures are normally beyond the means of all except established zoos. In an average studio, however, all the facilities necessary for small mammals, reptiles, amphibians, fish and insects can usually be installed. One approach is to rear the subjects from young, attempting to provide a permanent habitat in which they can lead normal, unstressed lives. Alternatively, the studio can function simply as a staging point, with animals that have been collected in the field brought in for a single photographic session before being returned undamaged to their natural environment.

Equipment

A wildlife studio is a combination of small zoo and still-life photographic studio. Its design can vary enormously, depending as much on personal styles of working as on the space and facilities available. Permanent living and rearing conditions for the animals are not essential, but their welfare must be paramount, and even temporary housing must be adequate.

Many of the basic techniques of photographic studios can be used. These can be quite sophisticated, but are not necessarily expensive. Lighting is an area of major improvement in recent years. There is no longer the inadequate choice between overheating photofloods and the stark, primitive illumination of a pocket flash unit. Mains-operated studio flash has quietly revolutionized studio work, combining high light output and continuous modelling lighting. Great depth of field is possible even with large camera formats, and the ability to make subtle refinements to the quality of light are taken for granted.

Studio space

Most studios have to conform to the available dimensions of an existing room, but there are certain minimum needs. Captive sets tend to be quite small, measuring less than a few square feet (one square metre) in plan, so that the studio does not need to be very large. The working surface, however, must be adequate. Typically, wildlife studio photography requires the use of a wide variety of camera angles. A free-standing table will be sufficient for most horizontal shots into a vivarium or aquarium, although an open frame would also allow shooting upwards through the base of a transparent tank. For vertical, downward shots, the floor or a low bench is usually used as the base.

Other important factors include the power supply –pumps, heaters and studio lights will often overload a single domestic circuit. In addition, plumbing for aquaria, provisions for making the room lighttight, ventilation and temperature control should all be considered.

Camera supports

In a studio, the camera support does not need to be particularly portable, but it should be versatile enough to cope with widely different camera positions. Some tripods have legs that can be spread to a wide angle for a low camera position. These are easier to work with and more stable than the alternative method, reversing the centre column. Some also can be fitted with a horizontal arm for vertical, downward shots to avoid including the tripod legs in the picture. For a large amount of vertical shooting, a copy stand may be more convenient. A table tripod or a clamp fitted with a ball and socket head are other possibilities. The most versatile and rigid of all studio supports is a camera stand, a heavy rolling column with an adjustable side arm that can hold the heaviest camera steady in a variety of positions.

Lighting

A studio flash unit is ideal. Single flash tubes have outputs ranging from 200 Joules (watt-seconds) to

The small size of the tube and reflector in a standard portable flash unit make it difficult to control the quality of the lighting to any great degree, particularly when the flash is mounted on the camera's hot shoe. However, for sheer convenience it can be invaluable, and the scale of small creatures (below) makes the light appear less harsh.
Nikon with 200 mm macro lens, Kodachrome 64, 1/60 sec at f16 with portable flash unit.

A large studio flash unit has several advantages. It is powerful enough to allow small apertures to be used, it can be fitted with a variety of reflectors and diffusers, and it has a tungsten modelling light to preview the effect. It can be used to mimic various types of daylight, as in the examples on the following pages, or for special effect, such as this strongly side-lit portrait of a hawk-eagle (below right).
Nikon with 180 mm lens, Kodachrome 64, 1/60 sec at f20 with 400 Joule (watt-second) diffused flash.

more than 5,000 Joules. The most powerful can be strongly diffused to provide softly shadowed illumination, yet allow aperture settings with fine grained colour film of as little as f64. A 400 Joule unit is adequate for practically all 35mm studio work. A variety of diffusers and reflectors is available, to provide every lighting style from a hard direct spot to a broad skylight. A photoflood modelling light gives a preview of the flash for focusing and composition, and can also be used as a main lighting source if necessary.

Studio flash units are of two types: integral units and those with power packs that are separate from the heads. The newer integral units are popular because of their convenient design, with few trailing leads, but are naturally heavier than a separate head.

A flash meter is indispensable for finely controlled work. Most function as incident light meters, measuring the light falling on the subject rather than light reflected from it. Some can also measure combined daylight and flash sources.

The lighting support system needs to be even more flexible than the camera support. One of the most useful lighting positions is directly overhead, but this is difficult to achieve with a basic lighting stand. Alternatives are a boom arm with counterweight, a short horizontal clamped arm, and a bar suspended between two vertical poles. Vertical supports can be either in the form of tripod stands or expanding poles that jam tight between floor and ceiling. Tripod supports for large lights are easier to move around if fitted onto a wheeled dolly.

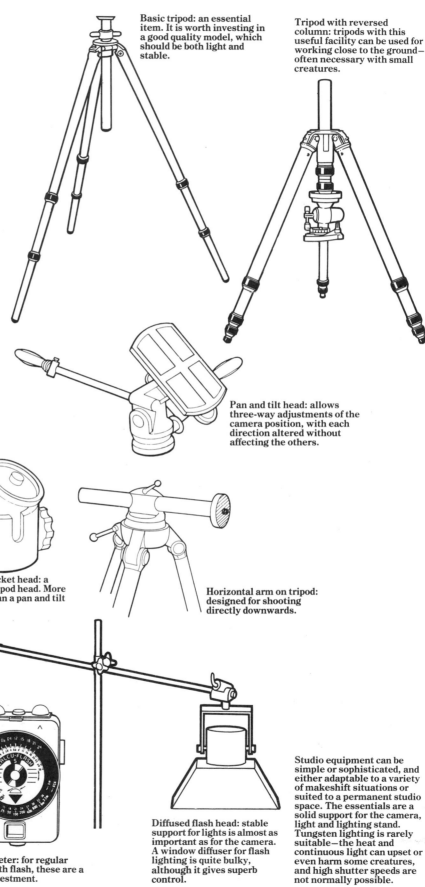

Basic tripod: an essential item. It is worth investing in a good quality model, which should be both light and stable.

Tripod with reversed column: tripods with this useful facility can be used for working close to the ground—often necessary with small creatures.

Pan and tilt head: allows three-way adjustments of the camera position, with each direction altered without affecting the others.

Portable flash unit: adequate illumination can be provided by such a small light source in close-up photography.

Ball and socket head: a standard tripod head. More portable than a pan and tilt model.

Horizontal arm on tripod: designed for shooting directly downwards.

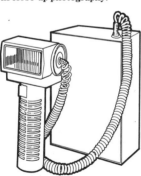

Portable flash with recycling battery: greater power and durability is offered by these models.

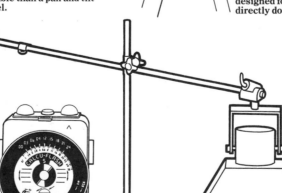

Ring-flash: for perfectly controlled, frontal lighting with close-up subjects.

Flash meter: for regular work with flash, these are a wise investment.

Diffused flash head: stable support for lights is almost as important as for the camera. A window diffuser for flash lighting is quite bulky, although it gives superb control.

Studio equipment can be simple or sophisticated, and either adaptable to a variety of makeshift situations or suited to a permanent studio space. The essentials are a solid support for the camera, light and lighting stand. Tungsten lighting is rarely suitable—the heat and continuous light can upset or even harm some creatures, and high shutter speeds are not normally possible.

Dry sets 1

There are two kinds of enclosed sets for photographing wildlife in the studio: those for terrestrial animals (vivaria) and those for water dwellers (aquaria). They have different requirements of construction and management, and they also demand different photographic techniques.

Dry sets can be used for small mammals, such as field mice and voles, a variety of lizards and other reptiles, and some insects. Although the special habits of many creatures call for custom built tanks or containers, a single basic design can be adapted to serve for the majority.

One method is to build a large vivarium, well stocked with the appropriate vegetation or other suitable material, and wait for the animal to settle into a routine. To a large extent, a substantial element of chance will remain with viewpoint and composition. You will almost inevitably have to shoot from a high position, and this kind of set is really only suited to creatures that will not attempt to climb or jump over the sides.

Designing a set

Much more control can be achieved by building a set that serves the camera. By angling the side walls towards the camera, a set can be constructed that covers exactly the angle of view of a chosen lens, no less and no more. Barring focusing problems, the animal will always be in the field of view. A simple housing to suit docile subjects can easily be built from plywood, board or perspex (plexiglass). Select the lens you will use—for example, a 55mm macro lens on a 35mm camera—and measure out the field of view on the uncut base. The base can then be cut to shape, and this makes the foundation for the remainder of the set.

A slightly more elaborate version has a hinged perspex (plexiglass) or glass lid and can thus be made escape proof. Here, to avoid degrading image quality by shooting through a glass front panel, a flexible sleeve puts the lens inside the vivarium, yet still provides a good seal. An additional sophistication is a scooped background, so no obviously artificial horizon line will appear in the shot.

In many cases the animals, despite all the preparations of a carefully designed set, will not adopt a photographic pose unaided, and you may need to encourage them into different positions. How much you can interfere with the animal depends on the species. Be careful not to confine the animal excessively or move it around too much. Beyond a certain point you will induce stress, and succeed only in photographing a display of fear, aggression or other extreme behaviour.

Backgrounds

Studio photography allows a great deal of control, including the opportunity to arrange the setting for the subjects and even to design the whole picture. One approach is to imitate the natural habitat as closely as possible, but this is by no means the only one. How you choose to present an animal is only partly influenced by its behaviour; the rest is up to the photographer. There may be one particular aspect that you want to highlight, such as the way a

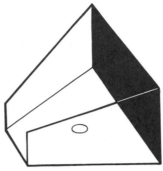

Vivarium shaped to match the angle of view of the lens.

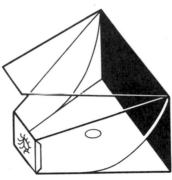

Shaped vivarium with angled 'scoop' and lid.

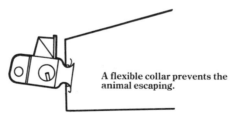

A flexible collar prevents the animal escaping.

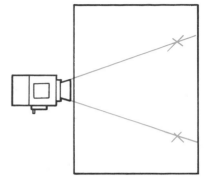

Wild flowers, mosses and grass were added to the set for this hedgehog, to imitate its natural environment. In order to give the impression of broad, even daylight, three flash heads were used, powered by the same unit, two in front and one behind the subject (J-P. Ferrero). Mamiya RB67 with 180 mm lens, Ektachrome 64, 1/125 sec at f16, with 800 Joule (watt-second) flash unit.

Rather than build a set for each photograph, it may be more convenient to use a design that can be adapted each time with new backgrounds, earth, rocks and vegetation. By planning it to fit the angle of view of the lens, there is no wasted space, and more importantly, no hidden corners.

One of the simplest and most useful lighting arrangements is a single, overhead light source, diffused through a 'window'—a box-like attachment fitted with opal perspex (plexiglass). Shadows are soft and there are no hard, bright highlights. In this photograph of a leopard gecko (far left), the area of the light is many times the size of the subject, imitating the effect of a hazy sun. Nikon with 55 mm macro lens, Kodachrome 64, 1/60 sec at f32, with 750 Joule (watt-second) flash.

On occasions when a clear straightforward portrait is required, look for an uncomplicated but relevant and natural background. The simple graphic pattern of a large, ribbed leaf complements the colour and detailed skin texture of a Phelsuma lizard (centre left). Nikon with 55 mm macro lens, Kodachrome 64, 1/60 sec at f22, 400 Joule (watt-second) flash.

For this lesser panda in a zoo in south India (left), the set of bamboo was created inside the animal's cage and lit by two flash units. A CC05 Yellow filter added a natural warmth to the photographic lighting (J-P. Ferrero). Mamiya RB67 with 180 mm lens, Ektachrome 64, 1/125 sec at f11, with two 200 Joule (watt-second) flash units.

Dry sets 2

For studio shots intended to show the behaviour of animals, captive specimens are ideal as they frequently become accustomed to humans and are unconcerned by the photographic process. This pet viparine snake, native to France, for example, was quite prepared to feed, despite the presence of camera, lights and photographer (J-P. Ferrero). Mamiya RB67 with 90 mm lens, Ektachrome 64, 1/125 sec at f11, with two 400 Joule (watt-second) flash heads.

A brown bandicoot in Northern Territory, Australia, responded to being provided with a suitable habitat in the studio set by digging a burrow, thus adding to the natural appearance of the shot (J-P. Ferrero). Mamiya RB67 with 180 mm lens, Ektachrome 64, 1/125 sec at f16, with two 200 Joule flash units.

gecko grips a vertical surface, and you may decide to treat this in a detached, scientific way. Or you may choose to treat the photograph as a studio portrait, with no pretensions to naturalism.

Natural backgrounds are the most demanding, simply because they need to appear accurate. A good knowledge of the real habitat is essential. If in any doubt, carefully examine photographs of similar environments. Once you have assembled the correct vegetation, rocks and other elements, start laying out the set, but avoid 'over-designing'. Being too neat is tempting, but the result will look artificial. Deliberate untidiness will help to give more naturalism to the picture.

Lighting

There are no rigid rules for lighting–no single quality or direction of light is 'correct'. Essentially, good lighting is that which gives an aesthetically pleasing effect, and this can be very subjective. Nevertheless, tastes in lighting are influenced by fashion and, in general, the present trend is towards naturalism with a general spread of diffused light in imitation of daylight. Remember, however, that if the animal is small in relation to the light source, the light will be greatly diffused. With small lizards, for example, a two foot square (0.6 metres) diffused light source may cast very little

shadow, producing almost no modelling. In this instance, a harder and more direct light may look better.

A single well diffused light source has many attractive qualities, and can be used as a basic form of lighting for most studio wildlife subjects. The shadows are relatively soft, without hard edges, and the overall effect is rounded and even. Used well, there is often no need for secondary lights, which nearly always create an artificial impression. Reflectors, such as hand mirrors, crumpled silver foil and pieces of white card, can be used to fill in the shadowed areas. If the diffused light is suspended directly over the set, pointing downwards, the result will be a good impression of hazy sunlight.

The most manageable design of diffuser is a box attached to the light head, fronted with opal perspex (plexiglass) or some other translucent material. With a studio flash unit placed close to the subject, use a low watt domestic bulb as a modelling light in the same position. This will have no effect on the flash output, but it will prevent overheating of the vivarium. Even so, take care that the lighting does not make the subjects uncomfortable–lizards or snakes that are accustomed to desert heat will thrive in the warm, drying conditions of studio lighting, but animals that

Camouflaged animals pose a special problem–how to show the effectiveness of their disguise while still giving a clear image of the subject. Unless a pair of photographs is taken, against different backgrounds, the best solution is normally a compromise, choosing a background–in this case the bark of a tree–against which the camouflage is only partially effective.
Nikon with 55 mm macro lens, Kodachrome 64, 1/60 sec at f27, 750 Joule (watt-second) flash.

Some small creatures, such as this mulgara, an Australian marsupial rat, are so active that it is very difficult to keep them sufficiently still for photography. In this case, the pet animal had to be confined by sheets of glass while the photograph was being taken, although the distraction of food also helped (J.-P. Ferrero).
Mamiya RB67 with 90 mm lens, Ektachrome 64, 1/125 sec at f22, with two 200 Joule (watt-second) flash units.

need high humidity may need extra moisture in the set. Also, some animals will not behave normally under continuous bright light—in these cases it may be better to switch the modelling lamp off altogether, working in semi-darkness and using the flash illumination above.

Animal welfare in the studio

Looking after animals is an important and difficult skill, and providing permanent accommodation for animals is almost a form of zoo-keeping, not to be undertaken lightly. With some protected or dangerous species, you will need a licence.

Even if animals are brought into the studio just for a photographic session—for a day or two only—check beforehand that you can provide at least the minimum facilities. These conditions vary greatly from species to species, but the following general points should be considered in the first instance.

1. General environmental needs Provide sufficient space and cover, including areas for retreat, feeding and nest building.

2. Temperature Domestic tungsten lighting may be sufficient but if the animals prefer darkness, an infrared lamp may be necessary. A thermostat is useful for critical temperature control.

3. Lighting Some animals are unaffected by the ambient light, but others, such as nocturnal species, have exacting demands. Many small mammals are most active at night, but it is possible, over a long period, gradually to alter the diurnal schedule so that the animal's night falls during the working day. This is usually more convenient.

4. Humidity A humidifier provides the most accurate control, but even a bowl of water or a wet sponge can be useful.

5. Ultraviolet light To stay healthy, many reptiles need the ultraviolet light that they would normally receive by basking in the sun. Fluorescent ultraviolet lamps can be used as a substitute.

6. Oxygen In aquaria, the oxygen content of the water can be critical. Aeration, through a small pump, is often necessary.

7. Minerals The chemical composition of water in aquaria is usually important, particularly for marine creatures. Even for freshwater aquaria, beware of chlorinated tap water.

As with larger animals, providing food is one of the easiest methods of encouraging insects to adopt natural attitudes. Here, a small moth was eagerly accepted by a South American mantis. Hasselblad with 80 mm lens with extension, Agfachrome 50, 1/125 sec at f 16, with ringflash.

Small frogs, such as this brightly coloured green tree frog found in Queensland, Australia, are on a similar scale to the larger insects and need the same extra attention to focusing and depth of field. This specimen was lit with a single flash unit, diffused and placed above the camera position (J.-P. Ferrero).
Nikon with 55 mm macro lens, Kodachrome 64, 1/60 sec at f 16, with portable flash unit.

Wet sets 1

Tight framing of marine subjects can avoid the problems caused by unnatural backgrounds and difficult lighting conditions in aquaria. This dragon fish, in an Australian zoo with no facilities provided for photographers, was photographed as it came close to the glass. Both the camera and the single flash unit had to be used hand-held (J-P. Ferrero).
Nikon with 55 mm macro lens, Kodachrome 25, 1/60 sec at f16, with one 200 Joule (watt-second) flash unit.

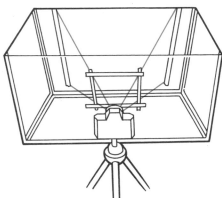

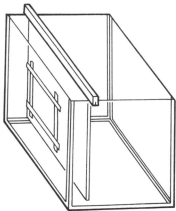

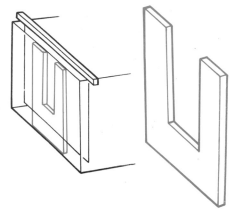

Marking the field of view

Close-up subjects

Controlling the subject's movement

Aquaria pose a special set of problems for the photographer, but they have one distinct advantage –they offer a great range of camera viewpoints. Aquatic creatures occupy a three dimensional world with great possibilities for interesting pictures.

Remember at the outset, however, that conditions such as temperature, chemical compostion of the water and oxygen content are generally critical, and constant monitoring is often even more important than with dry sets.

Converting aquaria for photography

Commercial aquarium supplies are usually the most convenient starting point. It is nearly always easier to adapt an existing tank for photography than to build one from scratch. Even in a fairly small tank, the water pressure near the base is high, and it can be surprisingly difficult to make an efficient seal.

Water and electricity are dangerous companions, and when water is brought into the studio, every electrical cable and component must be well insulated. It is also a good idea to raise all cables off the floor, where most spilled water will collect.

Most aquarium photographs are inevitably taken through glass, so check that the sides of the tank are free from defects. For the very best optical conditions, it may be worth replacing the front sheet with plate glass. To do this yourself, you will need fresh rubber sealant for the new glass. Once fixed, fill the tank immediately with water so that the pressure will make the seal watertight.

Not all water dwelling creatures need aeration– many small freshwater fish, for example, can live happily without it–but they will all be healthier if you provide it. The rising bubbles may interfere with the photography, but they can be turned off temporarily. In some cases, however, a few bubbles can improve the sense of movement in a picture. The most useful aeration system is a simple modular one, with a small pump, plastic tubing, adjustable valves and a variety of bubble generating heads. With a system like this, the rate and size of the bubbles can be adjusted to taste.

Some species, particularly marine ones, need running water–for which a water pump will be necessary. Seaweed makes a good background for marine photographs, and this also needs flowing

water to survive. If you collect water from a natural supply, which is safer than using tap water that is usually chlorinated, run it first through a filter to remove particles.

Controlling movement

The problem of focus and depth of field are even greater in water than in dry sets. Fish in particular have three dimensions in which to move about, and controlling their position in some way is usually necessary. Although it is possible with flash illumination to hold the camera by hand so as to follow movements, it can be frustratingly difficult. A more considered approach is first to fix the camera's viewpoint and then encourage the subject to move into position.

Arrange the camera position so that the background and reflections are under control–look carefully to see if the back edges of the tank are visible, with the aperture stopped down. Focus on a prearranged position for the fish, and then mark

Several methods can assist with focusing and framing. Marking the field of view: with the camera in position, use tape to mark the front and back of the tank with the limits of the field of view as seen in the viewfinder. Controlling the subject's movement: a separate sheet of glass can be suspended in the tank to keep the fish at the front of the tank. Close-up subjects: for the very precise focusing required with very small fish, a sheet of thick perspex (plexiglass) can be cut to have a central well. With another sheet behind, the subject can be confined in a narrow band.

This starfish (below) was photographed by natural light on the glass of its tank in Noumea Aquarium, New Caledonia (J-P. Ferrero). Nikon with 55 mm macro lens, Kodachrome 25, 1/30 sec at f5.6.

Wet sets 2

The choice of lighting positions is limited by the risk of catching reflections in the front sheet of glass. A straightforward arrangement (right) that can be used for most situations uses an overhead, diffused light in much the same way as a dry set. Any secondary reflections from the bright parts of the camera or the room can be eliminated by poking the lens through a piece of black paper, card or velvet. A white card reflector below the lens can be used to balance lighting on the undersides of fish and plants.

The duck-billed platypus (far right) was photographed in a zoo in Victoria, Australia. A long wait was necessary before the animal swam close to the front of the tank, at a point for which the focus had been pre-set. Two flash units were used—one above and one well to the side of the tank to avoid reflections in the glass (J-P. Ferrero). Mamiya RB67 with 180mm lens, Ektachrome 64, 1/125 sec at f16, with one 200 Joule (watt-second) flash unit above the tank, one 100 Joule unit to the side.

Quite apart from the need to aerate water in which fish are going to remain for a length of time, bubbles can add a sense of movement and realism to a tank photograph (below right). The most useful method is a small compressor fitted with a valve to control the pressure and a number of porous dispersers that fit on the end of a plastic tube and regulate the bubble size.

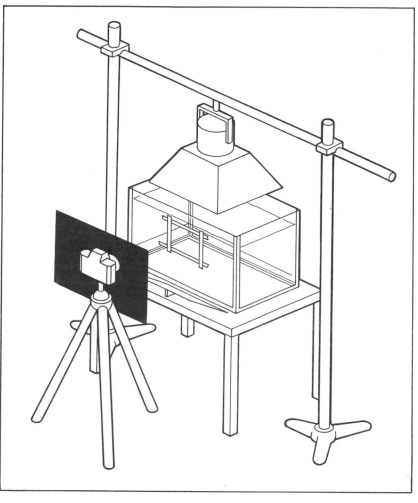

off the field of view on the tank front with a grease pencil or adhesive tape. You can then shoot without looking through the viewfinder, freeing you to control events inside the aquarium.

To confine the fish to the plane that you have already focused on, hang a sheet of glass inside the tank, close to the front. The fish now has little choice of moving out of focus, and whenever it swims into the area that you have marked off, you can shoot. If you need even greater control, you can block off the whole of the area surrounding the field of view with a perspex (plexiglass) insert. With this method, which virtually creates a small tank within the aquarium, the fish is compelled to stay inside the picture frame. Be careful, however, that this extreme confinement does not place the fish under noticeable stress, which will in any case make its movements unduly agitated.

Lighting

A common problem with aquarium photography is reflection from the glass sides of the tank. With a few commonsense precautions, however, this can be overcome. Any light source that is close to the camera position will be reflected by the glass into the lens and ruin the picture. Frontal lighting is in any case rarely the most attractive, however, and these reflections can easily be eliminated by

placing the light or lights further to one side, at a greater angle to the camera view.

More intractable is the reflection of the camera itself—the chrome trim and the numerals engraved on the lens mount may be particularly noticeable. Shade the lights so that very little spills onto the camera—this is also important for avoiding lens flare. An even more effective, simple solution is to hang a sheet of black paper, or better still black velvet, between the camera and aquarium. Cut a small hole in it sufficient for the lens. With these precautions, you will have a wide choice of lighting

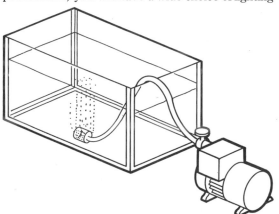

Wet sets 3

Black velvet

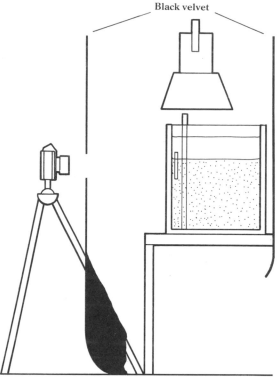

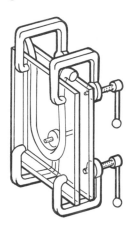

The arrangement at left is that used for the sequence of pictures showing the clam (left). It would be equally suitable for any small creature and has the virtue of great simplicity. For particularly small creatures in close-up, the arrangement below can be used to confine the subject to a shallow plane. In this arrangement, a U-shaped length of surgical rubber tubing provides a watertight seal between two sheets of glass clamped together.

positions. An overhead source, similar to that described for dry sets, gives the most natural illumination. If the bottom of the aquarium does not appear in the shot, a white plastic sheet can be weighted down to act as a reflector. Lighting from below, or obliquely from behind, can be dramatic, but also obviously artificial.

A special form of illumination is backlighting. For this, place an even sheet of diffusing material, such as opal perspex (plexiglass), behind the tank so that the entire field of view is covered. Put the light behind this, aimed directly towards the camera. Used on its own, the effect will be a silhouette. This can be very effective for animals that are at least partly transparent, but for a more balanced effect a supplementary top or side light can be used. To avoid flare, mask off the backlight to the edges of the picture frame with black paper or cloth held in place with tape.

Flash is essential to arrest motion, and a studio flash unit, as described for terrestrial animals, has sufficient power to allow the small apertures necessary for depth of field even when well diffused.

Background

In most situations, the background of the aquarium will be out of focus, even when the lens is stopped down to its minimum aperture. Nevertheless, care should be taken to make it appear right. For some subjects, you may choose a clinical, uncluttered setting so as not to interfere with the detailed appearance of the subject. In this case, a plain white background may be best. This can be created with the backlighting arrangement described above. Otherwise, you can provide a black or coloured setting either by hanging a velvet sheet behind the rear glass or, if there is a danger of reflections, by putting a sheet of black or coloured

For this sequence of a clam digging in to its normal feeding position (left), it was important that it move only downwards and stay close to the front sheet of glass, for clarity. A second, thin sheet of glass was pressed down into the sand to leave just enough space for the clam. Black velvet draped behind the tank simplified the background.
Nikon with 55 mm macro lens, Kodachrome 64, 1/60 sec at f16, with 750 Joule (watt-second) flash.

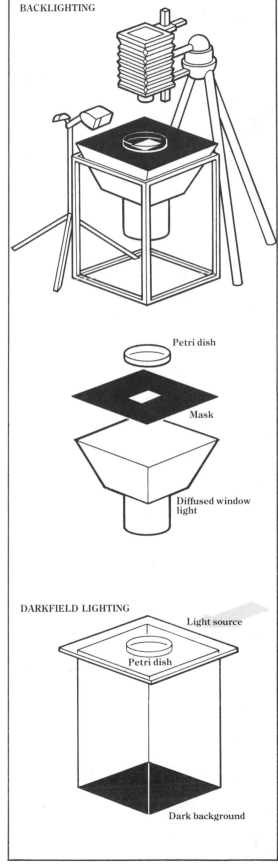

BACKLIGHTING

Petri dish

Mask

Diffused window light

DARKFIELD LIGHTING

Light source

Petri dish

Dark background

plastic inside the tank.

For a natural looking background, the habitat of the creature you are photographing will be the deciding factor. Water vegetation is a good, safe choice, but a blurred painted sheet of appropriate colours, such as green and brown, or blue and black, may be all that is necessary to give the right impression of depth.

Special settings

Small aquatic creatures need much closer control. Depth of field at a macroscopic level is very limited, and a normal aquarium is not very satisfactory. A simple miniature tank can be made with no more than two small sheets of glass, a short length of flexible plastic tubing, and clamps. The two sheets are held together with a U-shaped curve of tubing sandwiched between them. The tubing forms the seal, and its diameter determines the thickness of the tank.

Some creatures, particularly bottom dwellers, look best when photographed from directly overhead. In many ways this is easier to manage, as a shallow depth of water automatically keeps the right plane of focus. For small creatures, a laboratory petri dish is ideal. Overhead shots such as these can be backlit by placing the dish directly on top of a diffused light, or lit from the side by placing the dish on a sheet of glass. The background, of whatever colour, is then placed underneath. When using natural bottoms, the position of the light must be low, so as to avoid reflections from the water's surface.

The reverse of this position, looking directly upwards through the base of the tank, is awkward for photography, but poses few special difficulties. To keep the subject in focus, keep the water to a fairly low level.

To demonstrate the feeding mechanism of a mussel (above), which pumps through its body surprisingly large volumes of water, a red food dye was introduced with a pipette. Backlighting was the ideal way of showing this clearly (above right). The mussel was placed in position in a shallow petri dish with a small piece of plasticine, and the dish placed directly on the opal perspex (plexiglass) diffuser of the studio flash. To cut down flare, all the area outside the picture frame was masked off with black paper, and to add some modelling to the shell, a second light – a small portable flash – was directed from one side and synchronized with the main flash.
Cambo 4 × 5 in (9 × 12 cm) view camera with 150 mm lens, Ektachrome 64, f19, with 750 Joule (watt-second) flash.

Instead of lighting a dish from underneath, the flash can be positioned to one side, giving a choice of background colours. Coloured papers and cloths are best positioned some distance below the dish, so that any texture, shadows and creases are thrown out of focus. The background can be lit either by spill from the main light or, for more control, by a second, shaded light.

Zoos 1

For the photographer, zoos are in effect large captive sets. They offer many of the opportunities of a studio, but often lack the degree of control that is possible in a set that is specifically designed for photography. Ultimately, the outstanding advantages of zoos are that they are convenient and normally have good, healthy specimens of animals that might be impossible to photograph in the wild.

Nevertheless, a zoo, like all captive conditions, is never completely natural. It may be excellent for making a portrait of an animal, but behaviour patterns are likely to be distorted by captivity. This by no means invalidates zoo photography, but it creates problems for the photographer.

Natural settings

Zoos vary greatly in the settings that they provide for their inmates. Many are still handicapped with outmoded conditions, the animals in barred cages. Fortunately, modern zoo design tends towards naturalistic settings that are open to view, using moats and pits to replace bars.

The first step is to choose, whenever possible, a zoo that has good photographic possibilities. You cannot expect every exhibit to present a good picture, and finding a good camera viewpoint and lighting may involve an element of chance. The ideal is an isolated shot of an animal in a setting free from obtrusive and artificial elements. The background may be simulated, such as a bamboo

One of the simplest ways of avoiding the artificial surroundings of a zoo is to select a viewpoint with a plain background. Although this lion and lioness at London Zoo (far left) were photographed against a concrete wall, the absence of any identifying details, and the careful choice of lighting make it inconspicuous. Hasselblad with 250 mm lens, 70 mm Agfachrome ASA 50, 1/125 sec at f6.3.

Zoos vary greatly in the surroundings they provide for their animals. For the photographer, the best are those that attempt to reproduce the habitat of the species. Monkey Jungle, a small zoo in Florida (above), imported South American rainforest trees and plants, giving these squirrel monkeys conditions that are photographically indistinguishable from the real thing. Nikon with 400 mm lens, Kodachrome 64, 1/250 sec at f5.6.

Even in zoos which have the normal quota of railings and concrete, it is sometimes possible to make use of the occasional vegetation. Taken in Washington Zoo, this photograph of a lesser panda shows no evidence of artificial surroundings. The species of tree may not be realistic, but the setting is far more effective than the animal's ground level pen. Nikon with 400 mm lens, Kodachrome 64, 1/250 sec at f5.6.

Zoos 2

thicket in a tiger compound, or artificial cliffs for a herd of mountain goats, and this can be indistinguishable from the real thing in a photograph. More commonly, the background may be a plain wall. Even this can be made to look fairly natural, or at least inconspicuous, by using a wide aperture to achieve a shallow depth of field and throw it out of focus.

Choice of lens

In order to be able to control backgrounds in this way, and also to isolate the subject, a medium long-focus lens is often most suitable for zoo photography. The shallow depth of field at a wide aperture makes it possible to reduce inappropriate backgrounds to a blur. Shallow depth of field also provides a solution with barred compounds. Even closely spaced bars can be shot through with a long-focus lens – they become so far out of focus as to be unnoticeable. Lenses with very long focal lengths can occasionally be useful, but there is usually insufficient working distance to be able to frame the whole animal. Wide-angle lenses almost

inevitably include the zoo surroundings and spectators. Unless you are aiming for a general view of a zoo, they offer few possibilities.

Indoor zoos

In the indoor parts of a zoo, the lighting may be difficult to work with, particularly when using colour film. A pocket flash unit can be useful when it is permitted, but allow for some loss of light when aiming it through glass. Failing this, use a high speed film that is balanced to the colour of the ambient lighting. With tungsten lights (such as ordinary light bulbs), use a Type B tungsten-balanced film, perhaps with a slightly blue filter, such as a Kodak Wratten CC10 Blue. If fluorescent strip lighting is being used, choose daylight film with a CC30 Magenta filter – fluorescent lighting is unpredictable, but this filtration is a good starting point. In aquaria and vivaria, it is possible to use shutter speeds as slow as 1/4 sec without a tripod by pressing the lens up against the glass. This only works, of course, with slow moving animals, but such opportunities are surprisingly frequent.

A long-focus lens is useful in zoos not only to overcome the distance that separates visitors from animals but also because the narrow angle of view makes it possible to select small background areas and the shallow depth of field helps to keep them out of focus. This polar bear in London Zoo was in a moated concrete pit.
Hasselblad with 25 mm lens, 70 mm Agfachrome ASA 50, 1/60 sec at f5.6.

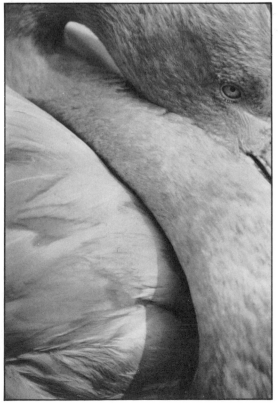

With subjects that keep relatively still, such as this shrimp (far left) or spider (above) it may be possible to use the available lighting. The light levels are nearly always low, so that with ASA 64 film, shutter speeds of between about 1/2 sec and 1/15 sec are necessary, depending on the maximum aperture of the lens. Always position the camera at a slight angle to the glass to avoid catching the camera's reflection, and be careful to watch for reflections of other illuminated tanks. Without a tripod, place the camera against the glass as a support.

Using a telephoto lens, interesting compositions are sometimes possible at close range, as with this flamingo (left).
Nikon with 200 mm lens, Kodachrome 64, 1/125 sec at f8.

Insects in flight

Legs extended in mid-jump, a desert locust launches itself towards the camera, both pairs of wings prepared for flight. With such a narrow depth of field, capturing a precisely focused image required electronic circuitry that could react to the signals of a sensor in almost a millionth of a second.

Further problems attended the photography of insects landing, as with this Pericopid moth in the Florida Everglades, about to alight on a leaf. Predicting the flight path is never a certainty, and Dalton must often use large quantities of film for a successful shot. For this photograph, a motel room served as a makeshift studio.

The studio is particularly convenient for photographing insects, for a number of reasons. Many of the technical problems encountered in the field, such as providing adequate lighting and making exposure calculations can be tackled more easily when the working conditions are controlled. The subjects themselves are relatively easy to capture and transport, and if insects are actually bred in captivity, the quality of specimens is likely to be much higher than in the wild, where wings and legs are frequently damaged.

The equipment and working methods differ very little from the studio sets already described, except that normally, everything is on a smaller scale. Even with minimum apertures, around f22 and f32, depth of field is no less of a problem than in the wild, and controlling the position of the insect to within a few millimetres is essential. As long as the subject is to be photographed whilst it is not moving, the problem is not too great—a twig or leaf can be arranged in a convenient position—and the insect can be encouraged to move into place.

Because the scale of operations is relatively small, lighting is easier to control. While the illumination from a pocket flash gun may be too harsh for

a large lizard or small mammal, the reflector bowl for the flash tube is larger than most insects, so that used close it actually gives a slightly diffused light, with softened shadow edges.

Stephen Dalton's insects

Photographing flying insects involves highly specialized techniques to overcome two severe problems—stopping on film the rapid wingbeats, and timing the exposure so that the insect is exactly in focus. Both problems call for precision and custom built equipment.

In-flight photography of insects has been largely pioneered by one man—Stephen Dalton. His first problem was lighting. Even a slow flying butterfly beats its wings eight times a second, whilst a midge has 1,000 beats per second. Ordinary flash units are far too slow to freeze movement within this range, and the short flash duration of modern thyristor units is achieved only at the expense of very weak intensity. Specifying a flash duration of no more than 1/25,000 sec, yet with enough output to give correct exposure 20 ins (51 cm) away from the insect at f16 on ASA 25 film at life-size reproduction, Dalton was only able to achieve

success by having a special flash unit built.

This was only part of the solution, however. Most insects fly fast and erratically, so that to catch them in precisely the right position calls for an ultra-sensitive trigger. This again involved more custom built electronics, using a photoelectric cell and an arrangement of small mirrors to make a criss-crossed web of light beams that would react to being interrupted even by a single antenna. This sensing mechanism was perfected so that the delay in activating the flash was practically one millionth of a second!

Even then, the camera needed modifying, with a special electronic shutter fitted in front of the permanently open lens. A standard shutter begins working far too slowly for this kind of work: Dalton's own shutter is open within 1/450 sec.

With this remarkable equipment, developed only with an equally remarkable persistence, Stephen Dalton's photographs are a major contribution to natural history, revealing for the first time the precise flight mechanisms of insects. With a subsequently developed stroboscopic flash unit, actual flight sequences can be recorded as the insect passes through a single frame.

Later developments in the equipment have allowed Dalton to record several images on one frame of film—here, the complete first cycle of wing beats as an Iron Prominent moth takes off from a leaf. With multiple exposures such as this, a black background must be substituted for the naturalistic settings that Dalton normally uses, in order for each image to stand out clearly.

Photomicrography 1

A dead water-flea has become the host for two types of small ciliates in this ×80 photomicrograph. When they have consumed all the tissue, they will form hard cysts and await their next meal.

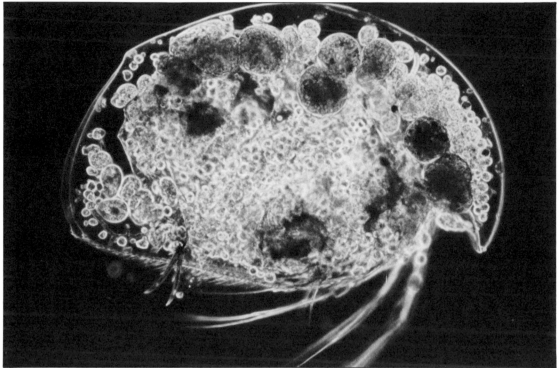

Most microscope work today involves photomicrography, either for teaching or for keeping a record. For the wildlife photographer, even the amateur, the variety of interest and lifeforms at the microscopic level offer exciting possibilities.

Choice of camera

In photomicrography, it is the microscope alone that should form the image. It is better equipped than any part of the camera system to do so, and it is important not to degrade a carefully enlarged image by using an additional, camera lens. For high quality photomicrographs, only a camera with a detachable lens is satisfactory, and a single lens reflex is much better than a direct viewfinder camera.

A 35mm camera body is light and compact enough to be supported directly on the eyepiece of the microscope, using a special adapter tube. Some stereo microscopes even have an additional vertical tube for a camera. These are known as trinocular microscopes, and can switch the image into either the viewing or photographic tubes by means of a prism.

With larger formats, principally 6 × 6cm reflex or view cameras, it is better to support them on a separate stand to overcome the problem of vibrations. A copy stand is ideal. Once again, an adapter tube replaces the lens and screws onto the end of the eyepiece.

The third category of camera is that purpose built for photomicrography. These can often be obtained as part of the microscope system. Most models use sheet film, usually 4 × 5in (9 × 12cm), because it allows a greater magnification, and the most sophisticated have adjustable bellows and a shutter with a wide range of speeds.

For microscopes that do not have light sources built into the base, the standard light source is a tungsten filament lamp, equipped with its own adjustable diaphragm and condenser. However, when photographing active specimens, such as the hydra overleaf a portable electronic flash unit is usually needed. To overcome the difficulty of positioning a small flash unit correctly, adjust it so that is is at the same angle and height as the tungsten lamp used to set up the shot, and then carefully slide it into the same position.

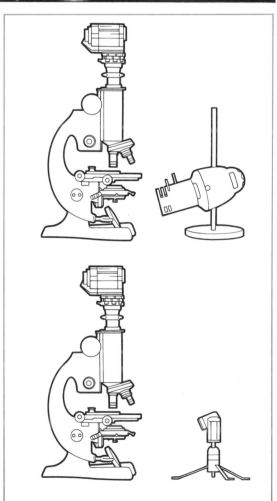

Choice of microscope

Microscope optics that are adequate for viewing may not necessarily be good enough for photography, particularly if colour film is used. Not surprisingly, the best microscope equipment is expensive, and the final choice is often a compromise between optical quality and price. For photomicrography, certain microscope components are particularly important.

Objective The principal lens in a microscope is called the objective. Its magnifying power is engraved on its mount, and is usually between 5× and 100×. The most important quality in an objective is its ability to resolve detail. The usual measure of this is known as 'numerical aperture', or NA, a figure calculated from the angle of a cone of light needed to fill the aperture of the lens. The higher the NA, the better the resolution. In air, the maximum NA is 1.0, but some objectives are designed to be immersed in a film of oil, which allows an NA of up to 1.40.

The most common, and least expensive, objectives arc known as achromats, and only partly correct the most common optical aberrations. Coloured fringes are usual at the edges of the image. The finest quality objective is the apochromat, which is corrected to a high degree.

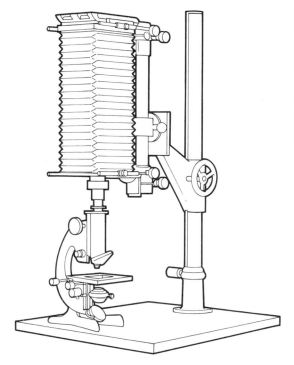

Although most photomicrography is done with 35 mm cameras, it is possible to adapt larger formats without too much trouble. Here, a copying stand is used to support a 4 × 5 in view camera. With large cameras, it is important that they be supported separately, to avoid vibration that would blur the photograph. An enlarger stand can also be adapted in the same way.

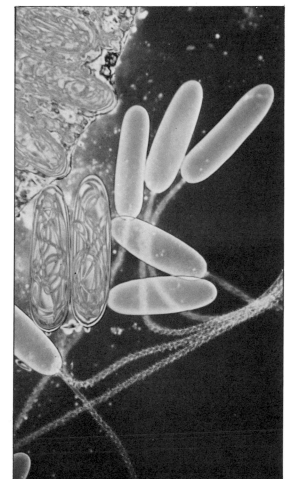

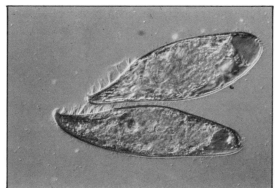

Photographed by the Nomarski technique that is favoured by many photomicrographers for living cells, these blepharisma ciliates have two sets of hair-like cilia—one for propulsion, the other for directing food into their mouths. Despite feeding normally on bacteria, cannibalism is also common.

A thin section of an anemone shows oval nematocysts at ×175 (far left). Inside two of the nematocysts the coiled threads are revealed by phase-contrast lighting (see pages 184–5); when fired at a victim, each thread uncoils inside-out to penetrate the tissue.

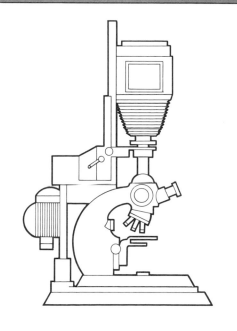

For the professional, combined microscopes and cameras are available, in this case taking 4×5 in (9×12 cm) sheet film and incorporating reflex viewing through a separate eyepiece. Apart from the large image size with its correspondingly good resolution, an advantage of the 4×5 in format is that it is possible to use Polaroid instant film, both as a test or for the final image.

Photomicrography 2

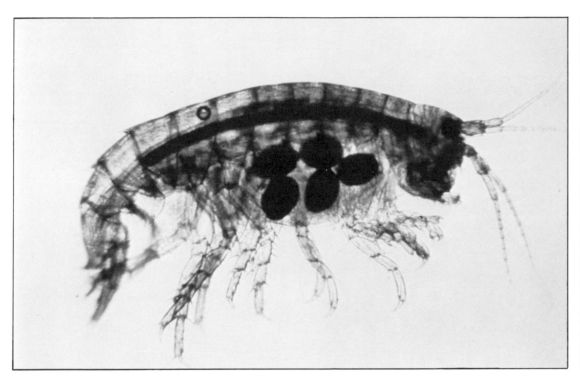

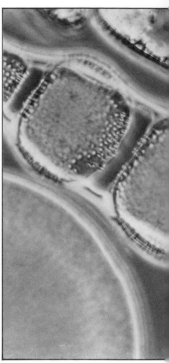

Eyepiece The secondary lens in a microscope is the eyepiece. It magnifies the primary image and projects it either to the eye or the film in a camera. For photomicrography, a 'compensating' eyepiece is needed – this corrects some of the defects in the objective. A matched pair of objective and eyepiece gives the highest quality image.

Condenser This lens, situated below the stage, collects the light from the lamp and converges it on the specimen. There are three types of condenser: Abbé, aplanatic and achromatic, and the latter is the most highly corrected for optical aberrations. It is thus best for photomicrography. Some method of centring the condenser is important for even illumination.

Mechanical stage For precise control of the position of the specimen and the composition of the image, a mechanical stage with micrometer drives, allowing much more precise movements than can be achieved manually, is a real advantage. If the stage can also be rotated, so much the better.

Basic operation

The simplest method of lighting a specimen is brightfield illumination, which as its name implies displays the specimen against a brightly lit background. The light is, in fact, passed through the specimen, which is thin enough to be translucent. Standard microscopes have a mirror beneath the subject, and this can be angled to project light upwards from a separate lamp. Some advanced models, however, have built-in light sources.

The principle of brightfield illumination is to focus an image of the lamp in the plane of the specimen, and in such a way that it falls on the centre of the field of view and covers the whole field evenly. The lamp, therefore, is an essential part of the optical system.

Light sources

The standard light source in photomicrography is a tungsten filament lamp, fitted with a condenser lens and diaphragm that can both be adjusted. A tungsten-halogen lamp is the best for colour photomicrography, as the glass envelope does not darken and discolour with age.

The disadvantage with this type of lamp occurs with active living organisms, with movements that need greater illumination to avoid blurring. In this case, an answer is electronic flash, using a pocket flash unit. An auxiliary tungsten lamp must be placed in the same position for viewing and focusing prior to photography, however.

Film

The ideal film for photomicrography is fine grained, with medium to high contrast. Speed is not usually significant, as static specimens can be photographed with long exposures if necessary and moving subjects are best illuminated with electronic flash. Most fine-grain films, therefore, are suitable but the following are among the best:

Black-and-white Kodak Ektapan 4162 in sheets for use with a view camera, Kodak Photomicrography Monochrome Film SO-410 in 35mm format, and Kodak Panatomic-X in 6 × 6cm/6 × 7cm and 35mm formats.

Colour Kodak Photomicrography Color Film 2483 in 4 × 5in (9 × 12cm) sheets and 35mm format, and Kodachrome 25 in 35mm format.

Exposure

Because microscope optics do not allow the use of an aperture diaphragm, exposure must be controlled by other methods. Altering the shutter speed on the camera gives one stop adjustments,

Essentially straightforward, brightfield illumination (above left), which has its large-scale equivalent in the backlighting used on page 173, is the basic textbook method. It is ideally suited to subspecies such as this live amphipod, whose internal structure (including eggs) has sufficient density to stand out clearly in silhouette. The magnification here is ×400.

For a close-up of colourless, transparent diatoms (above), interference-resistant lighting was used to heighten the minute differences in refractivity, and so enhance contrast.

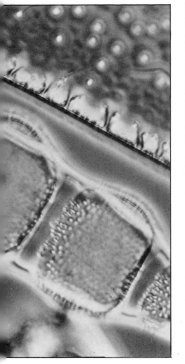

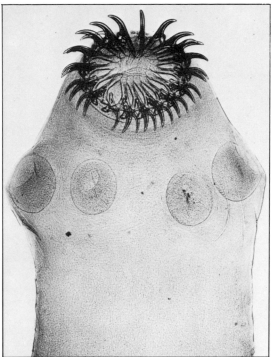

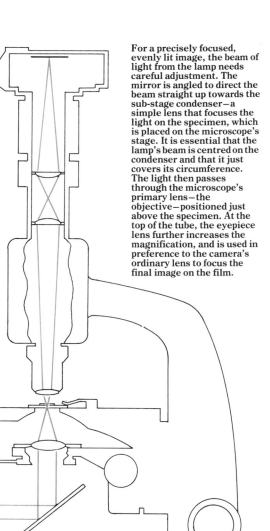

For a precisely focused, evenly lit image, the beam of light from the lamp needs careful adjustment. The mirror is angled to direct the beam straight up towards the sub-stage condenser—a simple lens that focuses the light on the specimen, which is placed on the microscope's stage. It is essential that the lamp's beam is centred on the condenser and that it just covers its circumference. The light then passes through the microscope's primary lens—the objective—positioned just above the specimen. At the top of the tube, the eyepiece lens further increases the magnification, and is used in preference to the camera's ordinary lens to focus the final image on the film.

but for finer control either the lamp position may be changed or neutral density filters may be used. Determining the correct exposure for one type of lighting situation usually means running a test film over a range of settings. As an approximate guide, shutter speeds for a typical brightfield arrangement using ASA 32 film, might run from 1/4 sec to 1/125 sec.

Standard brightfield illumination was also used for this photomicrograph of the head of a taenia tapeworm. Here again, there was sufficient density for the backlighting to show structural detail.

Staining

As thin transparent sections are necessary for brightfield photomicrography, many specimens would be invisible if not prepared in a special way. An integral part of much microscope work, therefore, is staining. Biological stains are available in all colours, and the choice depends partly on the specimen and partly on the type of film being used. Typically—on a tissue section, for example—two contrasting stains are used for different parts of the specimen. Two of the most common stains, frequently used together in animal tissue sections, are eosin, which is red, and hematoxylin, which is blue. More stains can be used in combination.

Colour films differ in how they record certain stains. Eosin, for example, reproduces well on Kodak Photomicrography Color Film 2483, but poorly on Kodachrome. Trial and error are necessary to match stains to a particular film emulsion.

Colour balance

Both microscope lamps and colour films are generally balanced at around either 3,200 Kelvins for tungsten light or 5,500K for daylight use. Any variation in the colour temperature between the film and the lamp can be compensated for by using an appropriate colour correction filter. These are available in different strengths, either to lower the colour temperature (that is, make the light more yellowish) or to raise it (make it more bluish). The table below gives a guide to the filters needed for most photomicrography, but individual tests may be needed to perfect the colour balance.

Apart from correcting the basic colour balance, some additional filtration may be needed to absorb unwanted ultraviolet radiation from zirconium arc, carbon arc or electronic flash—for this, a 2B filter will usually suffice. To compensate for slight colour differences between batches of film or chromatic aberration in the condenser, use CC05 or CC10 filters in Red, Blue, Green, Cyan, Yellow or Magenta.

Filters to balance colour

Colour temperature of lamp		Colour temperature of film		
		Tungsten type B 3,200K	Tungsten type A 3,400K	Daylight 5,500K
Xenon arc; electronic flash	5,500K	85B	85	None
Carbon arc	3,700K	81D	81B	80C
Zirconium arc; 6v coil; 12v tungsten halogen	3,200K	None	82A	80A
6v coil	3,100K	82	82B	80A+82
6v ribbon	3,000K	82A	82C	80A+82
6v tungsten	2,900K	82B	80D	80A+82B

Photomicrography 3

Because most microscope specimens are so thin that they are largely transparent, the greatest problem with photomicrography is to achieve sufficient contrast to record an image. In brightfield photomicrography, the answer is staining, but this may not always be possible, with living specimens, or sufficient, with some micro-organisms and cell structures. In this case, another method of increasing contrast must be found, involving different lighting techniques. Some of these are quite complex, at least in theory.

Darkfield

By arranging the lighting so that the background is dark rather than light, transparent specimens can be seen much more clearly, with enhanced contrast. To achieve this effect, a 'darkfield stop' is placed in the centre of the beam of light, below the condenser, forming the light into a hollow cone. When a specimen is placed on the stage, it scatters light up to the objective lens. Because so much of the light from the lamp is lost with this method, when photographing it is often necessary to use either a high speed film or electronic flash. At low power, however, it is ideal for marine organisms, such as plankton.

Phase-contrast

A more sophisticated lighting technique that can reveal internal details of completely transparent objects is the phase-contrast method. This uses the effect whereby the edges and fine detail in the specimen diffract the light passing through it–in effect, the specimen passes a portion of the light directly without modifying it, but scatters the remainder. In a phase-contrast microscope, a special coating behind the objective slows down the direct beam of light by one quarter of a wavelength. When the two beams, direct and scattered,

are drawn together again, they are no longer in phase–the peaks and troughs in the light waves are in slightly different positions. The light reaching the eyepiece is therefore less intense, but the small differences in the structure of the specimen have been enhanced.

Interference-contrast

In the phase-contrast system, detail is made visible because two beams of light create interference patterns that correspond with differences in the specimen. Other interference-contrast methods produce a similar result, but the light is split not by the specimen but by the microscope's optical system. The Nomarski system, for example, uses prisms to split the light, one beam of which is directed through the specimen, the other bypassing it. The first is called the 'object beam', the second the 'reference beam'.

Polarization

Another lighting technique that can produce spectacularly colourful results uses two polarizing filters. Light vibrates at different angles, but a polarizing filter passes only those waves vibrating in one particular direction. If a second polarizing filter is placed in the path of a beam that has already been polarized, it will only let the light pass through if it is oriented at the same angle as the first filter. If it is rotated through 90 degrees, the light is extinguished. Some specimens also polarize light, so that if placed in between the two polarizing filters–called the polarizer and the analyzer– they partly rotate the light which thus becomes visible again. Many growing crystals have this property, and because of slight variations in thickness, they polarize different colours by different amounts. The resulting interference colours can be very striking.

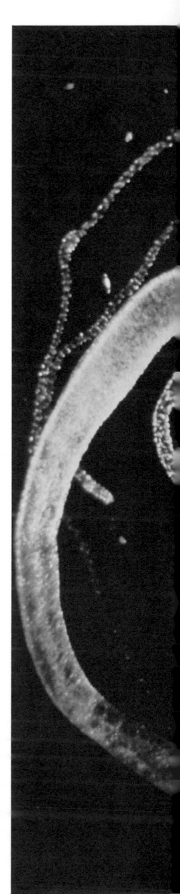

Crystals growing through the evaporation of a solution often make good subjects for polarized light photomicrography. Here the polarizer and analyzer have been crossed to block out all light from the background, leaving a vivid image of individual crystals.

The indirect illumination of the darkfield method is well-suited to giving a clear and bright image of this water-dwelling hydra (far right). At ×500 magnification, the hydra's open mouth is prominant.

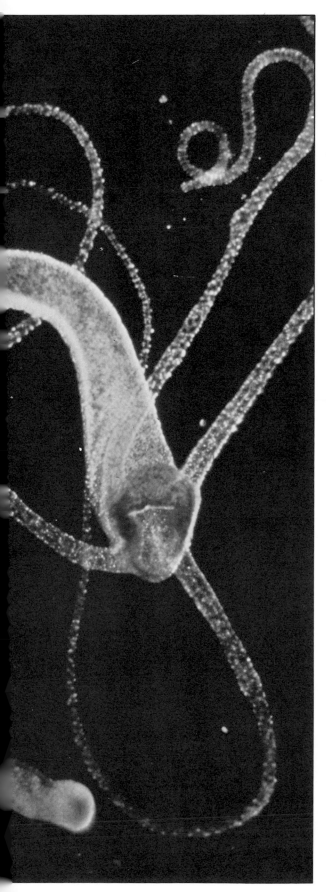

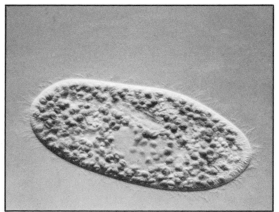

In this series of photographs, the same specimen—a common paramecium—is seen through different lighting techniques at a magnification of ×150. This first image uses the basic brightfield technique already described, but althought the general shape of the protozoa can be seen, and the green algae inside it stand out clearly, the positions of internal transparent organs can only be guessed at, and the cilia on the surface are hardly visible.

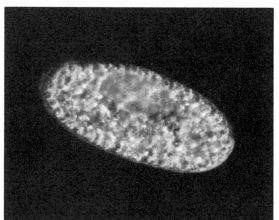

Under darkfield illumination, the internal structure acquires a luminosity that heightens contrast and at first glance seems to enhance clarity. However, although this technique, which uses oblique lighting, is good for small subjects, it can create too much optical confusion with larger specimens. As a result, there is little real detail visible in the shot.

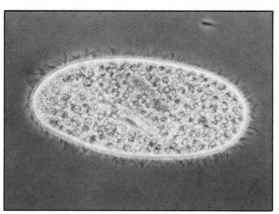

The phase-contrast technique, used here, makes fine differences in refractivity visible, and so is useful for small transparent and colourless subjects. The hair-like cilia are particularly prominent, and the internal structure is now clearer than in either of the two photographs above.

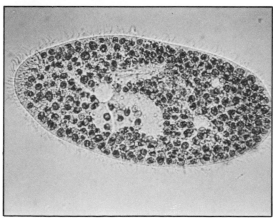

For this particular subject, interference-contrast (Nomarski) is probably the most successful. By isolating a very thin plane of focus, the confusing depth of the protozoa's structure is eliminated, and the individual organelles can be seen very clearly. The cilia, however, are rather less obvious than in the phase-contrast photograph.

Photomicrography 4

If photomicrography's considerable problems are largely due to the inadequacies of light waves at large magnifications, one answer is to look for shorter wavelengths as a way of forming an image. This should allow greater resolution and higher magnification, provided that the radiation can be guided and controlled in the same way that light can be refracted. This is the principle of the electron microscope, an instrument that can resolve detail down to two billionths of a centimeter, making it capable of over a thousand times greater magnification than the best optical microscope. Although such equipment is only found in specialized laboratories, the electron microscope has extended photography to new limits, and can produce strikingly beautiful images.

Using magnets instead of lenses, a beam of electrons is focused on the specimen. This beam knocks other electrons off the surface. These in turn are attracted to a sensor, which converts the data into a picture viewed on a television screen. This simplified explanation belies great technical sophistication, and the complete array of equipment would occupy most of a small room.

A further refinement to the electron microscope, developed only in the 1960s, is a means of moving the beam of electrons across the specimen. Each point on the surface of the object can then be resolved separately, permitting great depth of field. The scanning electron microscope can, especially at low magnifications, produce images with such depth of field that the eye finds it difficult to believe the scale. We are so accustomed to seeing shallow focus at close distances that a portrait of an ant, in sharp detail throughout, appears a little unnerving.

Because the scanning electron microscope displays its image on a cathode ray tube, photography is confined to taking pictures of this television-like screen. Ordinary black-and-white film with a moderately fine grain is normally used as colour, which is a function of visible wavelengths, is absent from the image.

This sequence of scanning electron micrographs demonstrates both the range and power of the technique. At low power (left), the point of a pin, magnified here 23 times, is quite recogniseable. At ×117 (right), the bluntness of its tip and its surface striations are obvious, while at the much greater magnification of ×580, clusters of bacteria can be clearly seen (far right). Continuing up the scale of magnification, the shape of individual bacteria are revealed at 2,900 times life-size, (below right), while finally, at the extremely high magnification of ×15,000 (below far right), even the details on the surface of each bacterium can be studied.

At a magnification of ×40, which is quite modest for a scanning electron microscope, this image of an earwig has the resolution, diffuse lighting and great depth of field that is normally associated with photography at more convential scales of reproduction. Because of the time taken for the narrow beam of electrons to scan the field of view, the subject must be immobilized by one means or another, which normally involves drying, freezing, and coating with gold or platinum. As electrons rather than light waves are used in this process, the image is inevitably without colour.

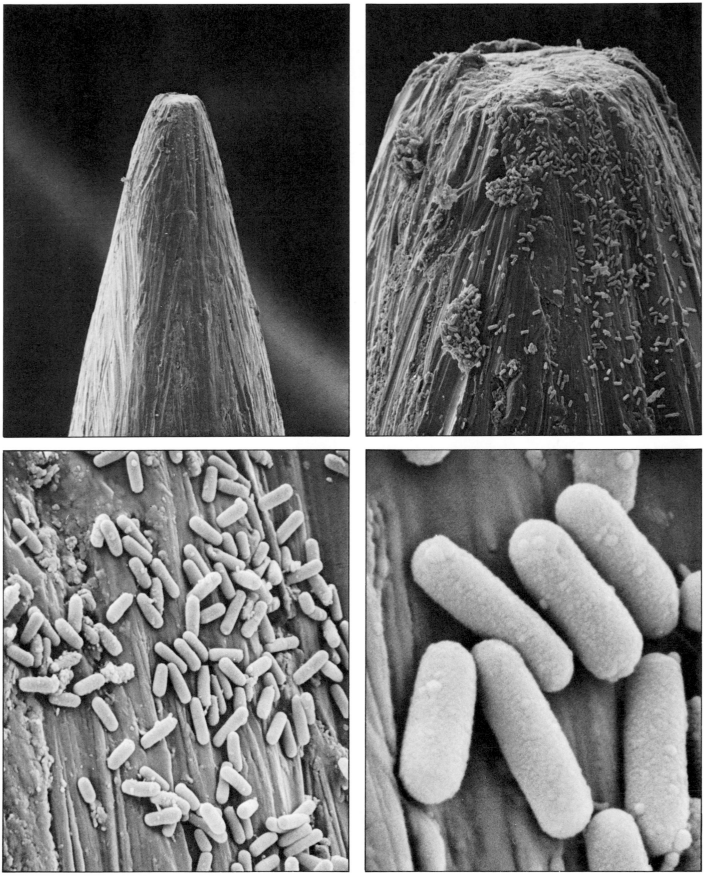

Fossils 1

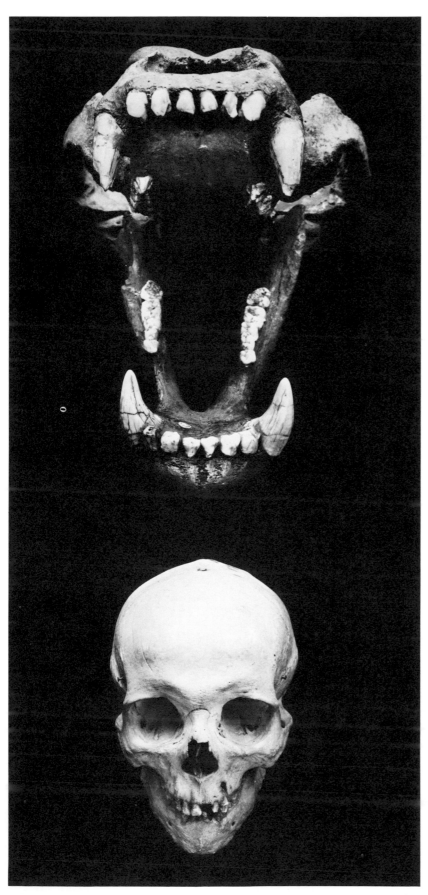

Fossils were formed in a number of different ways, but in practically all cases there were two prerequisites. First, the organism must have had some form of skeleton–the soft parts would have decomposed too quickly to allow the normal processes of fossilization and even shallow impressions of skin and organs are rarely found. Secondly, the animal or plant must have been quickly covered over with some material, before the skeleton could fall apart or be damaged. This requires that some form of deposition must have been in progress. Almost all fossils thus occur in sedimentary rocks and, as most of these were laid down in water, marine fossils are the most common. The pressure of the overlying sediment and later rock movements often deformed the fossils that did get created.

Very rarely, an entire organism is preserved –insects trapped in fossil resin (amber) are well-

known examples – but in the majority of cases only the skeletons have been fossilized. Some recent fossils, such as Pliocene shells, have lost only their organic content, and resemble skeletons of living species. Some plants have undergone carbonization, losing their nitrogen and oxygen content, as in the formation of coal. One of the most common ways in which fossils have been formed is through replacement, where the original materials are dissolved away in solution and replaced by minerals – fossil trees can be found in which even the cells and vessels are faithfully reproduced. This replacement occurs with different minerals, such as silica, calcite, iron pyrites and haematite. In other situations, the skeleton is dissolved away but not replaced, leaving simply a mould. This mould may later be filled with, say, glauconite or flint, producing a perfect cast of the original object.

The lighting set-up for the skull shot opposite. With a broadly diffused 'window' light positioned over the subject, even lighting is possible with just one light source with subjects this small. Black velvet is used for the background as this gives the most perfect black, although it is important to remove any specks of dust.

Frequently, the needs of fossil photography go little further than to provide a clear image of a specimen. It is nearly always possible, however, to improve the content of the shot and add graphic interest. The purpose of this photograph was to illustrate a point about the extinction of the cave bear. As this was principally at the hand of contemporary man, an ancient human skull was added. The comparison of the two skulls, and their symmetrical arrangement, made the shot more effective than the bear's skull would have been if shown alone. Hasselblad with 80 mm lens, ASA 125, 1/60 sec at f22, with 400 Joule (watt-second) flash unit.

Most fossils that are exposed either suffer natural erosion or are quickly removed by collectors. Nevertheless, there are occasions when it is possible to find remains that are in situ and relatively undisturbed. This 200 million year old fossilized tree trunk, its original composition replaced cell for cell by silicates from ancient falls of volcanic ash, has been gradually uncovered by wind and occasional rain. It owes its preservation to two conditions: the silica of which it is composed is much more able to withstand the mild erosion than the surrounding soft shale and clay, and it lies in Arizona's Petrified Forest National Park, protected by law from souvenir hunters. Panoramic camera with 90 mm lens, ASA 125, 1/4 sec at f45.

Fossils 2

From the sequence opposite these two contrasting treatments show the importance of carefully considered lighting. Neither is 'better' because each shows different qualities. The spotlight photograph defines the bone structure, while the shadowless treatment gives a clearer idea of shape and form.

The Tunisian trilobite (below) was lit through a sheet of opal perspex (plexiglass), by one overhead, diffused light. There was also a small amount of backlighting to keep the background light. If a fossil has been successfully removed from its matrix, it is usually important to show its shape as clearly as possible – hence the need for a plain background.

To appear at their best, most fossils must be carefully removed from the matrix or rock in which they are embedded. This is not usually easy to perform without damaging the specimen, and the operation demands patience and skill together with a good knowledge of the hidden parts of the fossil yet to be uncovered. Fossils that have already been prepared can be easily bought, however.

Photographing fossils

Although fossil animals and plants can sometimes be found exposed, the processes of erosion that brought them to light will usually have set to work on the fossils themselves, and it is not common to find them in good condition. Nevertheless, when good fossils are found in their natural setting, a marvellous opportunity for photographing them in relation to the surrounding rocks is provided.

The variety of ways in which fossils may have been formed demands a wide range of lighting techniques in the studio. Basically, however, the principles described later for shells apply equally well. A special situation is when the fossil is still partly embedded in the rock stratum. The back-

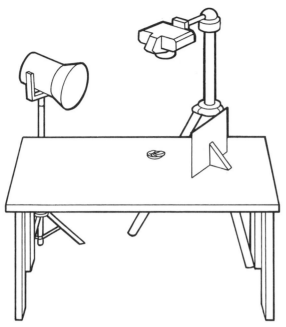

Spotlight with card reflector for sharp relief

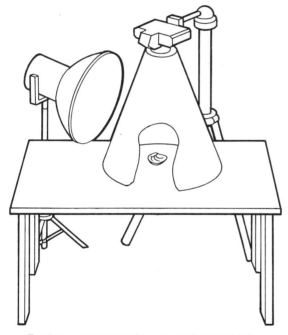

Tracing paper light tent for even, shadowless lighting

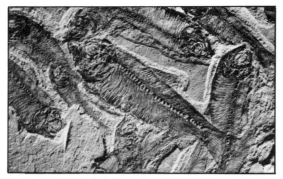

For sharp relief, a single spot light should be pointed at the subject from a low angle (illustration top left). Place a white card reflector opposite the lamp to prevent fall off of the light across the subject. To give an enveloping light, without shadows or bright highlights, a light tent is the most favoured technique (illustration below left). Basically a translucent cone, which acts as both diffuser and reflector, it can be made of any colourless milky material—paper, tracing paper or perspex (plexiglass). Used in the way shown, it should surround but not intrude on the picture frame at the base, and enclose the lens at the apex. Set up the camera, subject and background first, and then construct the light tent to those dimensions. Use a pattern similar to the one shown here. One or more lights can then be aimed through the tent.

Many fossils are too delicate to remove entirely from their matrix, and so are commonly displayed in low relief. How best to light fossils in this form depends very much on what aspects are to be given prominence. These Devonian fish provide an interesting test for lighting. While they stand up in low relief from the matrix, they are also darker in tone. Because of this, either the relief or the tone can be displayed. The standard technique for throwing low relief into prominence is a direct spotlight from a very shallow angle, throwing long, definite shadows. Conversely, the most effective way of showing tonal differences is to exclude relief by using shadowless lighting. The fossil fish were photographed under a range of lighting conditions between these two extremes.
For the first shot (top), a single spotlight was used, from the top left (more conventionally acceptable to a viewer than any other position). The effect is a very strong emphasis of relief, but the light level also falls off towards the bottom right.
In the second shot, a white card reflector, positioned on the opposite side of the specimen from the light, balances the light level across the picture without altering the definite shadows.
The third and fourth shots were taken with the light increasingly diffused, weakening the shadows and softening their edges.
Finally, for completely shadowless lighting (bottom), a light tent was constructed, as shown opposite.

ground is already provided, but there is little choice of viewpoint. In this form the fossils usually appear in low relief and the light is better set at a low angle to emphasize detail—raking the surface, the lighting will cast definite shadows. As strongly angled lighting also gives uneven illumination across the surface of the specimen, use a reflector on the opposite side. Concave fossils need a similar lighting treatment. If the depression is deep, move the light to a less acute angle, closer to the camera position. Again, use a stronger reflector to fill in the shadow.

Minerals and rocks

For small, static subjects that can be moved around easily, a straightforward camera set-up like this (illustration right) is the most useful.

When arranging the lighting, there are four considerations.
1. Intensity—This should be sufficient to allow a small aperture for depth of field.
2. Direction—Conventionally, the main light is normally aimed from the top left or top of the picture. Other lights can be added for fill.
3. Diffusion—Less diffusion reveals fine textural detail, more diffusion is better for overall shape and for tone.
4. Reflection—Reflectors (white card, silver foil, mirrors) are essential for fine control of shadows.

The most common way of presenting rock specimens is in cut sections, such as this small slab of ruin marble (below), so-called because of its supposed resemblance to a painting of ruined walls and columns. If the texture is important, then the lighting can be directional, but here, where the section has been polished to heighten tonal contrast, even illumination is called for.

The same specimen can be shown at different scales of magnification (far right below). In the top picture, the shape is most important, but below the texture of the crystals is emphasized by tight framing.

The properties of geological specimens vary greatly, for the conditions under which they were formed were never precisely duplicated. Each specimen must be treated on its own merits, and the lighting adjusted to show off its essential qualities. Try always to choose good specimens of their type—crystals of feldspar, for example, are often found twinned (that is, interlocked), and it is worth hunting for an example where this property is clearly visible.

Minerals are basic constituents of the earth's crust, each with a precise chemical composition. When minerals are allowed to solidify out of solution freely, they form crystals, with characteristic shapes and flat faces. Understandably, perfectly formed crystals are rare, and most minerals grow as aggregates of crystals, where the individual crystal shape is submerged in the form of a larger mass. These forms are also characteristic and enable the mineral to be identified—mica, for example, frequently occurs in flat, flaky sheets, haematite is often found in gently rounded shapes known as a mammilated form, and native copper is commonly found in a dendritic form, branched like a fern.

The way in which individual minerals break is another property. When the break is irregular, it is called a fracture; some minerals fracture very distinctively, such as curved surface of obsidian. Other minerals more frequently exhibit cleavage—this is a break that is closely related to the structure, usually close to where a crystal face would have been formed.

The optical properties of minerals include

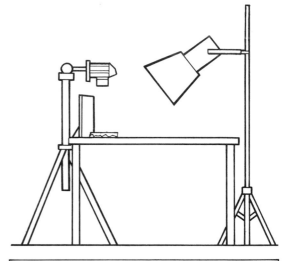

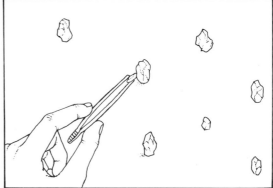

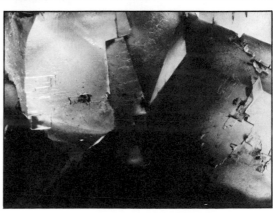

transparency, colour and lustre. Of these, lustre is usually the most challenging problem for photography, as it is essentially a subtle quality – the way in which a mineral's surface reflects light. Descriptions such as metallic, resinous, greasy, silky or pearly lustre are quite easy to understand and also easy to see when a specimen is turned in the hand to vary the play of light across it. In a still photograph, however, to make such refined differences apparent requires skilled lighting.

Rocks are accumulations of minerals, with much greater variety. There are three groups of rock – igneous, formed directly from molten lava; sedimentary, formed by the deposition of water or wind borne particles; and metamorphic, formed by the alteration of existing rocks under heat and pressure. Here, the important properties to convey are composition, texture and structure. How visible the composition of a rock is depends on the grain size of the individual minerals, and on how similar they are to each other. Granite displays its composition very clearly, as not only are the grains large and obvious, but the three constituents – quartz, mica and feldspar – have distinctively different colours and tones. The surface texture of the rock may also be very distinctive, from the fine smoothness of marble to the roughness of limestone. Its structure, on the other hand, is often on too large a scale to be seen in a small specimen, although some rocks, such as ropy lava and folded schists, show structural characteristics clearly.

Lighting

The same general lighting conditions apply to minerals and rocks as to shells and fossils, and many of the same techniques can be used. Knowing the essential properties of a particular specimen will help you to decide on the style of lighting. If a mineral has an interesting lustre, for example, such as the greasy or waxy look of chalcedony, then a well diffused light will reveal this most clearly. On the other hand, the same lighting would do nothing to display the compact powdery texture of loess, a clay deposited by wind, which would appear better with a hard, direct light. A low angled light reveals surface interpretation most clearly, but if the texture is unimportant in a specimen, more frontal illumination can be used.

Crystals are probably the most difficult of all minerals to photograph, as there are numerous reflections and refractions to contend with. The ideal is generally to display as many of the faces as possible and to keep the general appearance simple. The best way of achieving this is to vary the illumination on each face. Try to catch the reflections of a large diffused light source in at least two major planes, particularly when photographing transparent crystals. Reflectors of different strengths, such as foil and white card, can be carefully placed to give different intensities of reflection in each plane.

Gems combine two important qualities for photography – reflection and refraction. Reflection, from the different faces of the crystals, helps to define the outer surface. Refraction not only reveals inner details, but gives the essential sparkle. Capturing both in a photograph requires very careful positioning. For this group shot of some unusually shaped gems, a single, well diffused light was used, and a black background was chosen to enhance the refraction by contrast. The area light provided one bright tone for reflection, while a medium tone for other crystal faces came from a white card reflector. The light also displayed refraction. The key to success in a shot like this is the precise angle at which the stones sit. Plasticine cannot be used to prop up transparent stones, as it would show, and the answer in this case was to use small diamond chips, which are unnoticeable amid the play of light and colour. The arrangement is inevitably painstaking (see illustration opposite).

Shells

Shells make attractive photographic subjects in their own right, as objects rather than as part of the marine ecology. Controlled studio conditions are also the best for displaying their detailed form and structure.

The photographic problems are chiefly aesthetic, and in common with all still-life subjects, the most important element is lighting. As a general principle, one single main light source, partly diffused, gives good, uncomplicated modelling. Two lights aimed from different directions will, if positioned carelessly, cast conflicting shadows—not only is this ugly, but it confuses the detail in the shell. With a single light, the shadows can be filled in slightly by placing a white card or silvered reflector. Crumpled cooking foil glued to a card is a simple device for achieving selective fill-in.

Support the shell on plasticine or Blu-tack. The choice of angle will often depend on the key features of the particular specimen. Gastropods, for example, are usually positioned to display the aperture. An uncluttered background is usually best—if the shell is light in tone, black velvet can be very effective. The shell can be laid directly on the velvet or, to ensure that the velvet's texture is completely invisible, raise the specimen a few inches (centimetres) on a vertical rod. Take care that the camera is pointing vertically downwards so that the support remains hidden. Fluff on the velvet can be removed just before shooting by dabbing it with a strip of adhesive tape.

With dark shells against a light background, a plain white surface, such as white velvet, can be used, but the shadows underneath are likely to be deep. The light should be well diffused and reflectors added to provide fill-in. A hand mirror gives the strongest fill-in. An alternative background arrangement is the glass shot, where the fossil is laid on a horizontal glass sheet, which itself is

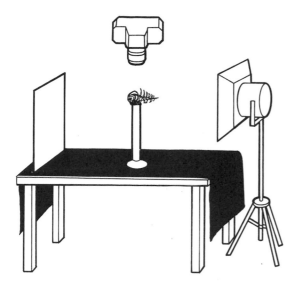

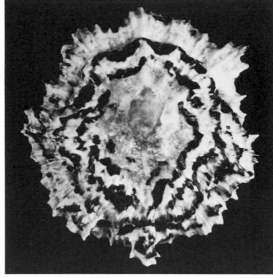

To emphasize the strong patterns of this small limpet from the Philippines (left), a black velvet background heightened contrasts. The same basic lighting was used as for the photograph of the wendletrap below, except that a stronger fill-in was used to reduce shadows and allow the jagged pattern to stand out.

raised above a white or coloured sheet of card. With careful positioning, the background card can then be lit separately, and no shadows are cast. Here, the effect is as if the shell 'floats'. The main light must not be so close to the camera position that it is reflected in the glass.

Shells with shiny surfaces–cowries, for example–need particular care, as they inevitably reflect the light source. A useful precaution is to increase the area of the light by diffusing it, preferably with a simple shape, such as a rectangular 'window' of opal perspex (plexiglass). There are also techniques for removing reflections, but use these with discretion as they can radically alter the shell's appearance. Dulling spray is a crude method that leaves a sticky film, easily visible in a high resolution photograph. A better alternative is

to cover the light with a sheet of polarizing material and use a polarizing filter over the lens. The two can be rotated until the reflections are killed. One occasional danger with polarizers crossed in this way, however, is a slight violet cast in the reflected highlight. An additional problem is that both polarizing filters and sheet reduce the light transmission by nearly two stops.

The colour of some shells can be intensified by wetting and a rather complex variation is to submerge the shell completely in water. The lighting must then be positioned very carefully to avoid reflections from the water's surface.

Some thin shells can be backlit effectively–showing internal features. Another method of displaying internal geometry is to slice the shell into sections.

Pale shells generally appear best against a dark background, and black velvet is one of the most useful of all background materials (opposite page, far left). The main difficulty with velvet is its tendency to attract specks of dust. These can be removed by dabbing it with a piece of sticky tape, and an extra precaution is to raise the shell a few inches above the velvet, using a short rod and plasticine (see illustration).

The translucency of many shells gives good opportunities for experiment. This chambered nautilus shell (opposite page, below) had already been sectioned to show the characteristic spiral of chambers, and for this photograph was placed in a wire holder over a single spotlight. A small amount of modelling was added by reflecting some of the light into the central whorl with a small mirror.

For dark shells (far left), a black background can merge with the edges. For clarity, a white background is usually the most effective. Here, the shell was placed on a sheet of opal perspex (plexiglass) and lit from below as well as from the side. The result is a clean background with no trace of shadow. The essential precaution with this method of lighting is to mask around the shell with black card, right up to the edges of the picture frame, so as to keep flare down to a minimum.

For the pale tones of this wendletrap (left), a black background was chosen to give full prominence to its shape. Using diffused sidelighting with a piece of cooking foil opposite to fill in shadows, the only significant problem was achieving the right tonal range. For a delicate impression, the tones were kept as light as possible.

Flowers 1

Most of the difficulties experienced when photographing flowers in their natural settings can be overcome if you can bring them into the studio. Here you can select whatever background you need to complement the flower, and their is no risk of a breeze moving it during a long exposure. Moreover, the appeal of flowers lies in their form and colour, and the graphic compositions that they offer are more easily worked out in the controlled environment of the studio.

Making the background work

In almost every case, it is best to have a background that isolates the flower and makes it as prominent as possible. The out of focus leaves and random blurs of flowers photographed in the wild or in gardens can be very distracting, but in the studio you can easily remove them.

Most flowers, particularly those with light tones, stand out more clearly against a dark background. For the darkest of backgrounds use black velvet, which absorbs light more efficiently than practically any other surface. Even coloured velvet is generally better than paper, which frequently shows creases and wrinkles. A second method of providing an isolating background is to use a colour that contrasts with that of the flower. So, a blue background for a yellow rose or a green background for a red hibiscus will give the greatest contrast of colours. The danger of this is that the result may be garish.

Depth of field

As with flowers in outdoor settings, one of the principal technical obstacles is the great depth of field needed to bring every part of the bloom into sharp focus. But by increasing the amount of light or by taking longer exposures, it is always possible in the studio to stop the lens down to its smallest aperture—usually f22 or f32. For larger flowers this will render every part sharp but with small flowers in extreme close-up, it is impossible. The only answer in this case are either to move back and accept a lower magnification, or to accept that some petals and leaves will be unsharp and focus on an important part of the flower, such as the stamen.

Lighting

It is much better to use electronic flash than tungsten lighting as the heat output of a tungsten lamp such as a photoflood bulb is enough to wilt a flower in a very few minutes. Even with a studio flash unit, you should dim the modelling light to preserve the bloom as long as possible.

The quality of lighting makes an important difference to the final image. Diffused lighting, such as from a window reflector, has a soft and natural quality to it. There are no hard edges to the internal shadows from petals. If the flower is very small, however, this diffusion of light may eliminate shadows too efficiently, to the point where there is almost no modelling.

Hard, direct lighting mimics strong sunlight, but carries an inevitable harshness and sometimes causes unpleasant highlights. Remember that the

Where studio work comes into its own with flowers is in the great control that can be applied. By testing the lighting and film in advance, considerable colour accuracy is possible, even with the difficult variations of red and purple in these two specimens (above and right). Composition can also be finely tuned, making symmetry possible, as in both these photographs.

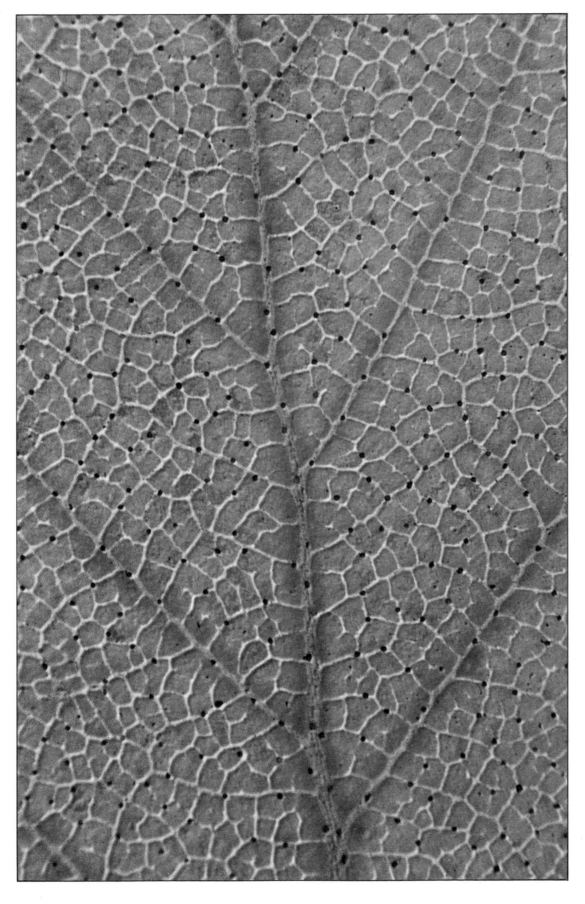

In the same way that it can be used to emphasize the structure of shells, backlighting can be used with plants to reveal veins and cells. To prevent the leaf or petal from curling, either tape it down onto a sheet of glass, or place another, clean sheet of glass over it. Mask down the area surrounding the picture frame to avoid the degraded image that may result from reflections.

THE STUDIO

197

Flowers 2

most saturated colours are achieved with diffused light – grass is at its greenest on a cloudy, overcast day.

The angle of the light can emphasize certain parts of flowers, and can also add atmosphere. A light placed behind the flower and to one side, out of the camera's view, can be adjusted to give a bright edge to petals and stamen. In this case, be sure to use white card or silver foil reflectors in front of the flower to lighten the shadows.

Recording colours faithfully

A flower's colour is one of its most important qualities, and you should take as much care as possible to render it accurately on film. For this, it is essential to run a series of colour tests for your studio lights and the batch of film you are using. To do this, choose a small studio arrangement that includes lighting such as you intend to use. Curve a large sheet of white paper as a base and background, arranging the light so that part of the paper falls off into shadow. Place a few objects under the light, including a Kodak Color Separation Guide (available at most photographic suppliers). Then run tests, taking several pictures with different colour compensating filters of weak strength – CC05 and CC10. Use blue, green and red filters to

To photograph these flowers in close-up, a studio setting was chosen to eliminate confusion and present the flowers as simple, uncluttered images. Orchids in particular are prone to appearing untidy in their natural environment. The graphic, luminous effect was achieved by carefully balancing backlighting and toplighting. The purpose of the backlight—an evenly illuminated sheet of thick opal perspex (plexiglass)—was principally to provide a white, shadowless background, but also to reveal something of the inner structure of translucent petals. The exposure and strength of lighting were set so that there was no more than a hint of tone in the background. Any brighter, and flare would have degraded the image. The toplight provided modelling and sparkle to the highlights. A fine spray of water contributed to these highlights, and also had a practical value—keeping the flowers fresh under the studio lights. The camera lens was masked with black card to cut out any stray light.

begin with, and judge the processed film on a light box. You will then be able to reproduce most colours with complete accuracy by using the filters that gave the most accurate colour in the test each time you use the studio arrangement.

Nevertheless, there will be some occasions, especially with flowers, when faithful colour reproduction may still be very difficult. This is because of the essential difference between colour films and the human eye's colour response. Films use dyes and these are designed to reproduce the most common hues best—flesh tones, blue sky and grass, for example. More unusual colours reproduce less well. Again, colour films are sensitive to a slightly different range of wavelengths than the eye. In particular, most films pick up reflections in the red and infrared part of the spectrum, where the eye has practically no sensitivity. Some flowers actually emit light in these wavelengths and for this reason some blue morning glory and ageratum blooms reproduce differently on film from the way we see them—to our interpretation, wrongly. Some additional filtration may help, but be forewarned that some flower colours just cannot be reproduced with total accuracy. But it should be possible to get close enough for all but the extreme perfectionist.

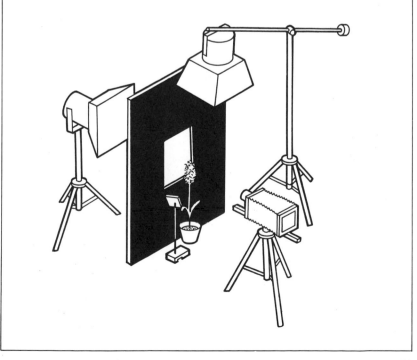

GAZETTEER

Behind many of the photographs in this book was some degree of planning. Studio work, naturally, is never casual, but even photography in the field needs to some extent to be worked out in advance. Although much of the book has been taken up with camera techniques and fieldcraft, wildlife and nature photography relies heavily on what could be called logistics—all the work that has to be done before using the camera. There are few arcane mysteries in wildlife photography, and sensible preparations will take care of most situations.

The first step is to research the subject: the more you know about the behaviour of a particular species and the conditions of its habitat, the better are the opportunities that you can make for yourself. This in turn suggests the kind of equipment and techniques you will need—the focal length of lens, type of film, whether to use hides or rely on stalking, and so on. It also gives some clue to the next, crucial step—finding the right place and being there at the right time.

This final section is a select list of places known for their good photographic opportunities. A thoroughly comprehensive gazetteer would need its own book, but in the space available personal favourites have been included. Guarantees in wildlife photography are impossible—fortunately so, as the uncertainty and the chance of discovering something new are part of the enjoyment. Nevertheless, the forty locations that follow are as rich in possibilities as any photographer could wish for.

Although the number of places is small, an attempt has been made to give a fair balance across the continents and among types of habitat. Two notable geographical gaps are the Soviet Union, which is likely to remain extremely difficult for political reasons, and China, which should become easier for naturalists to visit. Europe as a whole, despite strong efforts at conservation, suffers from its long history of settlement, and has few of the large unspoiled nature reserves that are abundant in North America and Africa.

Most of the best locations for wildlife and nature photography do coincide with reserves and natural parks, but what is good for conservation is not always good for photography, and vice versa. Some species are so endangered that even the intrusion of naturalists can be harmful, and some reserves cater so well for the animals' welfare that there are few opportunities for observation and photography.

On nests made of small stones, Gentoo penguins crowd the shores of Paradise Bay on the Antarctic Peninsula (F. Gohier).

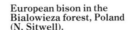

European bison in the
Bialowieza forest, Poland
(N. Sitwell).

Europe

Bialowieza, Poland

This splendid forest in north-eastern Poland is the
largest significant remnant of the great primeval forests
that once covered central Europe. Bialowieza Forest
itself covers some 500 square miles (1,300 square
kilometres), of which rather more than half is actually
across the border in Byelorussia. Of this, some 2,000
acres is strictly controlled as a national park–no timber
is removed, not even dead trees. It is a refuge for
characteristic forest wildlife, such as wolves, although
these do wander across into Russia where they are shot.
Beavers seem to wander in the reverse direction–to
safety. Red and roe deer and wild boar are abundant, and
there are a few elk. Bialowieza's pride and joy is its
unique herd of wild European bison. The most spectacular sight is perhaps the large number of giant trees.
Oak, lime, pine, spruce, and ash all soar to heights of 140
feet (40 metres) or more, and a great many of them are
at least 300 years old. More than 250 birds have been
recorded at Bialowieza, and the area is particularly rich
in fungi (over 500 mushrooms alone). There are many
small and some larger open areas spread through the
forest, so there is a great variety of habitats to be
explored. Bialowieza is easily accessible by road from
Warsaw or Bialystok (the nearest large city) and by rail.
Season Can be visited throughout the year, but central
Europe is best avoided in the depths of winter. The area
is a popular holiday resort, so July and August can be
rather crowded.

Camargue, France

The delta of the river Rhône, south of Arles–known as
the Camargue–is one of the most outstanding wildlife
areas in Europe. It is a land still in the process of
creation, built out of mud and silt brought down by the
Rhône from as far away as the Alps. A labyrinth of
shallow lagoons, large salt pans, and dry plains supports
a wealth of wildlife, especially birds, in a range of
different habitats. Though not really wild, the most
famous mammals are the cattle and the white horses.
Wild boar can be seen, while along tributaries of the
Rhône to the north there are still a number of the rare
European beaver. The great glory of the Camargue is
the host of flamingos, but there are innumerable other
bird species–waterbirds especially, but also a variety of
birds of prey and other smaller species. Of interest, too,
are several varieties each of frogs, snakes, and lizards.
The Camargue is easy to reach by road from Arles.
Season The Camargue can be visited at any time, but
the mid-summer period can be very hot, crowded, and
mosquito-ridden. Although winters are mild, there are
periods when the infamous mistral gusts from the north
and temperatures drop below freezing. Best for the
naturalist and photographer are probably spring and
autumn.

Coto Doñana, Spain

The Doñana National Park lies to the west of the Guadal-
quivir River where it meets the Mediterranean coast of
Spain. *Coto Doñana* properly applies only to the coastal
belt, though the whole 97,000 acres (39,000 hectares) is
often called the Coto. About half the park is an integral
reserve where no human activity apart from scientific
research is allowed. The area's special character is
caused by the huge sand dunes that have built up at the
mouth of the river, diverting it southwards, and by the
fact that the Atlantic Ocean holds back the winter floods,
which consequently cover a large area–the Marismas–
in fresh water. So the Coto Doñana is a wild land of
marshes, sand dunes, and lagoons. The vegetation includes scrub pine, cork oak, and marram grass. Histo-

rically, this wilderness was a network of hunting reserves owned by the crown and a few wealthy families. The park is a paradise for red and fallow deer, and is a last refuge for the Spanish lynx, although the visitor is unlikely to see one. It boasts a variety and number of birds the equal of anywhere else in Europe, dominated by waterbirds and raptors. The great prize is the Spanish imperial eagle, while huge numbers of cattle egrets and night herons are easily seen.
Season Open all year, and rewarding at all times.

Danube Delta, Romania
The Danube is Europe's longest river, and when it flows out into the Black Sea on the east coast of Romania, it disgorges millions of tons of silt. This rich load of nutrients, collected from distant mountains and plains, has created an enormous delta that is one of the richest areas for birds in Europe. Here, amid the marshes, lagoons, lakes, river channels, sandbars and floating reed islands are such specialities as the white pelican, as well as smaller numbers of the Dalmatian pelican. Glossy ibises breed nowhere else in Europe—here they are present in thousands. Great white egrets are common, and the pygmy cormorant outnumbers the common cormorant. Pinkfoot and greylag geese are regular winter visitors. Ducks and waders are plentiful.
Season All year, but early spring or autumn are best for migratory waterfowl.

Farne Islands, United Kingdom
Lying between two and five miles (three and eight kilometres) off the Northumberland coast, the thirty or so Farne Islands attract naturalists from all over Europe. Eider ducks are particularly tame and may even be stroked while on the nest—although visitors should resist this temptation. In fact, the eiders are locally known as 'cuddy ducks' after St. Cuthbert—a patron saint of animals—who spent some time here in the seventh century. Common and grey seals are also remarkably tame. The Farne Islands are one of the most accessible seabird colonies in Britain, with thousands of guillemots, razorbills, cormorants, puffins, fulmars, and terns of several species (including the rare roseate tern). Many of these can be approached close enough for photography. Access is from the coastal town of Sea-houses, where boats can be hired and landing tickets obtained.
Season Summer months.

Gran Paradiso, Italy
This splendid alpine national park is near Val d'Aosta in Italy, and close to both France and Switzerland—indeed part of it is contiguous with the somewhat similar Vanoise National Park in France. It is majestic country, with imposing peaks (the highest is Gran Paradiso itself at over 13,000 feet/3,900 metres), rivers, and glaciers. The most important mammal is the ibex, which is now rare elsewhere in Europe. Gran Paradiso is also noted for another sure footed mountain dweller, the chamois. Alpine marmots, mountain hares, and a variety of other mammals live here, but are not easy to see. Among the birds, the most prominent are golden eagle and eagle owl. Typical high altitude birds include ptarmigan, willow grouse and snow finch.

The flora is alpine, with many dwarf and creeping forms. Conifers dominate the landscape, and the alpine meadows are carpeted during the summer with a host of colourful wild flowers.

Gran Paradiso is dry and cold, and at 5,000 feet (1,500 metres) snow is present for six months of the year. At 11,500 feet (3,500 metres) there is snow for 11 months.
Season The park can be visited at any time of the year, without permission. The best time is June to September.

Ibex on a peak in Italy's Gran Paradiso National Park (J-P. Ferrero).

Puffins on a cliff top, Iceland
(J.-P. Ferrero).

Kittiwakes (bottom) on Noss
Island, Shetland
(J.-P. Ferrero).

Minsmere, United Kingdom
One of the most famous bird reserves in Britain, Minsmere is administered by the Royal Society for the Protection of Birds. Covering about 1,500 acres on the Suffolk coast, Minsmere comprises several distinct habitats—shoreline, freshwater marsh, mixed woodland, heathland and an area of shallow brackish water. More than 200 bird species are seen each year, and about 100 regularly breed here. Of this great ornithological wealth, two stars are the avocets and a few pairs of marsh harriers. Paths are marked, and you have to walk. Access is limited and the number of visitors per day strictly controlled. Havergate Island, another RSPB reserve a few miles to the south, is the only other place in Britain where you are likely to find avocets.
Season April to September. Permits should be obtained in advance for both Minsmere and Havergate.

Myvatn, Iceland
Lake Myvatn in Iceland is a Mecca for birdwatchers and photographers because of the incredible number of ducks that breed there. Some five miles (eight kilometres) across, Myvatn is set in a bleak, volcanic landscape of lava flows, geysers, sulphur pools and old craters. The shallow waters of the lake are alive with fish: multitudes of trout feed on the myriad midges, and they in turn attract fifteen breeding species of ducks. There are other birds, too, such as whooper swans, red-necked phalaropes, and Slavonian grebes. And the mighty gyrfalcon lords it over them all, at the top of the Myvatn food chain.

The name Myvatn in fact means 'lake of the flies', and although the midges do not bite their sheer numbers can bother some people. But it is worth putting up with the midges to see several ducks of American origin—Barrow's goldeneye, harlequin duck, American wigeon and great northern diver. The commonest bird is the scaup.
Season Late spring and summer.

New Forest, United Kingdom
Although wildlife is not spectacular in the New Forest—this is one of the largest areas of semi-natural common land in Britain, and many parts are only sparsely populated. There are nearly 50,000 acres (20,000 hectares) of woodland and heath. If the wildlife is not openly on display it is there nevertheless and worth searching for. The New Forest has the three native deer—red, roe and fallow—and the introduced muntjac. There are also badgers and the famous ponies, though these are only wild in that they wander across the Forest at will. Among birds, the area is a stronghold of buzzards, sparrowhawks, hobbies and the elusive Dartford warbler. The flora is rich, and species to look for are orchids, as well as rarities like the wild gladiolus, bog orchid and marsh gentian. It is also a place to find rare reptiles, such as smooth snake and sand lizard. Even scorpions are said to be found here. Butterflies and other insects are abundant.

The Forest has been 'new' since the time of William the Conqueror. Straddling southern Hampshire between Southampton Water and the Wiltshire Avon, it is one of five forests mentioned in the Domesday Book, and long before that was a hunting ground of the Saxon kings. In those days 'forest' meant any unenclosed land where the hunting was reserved for the king. Access is from a number of roads, such as the A31 and A35. The central town is Lyndhurst.
Season All year.

Shetland, United Kingdom
The Shetland islands are Britain's most northerly outpost—and a magnet for naturalists. These rugged

islands are sparsely inhabited, but they contain splendid seabird colonies, large rookeries of common and grey seals, and spectacular scenery. Great skuas (called bonxies), Arctic skuas, red-necked phalaropes, red-throated divers, kittiwakes, puffins, a large gannetry, an important greater black-backed gull colony, guillemots, fulmars, shags, and whimbrels, are among the avian attractions. A special treat is the chance of seeing snowy owls, which breed on Fetlar. Unst, Fetlar, and Noss are perhaps the most interesting islands, but there are many others worth seeing.

The Shetlands are in regular communication with the Scottish mainland by sea and air. There are some roads within the islands but the best way of getting around, and of seeing the seabird cliffs, is by boat.

Season All year, but best in spring, summer, and autumn.

The Welsh Islands, United Kingdom

Seabird enthusiasts will be thrilled by visits to three small islands off the tip of Dyfed (formerly Pembrokeshire)– Skomer, Skokholm and Grassholm. On Skomer Island there are spectacular breeding colonies of fulmars, puffins, razorbills, guillemots and kittiwakes, and it is possible to get good views of them from the clifftops. Skomer also has a breeding colony of grey seals and a unique sub-species of vole, larger and tamer then the mainland vole. Skomer and Skokholm between them hold the largest colony of Manx shearwaters in the world. Skokholm is also a stronghold of the storm petrel. The latter two birds are nocturnal, resting by day in burrows and rock crevices. Grassholm is farther out in the atlantic, and the smallest of the three. It has the only gannet colony in England and Wales–one of the largest in the world.

Access to Skomer is by boat from Martins Haven or Milford Haven, which is farther away. A small landing fee is payable. Skokholm, too, may be visited on a day trip from Milford Haven. Grassholm is more difficult to visit but landings can be arranged.

Season Summer months.

North America

Arches National Park, Utah

Desert erosion on the twisted layers of red sandstone in southeastern Utah has produced a spectacular array of natural stone arches, spires, windows and pinnacles. For unusual rock formations, Arches National Park is one of the most impressive sites in the world. Many can be seen by car, but the best, including Delicate Arch, the most spectacular of all rock arches, are on trails. Reached by car from Moab, the nearest town a few miles to the south, the park has one main road.

Season Any time of the year and although winter snow may make driving difficult, it also enhances the appearance of many of the formations.

The Everglades, Florida

Most of Florida's Everglades consist of a slowly flowing river of saw-grass, stretching from Lake Okeechobee 100 miles (160 kilometres) down to the Florida Bay. Dotted with small wooded islands known as 'hammocks', and changing gradually into a saltwater wilderness of mangroves near the sea, the Everglades has a rich variety of semi-aquatic life, much of it subtropical. Alligators, white-tailed deer, raccoons, snakebirds, ibises, storks and egrets are common, while manatee, flamingos and spoonbills can also be seen on occasions. The Florida cougar, American crocodile and Everglades kite are rare, but can sometimes be glimpsed.

The Anhinga Trail, a raised walk over the swamp near

Pine Tree Arch in Utah's Arches National Park.

Wood ibis silhouetted among the trees of Corkscrew Swamp, in the Florida Everglades.

**Sperry Glacier in Glacier
National Park, Montana.**

the Park entrance off State Road 27 from Miami, offers a
short introduction to Everglades wildlife, while Flamingo
is a good base for longer exploration. The Big Cypress
Swamp, in the western part, is easily visited at the
Audubon Society's Corkscrew Swamp Sanctuary, a 27
mile (43 kilometre) drive north east from Naples.

Although not strictly a part of the Everglades, the
Myakka River State Park, 24 miles (39 kilometres) east
of Sarasota on State Road 72, gives surprisingly accessible views of waterfowl, alligators and deer.

Season During the dry season, from the end of November until late spring or early summer, the flooded marsh-
lands are reduced in area and the wildlife is forced to
concentrate. The heat is also less intense, making the
winter months more comfortable as well as photographically more productive. The summer rainfall, which
determines the severity of the winter drought, varies
from year to year.

Glacier National Park, Montana
The state of Montana is called the Big Sky Country, and
the best place to see the big sky is surely in spectacular
Glacier National Park, 1,600 square miles (4,100 square
kilometres) of rugged territory in the Rocky Mountains
of north-western Montana. It is a land of sharp precipi-
tous peaks and knife edged ridges girdled with forests.
The American naturalist John Muir said, 'Give a month at
least to this precious reserve. The time will not be taken
from the sum of your life. Instead of shortening, it will
definitely lengthen it and make you truly immortal.'

There are glaciers in Glacier Park—about 48 of them—
and snow-fed lakes of almost every shade of blue and
green. The mountain vegetation is dominated by firs,
pines, and spruces, and wild shrubs like huckleberries,
service-berries, and raspberries are locally abundant. Of
the wildlife, bighorn sheep and mountain goats should
easily be seen, while hoary marmots, pikas, Columbian
and golden-mantled ground squirrels, golden eagles and
ptarmigans can also be found.

Glacier is bisected by the scenic Going-to-the-Sun
Road, the only route through the park. There are 750
miles (1,200 kilometres) of hiking trails, but camping is
allowed only at designated sites and these cannot be
booked more than 24 hours ahead; there should be no
problem early or late in the season. It is also possible to
explore on horseback, less strenuous, and enjoyable in
its own right.

Season Short, from mid-June to mid-September.
Before and after this the road is likely to be blocked by
snow.

Mount McKinley, Alaska
In the heart of the southern part of central Alaska lies
North America's highest mountain—Mount McKinley—
its 20,000 feet (6,500 metre) bulk dominating the 3,000
square miles (7,500 square kilometres) of national park
of the same name. It is a land of awesome grandeur and
spectacular wildlife, offering huge scope for the photographer, and it is comparatively easy of access.

Pure-white Dall sheep are a common sight, although it
is never an easy climb to get within camera range. Once
there, however, the animals are not especially wary.
Other species of note are barren ground caribou, moose,
and huge grizzly bears—the local variety are sandy
coloured and quite easy to spot. Hoary marmots, ground
squirrels, snowshoe hares, and red foxes are surprisingly tame. Wolves are not so likely to be seen, except at
the start and end of the brief summer season.

A good road from Fairbanks to Anchorage leads
directly to the park, and the Alaska Railroad stops daily
at the entrance. One American photographer describes
it as exquisite in June, when mount McKinley looms
surrealistically above while grizzly bears wade belly deep
in pink and purple wild flowers.

Season May 26 to September 10, the best time mid-June to end-July–unfortunately, also favoured by mosquitos.

Petrified Forest, Arizona
Located in the most colourful part of northern Arizona's Painted Desert, Petrified Forest National Park contains the world's finest exposed fossilized forest. As the park is strictly policed to prevent removal of specimens, it is possible to see many excellent examples along the posted trails. Formerly a low-lying swamp with trees and giant ferns, the area is now an elevated desert plateau with sands and mesas. The trees themselves, most of them lying as they fell but broken into sections, are composed of silica from volcanic ash falls, and are frequently many coloured.
Season All year.

Point Lobos, California
An established mecca for landscape photographers ever since the work of Edward Weston, Ansel Adams and others became known, Point Lobos, on the Californian coast south of Monterey, contains a remarkable concentration of varied scenery, together with interesting plant and animal life. The small, 1,250 acre (500 hectare) headland, topped with groves of gnarled and distorted Monterey cypress, has coves, small beaches and off-shore islands that are home to two species of sea-lion (California and Steller's), the California sea otter, cormorants, pelicans and other sea birds. In November, the grey whale begins its migration south to Baja California, and returns north in the spring. Point Lobos is an excellent vantage point, but the whales rarely surface close enough to land to be photographed with anything less than a 600 mm lens. Over 300 plant and 250 bird and animal species have been counted at Point Lobos–a truly remarkable concentration.

Its proximity to Monterey and Carmel has made Point Lobos understandably popular, and as a result access is very strictly controlled. Movement is restricted to a few well defined paths, but these are chosen so that practically everything of interest can be seen. Only a certain number of visitors are allowed in the reserve at one time, and at weekends and holidays the places are taken quickly.
Season Worth visiting at any time, particularly for its landscapes. Interesting views are possible under all weather conditions.

White Sands, New Mexico
Situated in the missile range east of the San Andres Mountains (and so closed occasionally for an hour or two) the White Sands National Monument contains the world's largest field of gypsum dunes. Formed by the slow erosion of gypsum rock in the mountains, deposited in the lowest part of the Tularosa Basin, the undulating dunes of glittering crystals make an unusual and disorienting landscape. During the day, the effect is as brilliant as snow, while the evening light can give subtle colours and shapes.
Season White Sands is worth visiting at any time. Although the park closes at sunset, there is a special late night opening on the few days around a full moon, with unusual possibilities for photography. Because the footprints of other visitors are visible over great distances and are usually an unwelcome element in photographs, the best time to go, if you are lucky, is after one of the irregular desert winds.

Wood Buffalo, Canada
The largest national park in both Canada and North America, Wood Buffalo is named after a subspecies of bison which still survives here–alongside much greater numbers of hybrid wood-plains bison. It stretches from the wild boreal plateaus of northern Alberta into the

Agate logs (top) lie scattered among the clay hills of Petrified Forest, Arizona.

Heavy surf at Point Lobos, California.

uplands of the Northwest Territories. Typical of northern Canada, the park encompasses great expanses of prairie grassland, endless taiga forests, marshes, bogs (called muskeg), and lakes large and small. Other large mammals include moose, woodland caribou, and black bear. Four migration flyways overlap at the Peace-Athabasca delta, and swans and geese are among over 200 birds recorded. The autumn accumulation of water-fowl is rated one of the great ornithological spectacles of North America. It is notable for great numbers of Ross's geese. But the most important bird is the whooping crane, still one of the rarest species in the world, which only nests in Wood Buffalo park.

The park is close to both Lake Athabasca and the Great Slave Lake, and access is via Fort Smith.

Season All year, but best in spring to autumn.

Yellowstone

Yellowstone National Park, straddling the borders of Wyoming, Montana and Idaho with 3,400 square miles (8,800 square kilometres) of northern forest, hot springs, geysers and canyons, was the first national park in the United States and the world. Interestingly enough, it was the photography of Yellowstone's natural beauty that persuaded Congress to conserve it.

The remains of an ancient collapsed volcano–a caldera–Yellowstone is one of the best places in the world to see the whole range of geothermal activity, including geysers (Old Faithful is only one of many), brightly coloured hot springs, mud volcanoes, sinter terraces (the Minerva Terrace in Mammoth Hot Springs is the most famous), paint pots and fumaroles. The Park's wildlife is also abundant: elk, moose, bison, pronghorn and bighorn can all be seen, as well as smaller animals such as marmot and squirrels. Birds include ducks, geese, trumpeter swan, osprey and eagles.

Yellowstone is the country's busiest national park, and during the height of the summer holidays traffic jams are frequent, despite 500 miles (800 kilometres) of good roads and the efficient Park Service. Hiking and horse trails have considerable advantages at this time of the year.

Season The main season is May to October, when all the facilities are available. June, July and August are the busiest months, and are probably best avoided for serious wildlife photography. The other seasons are less well catered for, but do offer relative solitude. Spring gives opportunities for photographing newly born animals, while those that have been hibernating are especially active. In autumn, animals that have spent the summer on the high plateaus return to the lowlands. The winter scenery is spectacular, and snowmobiles are available locally.

A gypsum dune (top) **in early morning sunlight, White Sands, New Mexico.**

A bison (above) **in the Hayden Valley, Yellowstone, Wyoming.**

Condor (right) **soaring over the Aguada Blanca, Peru** (N. Sitwell).

South America

Aguada Blanca, Peru

Though officially named the Reserva de Pampa Canahuas, this magnificent reserve to the north of Arequipa in Peru is generally known as Aguada Blanca after the river Blanco which runs through it. Not too difficult to visit by car, it is approached along a zigzagging road that rises out of Arequipa between the 18,000 feet (6,000 metre) volcanic cones of Chachani and Misti. The latter's slightly active state is betrayed by wisps of steam. Behind the mountains lies a beautiful high plateau of pampas and lagoons, some 1,400 square miles (3,600 square kilometres) in area.

The vegetation is sparse–largely coarse ichu grass–but there are oddities including polylepis trees and at 15,000 feet (5,000 metres) a curious hard umbellifer with tiny flowers, called *Azorella*. Most of the reserve is between 12,000 and 14,000 feet (4,000 and 4,500 metres), so altitude sickness may cause headaches. But the wildlife is worth any temporary discomfort. All four South American camelids are here–the graceful vicuña, with the most valuable wool in the world; a few guanacos; and the domesticated alpaca and llama. Viscachas leap about the rocks–photographers need swift reactions–and if you are very lucky you may see a herd of the rare Andean deer.

Bird life is especially rich. Highlights include flamingos and an almost certain chance of seeing condors in the early morning as they climb the thermals at Croce de la Condor, just north of the reserve. Torrent ducks, ibises, Andean geese, giant coots, burrowing owls, and caracaras and falcons are also likely to be seen. The scenery is spectacular, and just north of the reserve is the Canyon of the Colca, deeper than the Grand Canyon.

No good maps are available, so a guide is essential. There are a number of rough but serviceable roads and tracks. Laguna del Indio and Salinas are especially good bird sites.

Season Any time, but avoid the rainy season from December to March. At all times take a warm sweater and perhaps a poncho to ward off the high-altitude chill. However, it is mostly sunny and the climate is invigorating. Flamingos are more likely to be seen around September.

Galapagos Islands

Possibly the most famous and certainly one of the most scientifically important archipelagos in the world, the Galapagos lie on the equator 600 miles (960 kilometres) west of Ecuador. The name comes from the Spanish for tortoise–the giant tortoises that exist in a variety of different forms on different islands. They, the iguanas and Darwin's finches provided the original inspiration for Charles Darwin's theory of evolution through natural selection.

There are 13 major islands, six minor islands, and a number of islets. All have fascinating and unique animals and plants. Two thirds of the birds and all the reptiles, apart from one species of gecko, are only found in the Galapagos. Some 5,000 people live in the islands–which are a province of Ecuador–and are divided between two large and several small communities. The islands are a photographer's paradise. Almost all creatures are confidingly tame: lumbering, three foot land iguanas amble up, while a mockingbird may perch inquisitively on a telephoto lens. Boobies of three species nest unconcernedly on the volcanic rocks, while a swim in the cool waters of the Humboldt current can be interrupted by the friendly attentions of sea-lions.

The archipelago is a national park, and the park service strictly regulates the total number of tourists, and lays down a code of conduct. No visitor is allowed ashore without a trained guide. You may not stray from the marked trails, but this is not onerous as they generally lead through the most interesting areas. No litter is allowed–even cigarette butts must be pocketed for shipboard disposal. Care must be taken not to transfer plant seeds from one island to another. Above all, the wildlife must be disturbed as little as possible, and preferably not at all.

Do not be deterred by these regulations, for most visitors quickly see their point and even help the guides enforce them. And the wildlife almost seems to want to pose for the photographer. Seldom is anything more than a 135mm lens needed. But what is most definitely required is a plentiful supply–and more–of film. One cautionary note: most tourists only manage to see giant tortoises in captivity at the Charles Darwin Research Station. But there is an abundance of other interesting animals and some very odd plants. The landscapes,

Alpaca of various shades (above) **by a lagoon on the plateau of Aguada Blanca (N. Sitwell).**

Land iguana (left) **on Fernandina Island, Galapagos (N. Sitwell).**

especially the lava flows and volcanic rocks are photographically rewarding.

Seasons Any time is good, but some times are better than others for migratory birds. The waved albatross, which breeds only on Hood Island, is not present between about December and March. Similarly April to November is the best time to see the male frigatebirds displaying their scarlet gular pouches.

Paracas, Peru

Deserts are not always as devoid of life as they may first seem, and this applies particularly to the coastal desert of Peru. The Paracas National Reserve, some 150 miles (240 kilometres) south of Lima (about four hours drive down the Panamerican Highway), encompasses an area of 1,300 square miles (3,350 square kilometres) of which about two thirds is sea. The land part is true desert for it only rains a few drops about once a century. But around its fringe the cold Humboldt current is rich in fish—especially anchovies—which in turn support a rich variety of resident and migratory birds. Outstanding attractions are Andean condors and guano birds (cormorants, boobies and pelicans) in thousands on the offshore guano islands. The beautiful Inca tern is much in evidence. Also likely to be seen are Chilean flamingos, turkey vultures, skimmers, ospreys, Humboldt's penguins, and a variety of shorebirds. Fur seals and sea-lions can be seen around the coast and on the islands. The sea-sculpted cliffs and wind-blown desert scenery are very photogenic, and there are fascinating remains of pre-Inca civilizations—including the enormous candelabra on a sandy slope facing the Pacific.

Season Any time, though sun is most likely from October to February during the Peruvian summer. At this time condors are particularly in evidence, as they come to feed on the new-born sea-lions, but some are there all year. At other times, it tends to be cloudy or misty, but not cold.

Trinidad and Tobago

Ten miles off Venezuela's Orinoco delta, Trinidad and the smaller Tobago belong ornithologically to South America—and this part is the world's richest area for birds. Trinidad has about 300 species in an area 50 by 37 miles (80 by 59 kilometres). The islands are also a haven for that remarkable New World family, the hummingbirds. Trinidad has 17 species and Tobago seven. But the two outstanding spectacles in Trinidad are at the Caroni Swamps and the Springhill Estate.

Caroni Swamp is on the west coast, south of Port of Spain, and the highlight is the evening flight of the scarlet ibis as they come to roost in the mangrove trees. Like flamingos, the scarlet ibises' colour derives from the crustaceans in their diet. Roseate spoonbills are among the many other birds, especially herons, to be seen.

On the road from Arima to Blanchiseusse, near the north coast, lies the Springhill Estate, which harbours the world-famous Asa Wright Nature Centre. There are many interesting walks, but none with quite the excitement of a visit to Diablotin Cave and its oilbirds. These large and curious birds live in caves and tunnels, are completely nocturnal, have an excellent sense of smell, and navigate by echo-location. They fly out at night to feed on palm nuts. Those at Diablotin are accustomed to humans and not disturbed by flash photography.

Season Any time, but August to October is especially good for scarlet ibis as it is their breeding season. Most rain falls during August.

Valdes Peninsula, Argentina

About halfway down the coast of Argentina, the Valdes Peninsula is perhaps the richest area for wildlife in Patagonia. Mainly covered in brush and scrub and with

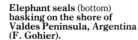
Elephant seals (bottom) basking on the shore of Valdes Peninsula, Argentina (F. Gohier).

Pelican skimming the waves (below), off Paracas, Peru (N. Sitwell).

gravelly beaches, Valdes also has some imposing cliffs on its southern shore. It is a haven for sea mammals and seabirds, and by its very shape a natural nature reserve. The wildlife arrives at Valdes during the spring and summer to breed. Among the species likely to be seen are elegant guanacos on the downs near the coast, where they mingle with the uncommon Darwin's rhea. Maras should be seen in large numbers, and you may spot a Patagonian skunk or a pampas cat. But the great sights are of marine mammals. Southern right whales come in very close to bear their young, while there are large numbers of southern sea-lions, and the colonies of the gigantic elephant seals are the only ones in South America. The intrepid or more experienced visitor can swim among them. The peninsula is quite large – 60 miles (95 kilometres) from north to south and 40 miles (65 kilometres) from east to west – but there are roads and tracks across it. The whales congregate in Golfo Nuevo, off the isthmus connecting the peninsula with the mainland. The place to head for is Puerto Madryn on the mainland, where there is a helpful tourist bureau.

Season Hard to get to in the southern winter. Best time is spring and summer, beginning in September when seals, sea elephants and sea-lions will have formed harems on the beaches. Whales will be breeding in September.

Asia

Bharatpur, India

Described by the Audubon Society as 'perhaps the best breeding sanctuary for waterbirds in the world', the Keoladeo Ghana reserve at Bharatpur covers just 11 square miles (28 square kilometres) of flooded acacia forest between Jaipur and Agra. Previously owned by the Maharajah of Bharatpur as a private shooting preserve, but now a state sanctuary, Bharatpur is a nesting and breeding ground for more than 250 species of birds, many of them in extremely large numbers. Apart from black-necked storks, painted storks, spoonbills, white ibis and others, Bharatpur is particularly well known for the indigenous Sarus crane and the rare migratory Siberian crane, whose only known winter home it is.

As well as birds, sambar, chital and nilgai are common.

Season The start of nesting depends on the timing of the north east monsoon, which can never be forecast precisely, but is usually around mid-September. The most spectacular months are November, December and January, when winter migrants swell the numbers. Most birds leave by March.

Bohorok, Sumatra

The great apes are fascinating, no doubt because they are man's closest animal relatives. But they prefer to live in dense forests so they are not easy to observe. Orang utans, in particular, are wholly arboreal, which makes it virtually impossible to see them – except in a place like the Bohorok Rehabilitation Centre in northern Sumatra. Here young orangs which have been confiscated – it is illegal to own one as a pet – are gradually reintroduced to life in the wild. Each day in the morning and afternoon they are fed bananas as part of the rehabilitation process. The rest of the time they are out of sight in the forest canopy. It is extraordinarily exciting to see the young orangs, and occasionally an older one or even a truly wild adult, come down towards the feeding platform. There are plenty of opportunities to photograph the apes as they swing through the branches.

Bohorok can be reached by road, about a three hour drive from Medan. It is worth staying overnight, as the surrounding forest is rich in creatures like hornbills, gibbons, siamangs, and other rain forest fauna. You may

Acacias and palm trees (above) **in the Baratpur sanctuary, near Agra, India.**

Young orang utan (left) **at Bohorok, Sumatra.**

211

Indian one-horned
rhinoceros, Kaziranga
sanctuary in Assam
(J-P. Ferrero).

be lucky enough to hear an argus pheasant. Bohorok is on the edge of the mighty Gunung Leuser National Park, the largest rain forest conservation area in South-East Asia. Special arrangements should be made to explore the forest with a guide.
Season Visit between April and September to avoid the rainy season. Weekends can be busy, so aim for mid-week.

Chitwan, Nepal
The Kingdom of Nepal may be best known for Mount Everest and the elusive yeti, but for the wildlife photographer it has something even better, and certainly easier to locate. South from Katmandu, in the *terai*, lies one of Asia's richest wildlife areas, the Royal Chitwan National Park. A well watered region of swamp, elephant grass and sal forest, Chitwan is noted for its tigers and one-horned Indian rhinos. It is also a sanctuary for the gharial, a rare Asian crocodile with a pronounced elongated snout. The Gangetic dolphin is occasionally sighted. Other mammals include four species of deer and animals such as nilgai, gaur and wild boar. The birds are many and varied. Baits are sometimes put out for the tigers here, to ensure the visitor a reasonable chance of a sighting. Another feature is the possibility of safaris on elephant-back.
Season Avoid the rainy season from June to September. Best time is in the cooler weather from November to April. Later in the season the vegetation dies down, allowing better views of the wildlife.

Kaziranga, India
India's most spectacular and rewarding sanctuary, Kaziranga lies in flat, swampy country on the southern bank of the Brahmaputra river in Assam. There is every chance of seeing the Indian one-horned rhino as this is the species' main stronghold, swamp deer, hog deer and wild buffalo. There are also wild elephants and a variety of waterbirds. A special feature is game-viewing on elephant back, which gives a better view and is safer as rhinos are not likely to attack.
    Kaziranga is reached by air to Gauhati, and then a drive of 135 miles (220 kilometres), or by air to Jorhat, followed by a drive of 60 miles (95 kilometres).
Season All year, but best November to April. There are floods from June to August.

Periyar, India
As far as the visitor is concerned, the most interesting part of this sanctuary in southern India is the 10 square mile (26 square kilometre) Periyar Lake. This was artificially created in 1900 to provide irrigation water for Tamil Nadu state—although Periyar is just across the border in Kerala. The lake is well provided with attractive vistas and intriguing creeks, and the whole area is noted for its scenery. Wild elephants are plentiful, and you are more likely to see them from a boat on this lake than anywhere else in India. There is a troupe of the rare Nilgiri langur around the main lodge, which any visitor should see. The sanctuary also has gaur, sambar, muntjac and a wide variety of birds, especially waterbirds. Periyar is 120 miles (190 kilometres) from Cochin on the Cochin-Madurai road.
Season Open all year; best months March to May.

Ujung Kulon, Java
One of the most celebrated of all rare animals is the Javan rhino. And the only place in the world it can be seen is Ujung Kulon, a reserve of about 200 square miles (500 square kilometres) on the westernmost tip of Java. This is a true lowland forest reserve, only accessible by sea. The chances of seeing a rhino are small—but this, combined with the wealth of other wildlife to be seen,

make a visit very appealing. There are watchtowers from where one can observe animals on the 'grazing grounds'–banteng, rusa deer, wild boar and pea and junglefowl. Ujung Kulon boasts some 250 bird species in the forest and swamps, and the surrounding waters are rich in marine life. A canoe trip up one of the jungle streams offers the chance of spotting monitor lizards, pythons and many birds.

Special permission is needed to visit Ujung Kulon, and it is cheaper to go in a group. It is reached by driving for about four and a half hours from Jakarta to Labuan, then going by chartered fishing boat for the seven hour journey to Pulau Peucang, a little island just off Ujung Kulon itself. The boat trip can detour to pass by Krakatau.
Season Best when it is not raining, from May to September.

Wilpattu, Sri Lanka
Sri Lanka's largest national park with some 400 square miles (1,000 square kilometres), Wilpattu is one of the few places in Asia or Africa where leopards both exist and are very likely to be seen. The western part is a flat sandy area with numerous shallow lakes, while the eastern section has many streams and richer forest, although this is still rather straggly due to the area's long history of human habitation. Wildlife attractions include Asiatic elephants, wild boar, sambhar, barking deer, crocodiles and abundant birdlife on the lakes and lagoons.

In the eastern section there are other attractions for archaeologists of ancient cave temples, stone columns, and remains of Buddhist civilizations.
Season Open all year, and both wet and dry seasons have their own advantages and disadvantages. The heavy rains of February to March and August to September are best avoided. The best time is probably May to June. In January the park becomes a great garden of wild flowers.

Africa

Aberdare National Park, Kenya
This national park in Kenya is a rarity in the tropics, with its rich alpine and sub-alpine flora. It ranges from 6,000 to 13,000 feet (2,000 to 4,000 metres) above sea level. Cradled in the forests and moors of the Aberdare Mountains, it is crossed by many streams, some of which cascade to the bamboo forests in the foothills. A sanctuary for the more elusive forest species, Aberdare National Park is reached from Nairobi by way of Nyeri. A well-frequented waterhole and saltlick at Treetops Hotel is floodlit at night, providing good chances of seeing elephants, rhinos, buffalos, and warthog–plus rarer or shyer forest animals such as bongo antelope, bushbuck, and the giant forest hog.
Season All year; the best time January and February.

Etosha, Namibia
Ranging from desert to semi-arid, Etosha National Park in Namibia is primeval and relatively little visited. At its heart lies Etosha Pan, a 2,300 square mile (6,000 square kilometre) inland sea which acts as a magnet for migratory game. Etosha is noted for blue wildebeest, springbok, Burchell's zebra, bat-eared fox, black-faced impala, eland, and one of the smallest antelopes, the Damara dik-dik. Birds include ostriches, cranes and flamingos. The area has never been densely populated, and when the game was practically exterminated by rinderpest at the turn of the century, the local tribesmen went elsewhere. But the wildlife has now recovered, and the park offers a fine chance to see desert fauna and flora.

An old male Indian elephant leads a herd along the shore of Periyar Lake, southern India (J-P. Ferrero).

Etosha can be reached by car and bus–it is around 300 miles (480 kilometres) from Windhoek. It is also accessible by light aircraft.
Season Avoid the wet seasons–although there is little rain–in April and October to November. The camps are open from May to mid-October, with August and September the best time. The climate in the open season is moderate to cool, and dry.

Luangwa Valley, Zambia

Zambia's Luangwa Valley is part of the great Rift Valley, the 6,000 mile (9,000 kilometre) gash that runs from the Middle East to Malawi. The Luangwa itself is some 400 miles (640 kilometres) long and 60 miles (96 kilometres) wide, of which about half is national park. Much of the landscape is parkland, featuring grassy plains and mopani woodland. The Lungwa River has created many oxbow lakes and islands which are rich in vegetation. Crocodiles can be seen, as well as elephants and hippos. The rich birdlife ranges from brilliant bee-eaters and sunbirds to majestic fish eagles.

Walking safaris are a special attraction. You can choose daily trips, of a few miles, with the nights spent in a lodge, or longer safaris, using temporary bush-camps. More conventional game-viewing drives by Land-Rover are also available. A new departure is the night safari–viewing game with the aid of a spotlight mounted on a vehicle.

While photography of the larger mammals is probably best done from a vehicle as the animals tend not to associate cars with human beings, photography during a walking safari can be more rewarding. One has to exercise that much more care–it becomes a real hunt with a camera. And flowers, insects, and the like can only properly be photographed on foot.
Season The park is open all year, but the best time is during the dry season, from May to October.

Okavango, Botswana

The mighty Okavango river rises in the mountains of Angola near the Atlantic coast of Africa and does something few other rivers do: it flows inland for thousands of miles to eventually falter and lose its way among the hot sands of the Kalahari desert in northern Botswana. The Okavango Delta is a unique natural phenomenon–a 6,000 square mile (over 15,000 square kilometre) inland delta. The life-giving waters flow through a myriad twisting channels, many of which change their course from year to year, and support a luxuriant variety of plants and animals.

The Moremi Wildlife Reserve was once the traditional hunting ground of the Batawana tribe, who in 1963 declared it a wildlife sanctuary. Moremi is noted for aquatic birds, and there is a world-famous heronry at Txatxanika. Mammals are abundant, including hippos and crocodiles, but specialities include three uncommon antelopes–sitatunga, Chobe bushbuck and the red lechwe.
Season Annual rains fall between November and March, but the peak safari season is from April to October.

The Selous, Tanzania

The word 'safari' evokes an instant picture of teeming herds of East African big game. This is not surprising, perhaps, for the word is Swahili, the common language of East Africa, and means simply a journey. Adopted first in colonial times to mean a hunting trip, it now describes a holiday to watch and photograph wildlife. East Africa is still–with justification–the home of the safari.

With the enormous growth of tourism in the past two decades, it is exciting to think that the greatest of all African wildlife conservation areas, the Selous Game

An elephant in the Selous reserve, Tanzania (N. Sitwell).

Reserve of southern Tanzania, is still practically unknown and awaiting discovery by the ordinary visitor. There is a certain romance, too, in the realization that the Selous was always a hunting reserve, and still is today, in its southern portion. At 21,000 square miles (about 45,000 square kilometres) it is the biggest wildlife conservation area in Africa and the second largest in the world. it is two and a half times the size of Wales, and about a third bigger than Denmark. And in all this huge, almost pristine wilderness, there live no more than a handful of people.

Much of the Selous is woodland of various kinds, especially *miombo* woodland, which can be poor for game viewing. But there are plenty of places where the woodland is broken up with grassland, swamps and rivers. The northern sector is the richest, and also the most accessible. The Selous has some 100,000 elephants, among them encouraging numbers of heavy tusked bulls. There are 2,500 or so black rhinos, 150,000 buffalo and large numbers of antelopes of many kinds. There are also a few of the very restricted Nyasa wildebeest, distinguished from its northern relative by a white chevron on its forehead.

Because the Selous is a game reserve not a national park, foot safaris, with an armed guard, are allowed—though it must be said that photography is easier from a Land-Rover.

Season It is best to avoid March and April, and perhaps May, when the 'long rains' make tracks impassable. The 'short rains' come in November to December, and this is not an ideal time to visit, although possible. From June to October, the Selous is cool and dry, and the grasses are short, making for easier game spotting. January and February, between the rains, is an interesting time, with everything green and lush.

Serengeti, Tanzania

Home of the largest and most spectacular concentrations of plains game in the world, the Serengeti National Park in northern Tanzania is probably the most famous of all national parks, apart from America's Yellowstone. Recent estimates suggest some 1,750,000 animals within its 5,700 square miles (14,763 square kilometres). Of these, perhaps 800,000 are wildebeest.

The Serengeti is best known for the annual migration of wildebeest and zebras. In late May and June, at the start of the dry season, hundreds of thousands of animals begin their trek, from the central plains to the park's western corridor—one of the most remarkable sights in all Africa. And these great herds attract prides of lions, as well as leopards, cheetahs, hunting dogs and other carnivores and scavengers.

The Serengeti is open, largely flat, and to a great extent treeless. But it is amazingly rich in wildlife, including birds, and photographic opportunities are virtually unlimited.

Season Any time except perhaps April and early May, when heavy rains can cause problems. The driest season is June to December, but the best time is late May and June, the start of the migration.

Seychelles

This island group in the western Indian Ocean, 1,000 miles (1,600 kilometres) east of the Kenyan coast, is the ideal place to combine natural history photography with the more conventional holiday activities. Lying just south of the equator, Seychelles comprises 40 granite islands, lush and tropical, with dense forests and thick undergrowth, and about 50 coralline islands, which are more barren and low lying, but covered in coconut palms and often rich in seabirds.

Seychelles boasts many unique birds, much unusual vegetation and is one of the best places in the world for

A herd of wildebeest (below) **on the Serengeti plains, Tanzania** (N. Sitwell).

A pride of lions (bottom) **in the Serengeti** (N. Sitwell).

215

A green turtle (above) on
Heron Island, Great Barrier
Reef, Australia
(J-P. Ferrero).

An Australian sea-lion on a
Kangaroo Island beach,
Australia (J-P. Ferrero).

snorkelling and underwater photography. Not all the
birds present themselves readily for photography,
though the distinctive black paradise flycatcher, once
thought to be extinct, conveniently builds its nest
hanging across paths on La Digue Island. Do not miss the
Vallée de Mai on Praslin Island, only home of the giant
coco de mer palm. There are many excellent areas for
underwater exploration, but the clarity of the water at
the various sites depends greatly on the monsoon which
prevails at the time. There are always some good places
to go.

If the atoll of Aldabra should be opened again to non-
scientific visitors it is an essential place to visit, especially to see the unique flightless rail and the 150,000
giant tortoises, the only ones in the Indian Ocean.
Season All the year round.

Australia

Heron Island

Australia's Great Barrier Reef is the largest coral reef in
the world, and Heron Island is the best place in all its
1,200 mile (1,900 kilometre) length from which to
explore the reef's spectacular marine life. Heron Island
lies some 45 miles (70 kilometres) off the Queensland
coast, and is the only inhabited coral cay catering
specifically for divers and underwater photographers.
Quite small in surface area, the island is a marine
sanctuary. Some of the fish are tame enough to feed by
hand.

Heron Island and other nearby reefs and islands offer a
rich assembly of fishes, corals, and other marine
creatures. But on land, too, there are things to
photograph. The lush green Pisonia forest harbours
many seabirds and waders, and white-breasted sea
eagles nest here. Throughout the island are extensive
burrows made by wedge-tailed shearwaters, or mutton
birds.
Season Best from April to November. But around
October the mutton birds are nesting, and green and
loggerhead turtles haul themselves ashore at night to lay
their eggs.

Kangaroo Island

Seventy miles south-west of Adelaide, Kangaroo Island
is a large natural sanctuary of some 90 by 30 miles (145
by 45 kilometres). Many of the animals are as tame as
they were when the island was discovered by Matthew
Flinders in 1802. Part of the island has been declared a
national park and named Flinders Chase in his memory.
There is a fascinating variety of animal and plant life on
Kangaroo Island, and many species have developed into
distinctive island forms. The vegetation is largely
tangled scrub, thorny acacias and towering eucalypus
'gums'—and is not always easy to penetrate. But
persevere, for among the wildlife treasures are emus, a
strong colony of koalas and several hundred Cape Barren
geese—one of the world's rarer birds. Some believe the
grey kangaroo found here is a separate species from that
on the mainland. There are also wallabies, spiny ant-
eaters, and two species of goanna or lace monitor, one of
which attains a length of seven feet (two metres). Fairy
penguins breed here, as do Australian fur seals and
Australian hair seals. Wild flowers bloom all year round—
especially outstanding are the various orchids and the
remarkable scarlet bottlebrush.
Season All year, but August to about January or
February—spring and summer—are particularly good
times for breeding animals and wild flowers.

Phillip Island

One of the richest wildlife areas in the Australian state of

Victoria, Phillip Island is famous for its mighty 'penguin parade'. The fairy penguin is the smallest of the penguins, and its small size makes it vulnerable to larger, predatory birds. So it has taken to nesting underground in burrows and also comes ashore to the rookeries after dark. Thousands of tourists every year come to witness this remarkable sight. As darkness gathers, visitors are confined behind two parallel fences which run down to the shore. Floodlights illuminate the scene, but the penguins seem quite unconcerned.

Phillip Island is easily reached by road from Melbourne, about 70 miles (110 kilometres) away. A bridge connects the island with the mainland. Other attractions on the island include a variety of birds, koalas and Australian fur seals.

Season Some penguins can be seen all year round, but the best time is between October and May.

Antarctica

The Antarctic continent is one huge wildlife refuge of five and a half million square miles (14.2 million square kilometres). No human beings live there permanently, though there are some permanent scientific research stations. Certainly, no human being has ever been born in Antarctica, so far as is known. The expanse of barren ice is huge, yet around the edges, where it is lapped by the Southern Ocean, there is an abundance of life. There are seals and sea-lions of half a dozen species, penguins by the million, cormorants, petrels, skuas, and several albatrosses–above all the wandering albatrosses, with their eleven foot (three metre) wingspan, the largest birds in the world. And in the sea itself there are whales, including the blue whale, the biggest of them all.

We tend to think of Antarctica as dangerous, but it can be a land of sunny skies and mild temperatures; the winter is another matter. Naturalists speak of it as a magical place, a land of awe inspiring beauty and overwhelming romance, the last great wilderness.

It is, however, difficult and expensive to visit. About the only way is to become attached to one of the official scientific teams, or travel there aboard one of the few cruise ships that venture there during the brief Antarctic summer.

Season Approximately December to February.

Wandering albatross on the coast of South Georgia, an island in the Atlantic Ocean off Antarctica (F. Gohier).

217

Using your photographs

Unlike many types of photography, wildlife and nature are not dominated by professionals. Even with the most careful planning, good wildlife pictures can never be guaranteed, and many of the great photographs are a combination of quick reactions, a good visual sense, being on the spot, and a large element of luck. Such uncertainty is one of the real delights of the subject, but one that more readily appeals to the amateur than to the professional on assignment, committed to delivering sucessful pictures at the end of it. While lack of funds may limit the scope of the amateur wildlife photographer and the possible subjects and locations may not be so wide-ranging, the absence of commercial pressure gives valuable freedom to experiment. Often, it is only the amateur, working for love rather than profit, who can afford the time and effort needed to capture shy and difficult subjects on film. However, even if not sought initially, financial rewards can, and often do, follow.

Because it is so difficult to guarantee success, magazine and book publishers lean heavily on stock photographs obtained from picture agencies rather than commission. On the picture editor's light box, professional status counts for little—what matters is the worth of the individual photograph. Note that colour transparencies, rather than prints, are always more acceptable for publication purposes.

The market

The demand for wildlife and nature photographs is high, not through any current fashion or bout of enthusiasm, but because of the very basic interest that these subjects have for the general public. The greatest commercial use is in books and maga-zines. Book titles that need this kind of material are usually specific to wildlife and nature, although there is also a substantial demand among more general titles, with geographical or travel themes for example. Both general interest and wildlife magazines exist as markets for photographs, although the latter have much smaller circulations. Subsidiary uses are advertising, calendars and postcards.

Stock agencies

Many photographers keep their own libraries and deal directly with publishers, relying heavily on their reputations for potential clients to contact them with picture requests. For the majority of photographers, however, it is more convenient to leave the handling and sale of pictures to a professional stock agency. Picture researchers and picture editors deal regularly with agencies, who are therefore in touch with a much larger market for photographs than any individual photographer. Although most agents subtract a 25 per cent commission from sales, they can nearly always make much better use of material than the photographer, simply because it is their full time business. They can also take care of the tedium of administration, and are generally better equipped to handle the complexities of reproduction rights and legal problems.

Most stock agencies prefer to see a selection of photographs before committing themselves to taking on a photographer's work. Generally, it is not worth an agency's while to accept less than 100 pictures as a first selection. But when you have a sufficient number of photographs of good quality to offer, perhaps on a particular theme, you may be wise to take them to some picture agencies. Addresses can be found in publishing and journalistic year books or trade magazines.

Bibliography

The 35 mm Handbook, *Freeman, Michael.* Windward, 1980.

Alaska, *Brown, Dale.* Time-Life Books, 1972.

The Amazon, *Steding, Tom.* Time-Life Books, 1973.

The Andes, *Morrison, Tony.* Time-Life Books, 1975.

Andreas Feininger, *Ralph Hartersley.* Morgan & Morgan, 1973.

Ansel Adams. Morgan & Morgan, 1972.

The Audubon Society Book of Wild Animals. Harry N. Abrams.

The Audubon Society Book of Wild Birds. Harry N. Abrams.

The Audubon Society Book of Wildflowers, *Live, Les & Hodge, Walter Hendricks.* Harry N. Abrams, 1978.

The Birds, *Peterson, Roger Tory.* Time-Life Books, 1964.

Desert Survival, *Nelson, Richard & Sharon.* Tecolore Press, 1977.

Field Guide to the Butterflies of Britain and Europe, *Higgins, L. G. & Riley, N. D.* Collins, 1970.

Field Guide to the Mammals of Britain and Europe, *van den Brink, F. H.* Collins, 1965.

Flights of Discovery, *Gorster, Georg.* Paddington Press, 1978.

The Forest & The Sea, *Bates, Marston.* Museum Press, 1961.

In-water Photography: Theory & Practice, *Mertens, L. E.* Wiley-Interscience, 1970.

Land Above the Clouds, *Morrison, Tony.* André Deutsch, 1974.

Lapland, *Marsden, Walter.* Time-Life Books, 1976.

Magnifications: Photography with the Scanning Electron Microscope, *Scharf, David.* Schocken Books, 1977.

Photographing Nature. Time-Life Books, 1973.

Photographs of the Southwest, *Adams, Ansel.* New York Graphic Society, 1976.

Photography as a Tool. Time-Life Books, 1972.

Photography on Expeditions, *John, D. H. O.* Focal Press, 1965.

Photography Through The Microscope. Eastman Kodak, 1974.

South America, *Bates, Marston.* Time-Life Books, 1969.

The Technique of Wildlife Cinematography, *Warham, John.* Focal Press, 1966.

Underwater Photography for Everyone, *Schulke, Flip.* Prentice-Hall, 1978.

View Camera Technique, *Stroebel, Leslie.* Focal Press, 1967.

Voyage of the Eye, *Brett Weston.* Aperture, 1975.

Wildlife Watcher's Handbook, *Hanenkrat, Frank.* Winchester Press, 1977.

The Wild Places, ed: *Rogoff, Milton & Guilfoyle, Ann.* Harper & Row, 1974.

Index

Page numbers for illustrations are given in italics.

Acknowledgements

The author would like to thank Francesca Serpell for the picture research and Wayne Irwin of Custom Flying Tours Inc., Merced, California, for help with the aerial photography.

The photographs are by Michael Freeman except where indicated in the captions. In addition, the photomicrographs on pages 180 to 186 were supplied by Dr David Patterson, Dr Brad Amos, James Bell and Gene Cox/Science Photo Library. The photographs of insects in flight on pages 178 and 179 are by Stephen Dalton.